Emotional
Expression
in
Psychotherapy

Emotional Expression in Psychotherapy

Robert A. Pierce, Ph.D.
Michael P. Nichols, Ph.D.
Joyce R. DuBrin, M.A.

GARDNER PRESS, INC
New York and London

Copyright © 1983 by Gardner Press, Inc.

All rights reserved. No part of this book may be reproduced in any form,
by photostat, microfilm, retrieval system,
or any means now known or later devised, without the prior written permission of the
publisher:

GARDNER PRESS, INC.
19 Union Square West
New York, New York 10003

Library of Congress Cataloging in Publication Data

Pierce, Robert A.
    Emotional expression in psychotherapy.

    Bibliography: p.
    Includes index.
    1. Psychotherapy. 2. Emotions. 3. Expression.
I. Nichols, Michael P. II. DuBrin, Joyce R.
III. Title. [DNLM: 1. Psychotherapy—Methods.
2. Emotions. 3. Catharsis. WM 120 P617e]
RC480.5.P53 1983   616.89′1   83-5604
ISBN O-89876-015-1

For Our Children
Carl, Debi, Doug, Drew, Laura,
Paul, and Sandy

Acknowledgments

We with to thank first those who gave us our start as psychologists and clinicians: R.A.P. thanks Drs. Henry Paar, Emory Cowen, Melvin Zax and Leonard Salzman for their interest and encouragement. He wishes to thank J.R.D. for sharing, on countless occasions, her uncanny sensitivity to people and their feelings, and M.P.N. for urging him to write this book. M.P.N. thanks Drs. Jay Efran and Rodney Shapiro and R.A.P. J.R.D. thanks Ms. Rosina Raymond, her first mentor, for permission to feel, and Ms. Elizabeth Friauf-Struever, Dr. Charles Solky and especially R.A.P. for their contributions as teachers and psychotherapists.

Harvey Jackins was the first to show us how to elicit strong feelings in clients and in ourselves and he gave us our first theory about how feeling-expression helps. We thank him for that.

We appreciate help from our colleagues who read and commented on parts of the manuscript—Drs. Raymond Babineau, Allen Roach, Diane DePalma and Trudy Baran. We wish to thank Dr. John Thibideau for his generous and long-suffering help with the statistics for the research chapter.

M.P.N. thanks his wife, Melody Nichols for her wise and insightful comments about the book in its various stages.

We appreciate Henrietta Levine, our typist, friend and mood enhancer for her frankness, help and humor.

We are grateful to our families and friends for their encouragement and love even when working on the book meant being away from them.

Our publisher, Gardner Spungin, has been patient, encouraging and helpful. His high standards have made this a better book than it otherwise would have been, and his friendship has made it possible.

Finally, we wish to thank our clients who, in sharing themselves with us, and in responding to our interventions showed us that worked and what did not. We appreciate their trust in us as well as their willingness, on many occasions, to supervise our work, letting us know when we were being helpful and when we were not.

Contents

Preface

All psychotherapies attempt to alleviate emotional pain. Unhappy
people, frustrated with their inability to make their lives work for them,
turn to psychotherapists for relief from their suffering. Unfortunately,
psychotherapists all too often respond to painful feelings by trying to
ignore, analyze, or block them. Mistaking the expression of feelings for
the pain itself, they unwittingly abort the natural therapeutic process of
feeling-expression. Although people feel and act, as well as think, most
often they have been treated with thought-oriented therapies. These approaches may involve much talk *about* feelings, but the full, vigorous
expression *of* feelings is rare; in fact, therapists seldom seek such expression. We believe that when this imbalance is corrected, psychotherapy
will be of more help to more people. Our own approach, feeling-expressive
therapy, does not attempt to replace thinking with feeling, but rather, to
provide a useful integration of feeling, thought, and behavior.

This book was written to explain why intense emotional expression
is important in psychotherapy, how to elicit such emotional expression,
and how to integrate feeling, thinking, and acting in psychological treatment. Since theory and technique build on and reinforce each other, we
have interspersed clinical examples from our own practice throughout this
volume. All names of clients, therapists, and others mentioned in these
case examples have been changed to protect their privacy.

There are many cathartic therapies, the most influential of which are
described and discussed in Chapter 2. Our own approach springs in part
from these and in part from our own clinical experience. Most of the book
tells how and why we work with feelings, and how we integrate feeling-
expression with insight and behavior change. This book aims to reach not
only current and prospective feeling-expressive therapists, but the many
therapists working in other styles who would like to elicit more feeling
in their clients and to use the expression of that feeling for therapeutic
gain.

The authors and their colleagues have worked actively with cathartic
methods for over a dozen years at the University of Rochester, Emory
University, Albany Medical College, and the Therapy Center in Rochester, New York. We present here what has worked for us and what we
believe will work for others.

The book is divided into three parts: Introduction, Clinical Issues,
and Special Issues. The first chapter examines catharsis in the context of
cultural inhibitions of feeling-expression. Case vignettes are used to illustrate various types of feelings. Chapter 2 describes the history and
current use of catharsis in healing and psychotherapy while Chapter 3

describes specific techniques we use in working with feelings, in relation to both the objective of the intervention and the specific method used by the therapist.

In Chapters 4, 5, and 6, we use three long, detailed cases to illustrate the beginning, middle, and termination phases of treatment. The various tasks of each phase are described and illustrated in the case examples.

The very important community aspect of our work is treated in Chapter 7, where we describe how clients help each other in weekly therapy groups, workshops, and peer-counseling. Chapter 8 presents a rationale for our use of feeling-expression in work with couples and suggests emotive methods of helping couples to change.

In Chapter 9, we discuss various methods therapists and students can use to increase their comfort and familiarity with their own feelings, and their skill in working with their clients' feelings. Chapter 10 reports our research findings from a series of studies we have carried out to assess the usefulness of feeling-expression in psychotherapy. Finally, in Chapter 11, we seek to place feeling-expressive therapy in the context of humanity's long history of efforts to heal pained and dysfunctional people. In this historical perspective, we believe our emphases on community and on emotional expression are very much in the mainstream, and are considerably less radical than they may appear in the contemporary context of highly cognitive and individualistic psychotherapies.

As we wrote this book, we were frequently faced with the question of how much to focus on feeling-expression specifically as opposed to dealing more broadly with general therapy issues. For example, in describing the beginning phase of treatment, should we write only about how to deal with feelings or, more generally, about the various issues involved in beginning a course of treatment? We decided to include some of our basic assumptions about each area, but to concentrate on the unique perspectives we have about working with feelings. In other words, we spent most of our time writing about our particular slant on these topics, rather than repeating generally known facts or widely shared beliefs.

We hope this book conveys something of the excitement we feel as we learn more about intense feeling-expression and as we seek to find the most useful integration of feeling, insight, and behavior in psychotherapy. If we succeed in making the treatment of emotional problems even a little more emotional, we will be pleased.

Part I

INTRODUCTION:
THEORY,
HISTORY AND TECHNIQUES.

Feeling-Expression:
What It Is
and What It Does

Funny about feelings, they seem to come and go in a flash yet outlast metal.

John Updike
Rabbit Is Rich

People feel, think and behave. Most psychotherapies focus on one of these functions and give less importance to the other two. Even therapy systems that attempt to integrate all three seldom do so successfully. We believe that most mainstream therapies have sought an integration with too little attention to the role of feeling-expression. This chapter shows how emotional expression leads to personal change. To understand this process, however, we must first examine the widespread tendency in our culture to inhibit the expression of feelings.

CULTURAL INHIBITIONS OF FEELING-EXPRESSION

Emotional suppression is everywhere. Because people do not want to feel pain, many give up feeling anything. In the most dramatic cases, emotional suppression is easily recognized. The obsessive-compulsive person's colorless life is an example of what happens when one gives up joy to avoid the risk of pain. While the lack of feeling in the obsessive is obvious, it is only an extreme version of a universal fear of strong feelings.

The social groups we live in—family, friends, work groups, and neighborhoods—make frequent demands on us to curb feeling-expression. These demands, rational and irrational, are frequent, at times subtle and often extremely persuasive. Growing children learn under what circumstances feelings can be expressed fully, covertly, or not at all. Even the freest children quickly learn that many feelings must be at least partially suppressed. For example, if a child gets angry and begins to yell in a supermarket, her parents are liable to become extremely embarrassed. Other customers are likely to be anxious in the face of so much rage. In most cases, parents will forcibly stop the child from yelling. Few will be so composed as to explain, "I need you to stop yelling. Feel angry if you want but don't show it." Fewer still will think of suggesting an alternate expression of anger, such as "Show me a mad face" or "Look mean at the faces on the cereal boxes." A more likely response will be, "Be quiet!" or "Shut up!" In giving such a response, the parents seek to control their child's *actions* by blocking or distorting the child's *feelings*. Parents who are estranged from their own feelings cannot make this discrimination and so play a role in the emotional blunting of their children. This blunting and distortion does not happen all at once or in a few traumatic scenes. It happens slowly as children grow up and learn to expect punishment for expressing feelings. In response, they suppress and distort their emotional experience to avoid painful criticism. The price they pay is losing touch with what they feel.

Some indictments of parents for interfering with their children's feelings probably make matters worse. Often parents who are unable to differentiate between accepting their children's feelings and giving in to their whims give in repeatedly until they exhaust even their ability to listen empathically. Many critics of child-rearing practices imply that it is wrong for parents to try to control their children. Such critics equate controlling children with suppressing their feelings. Nothing could be further from the truth. Once parents are able to control their children's behavior sufficiently, they can be more attentive to, and accepting of, their children's feelings.

When they express feelings, children are asking both to be understood and to be allowed to do something. A common arena in which the struggle between parents and children takes place is bedtime.

Daddy: It's time for bed.
Child: I don't want to go to bed. I'm not tired.

The parents may have decided that their need for privacy in the evening is more important than their child's wish to stay up until she is tired. If they respond by accepting the feelings while maintaining firm control over the actions, this need not become a problem. "I understand that you are not tired, but you still have to go to bed." Problems arise when parents feel threatened or unable to establish firm control. Unless a three-year-old has very big muscles from lifting blocks all day, most parents will be able to make her go to bed on time. If so, it will not be necessary to argue that a small child feels something she does not feel (tired) in order to get her to do something she does not want to do (go to bed). This is also good training for adult behavior: "I can feel whatever I want, but I can behave only in certain ways. I do not have to control my behavior by fooling myself about what I feel."

Unhappily, children who are punished or ignored when they express what they feel, conceal and submerge their feelings. Eventually they do not even recognize them. Instead, they feel only the residues of suppression: boredom, anxiety, and apathy. Furthermore, when parents yell at their children, the children develop the idea that their feelings and impulses, and thus they themselves are not acceptable. ("If Daddy yells at me, I must be bad for wanting to stay up late.")

Emotional suppression is only half of the problem; the other half is that mystifying web of rules about what *can* be expressed and how. For example, a child could easily learn the following:

If I yell in the store, I'll get hit; if I stop yelling, I'll get a cookie; but if I don't yell at all, I won't get a cookie.

When I play with my wee-wee, my mother pushes my hand away, my father doesn't notice, and my brother laughs.

When I'm afraid, my mother is nice and holds me, but my father gets mad and says, "Cut it out!"

When I'm mad, they tell me I'm really tired; when I'm sad they say I must be hungry and offer me food.

Unfortunately, only the most clear-headed child would actually see these things so clearly. Mystification usually occurs more subtly; it is the inability to stand back and look at the process which makes it both so compelling and so hard to change. It often takes adults a long time to rediscover when they are really hungry and when they are not hungry but feel driven to eat by anger, sadness, or loneliness. There are many similar distorted expressions of feeling that must be unlearned. What feels like sexiness is sometimes a wish to be touched. What feels like fear may in fact be anger.

When feelings are suppressed, they are mislabeled, denied, and masked, only to reappear as illness, fatigue, deadness, or argumentativeness. To make matters worse, true feelings (e.g., anger, sadness) are frequently confused with what might better be called appetites (e.g., hunger, sexiness). Since the word "feel" is used for both ("I feel sexy"; "I feel sad") our language, too, conspires in our mystification.

CATHARSIS

Many writers agree that emotional suppression and mystification are widespread, but few accept the idea that catharsis provides definitive leverage to reverse this pattern. Catharsis is most commonly described as a trivial and incidental feature of psychotherapy—hardly a sufficient force around which to build a powerful form of treatment (Patterson, 1966; Wolberg, 1977).

One reason for underestimating the value of catharsis is that many writers use the word very loosely to mean simply speaking freely and with some feeling. When Freud (Breuer and Freud, 1957) wrote about catharsis, he referred to *vigorous expression of feelings* about *experiences which had been previously unavailable to awareness.* Thus, there were two central components to catharsis: recall of repressed material and strong expression of feeling. Some writers (e.g., Nichols and Zax, 1977) still reserve the word for its original meaning—vigorous expression of feelings about repressed events—but many use the term to mean simply speaking freely, without any implication of vigorous expression of feelings or recall of repressed experiences.

Thus, "catharsis" is either a relatively insignificant feature of psychotherapy or a powerful agent of significant personality change, depending upon whether one is referring to just talking spontaneously about experiences with some feeling, or engaging in prolonged and intense expression of affect about events near the margin of awareness. One reason that this distinction has been blurred is that many traditional psychotherapists do not make interventions that produce intense feeling-expression; therefore their evaluations of catharsis are likely to refer simply to nondirected talking.

In feeling-expressive therapy, we provide both types of "catharsis": the spontaneous talk about feelings that occurs in almost any therapy and the intense affective release that occurs only with a concerted effort. (We shall reserve the term "catharsis" for the latter.) Although the benefits of simply speaking freely about feelings are less than those of strong emotional release, it is important to encourage the former before pressing for the latter.

WHAT FEELINGS ARE AND ARE NOT

Most discussions of catharsis are muddled by unclear thinking about the nature of emotions. When psychotherapists write about feelings, they usually resort to metaphor and analogy; their discussions tend to revolve around the idea that unexpressed feelings "build up" inside and need to be "gotten out." This explanation is predicated on the assumption that repressed affects are accumulated and stored, and must be drained or harm will result. Critics of cathartic therapy use exaggerated versions of this metaphoric description to ridicule catharsis while proponents use similar but more appealing versions of the same metaphor to support cathartic therapy. In fact, the idea that emotions are stored and should be discharged is based on a common but misleading notion of what emotions are.

Implicit in most discussions of emotions is the idea that they are concrete entities capable of being stored and requiring a container (Ayer, 1946; Shafer, 1976). Thus, people say that anger is "kept inside," "let out," or "discharged." Likewise, it may be said that "primal pain" is stored from early childhood until it is finally released many years later. This hydraulic model (variously known as the "hydrolic," "pimple," or "toxic chemical dump" model) would not be so widely used if it did not capture something real in people's experience. It has some problems, however. One is that such descriptions legitimize psychoanalytic metaphors of inner and outer space, and tend to portray people as passive recipients of their feelings. When people are said to "struggle with their feelings," it seems that the feelings are somehow outside or inside them, but not of them.

A brief clinical vignette illustrates how commonly and unthinkingly we treat emotions as objects.

Shortly after the birth of their second child, Mr. Jones's wife died. This tragedy was such a great shock to him that he could not accept it. So he repressed his grief (and anger at being abandoned) and kept his feelings buried deep inside. During the ten years since her death, Mr. Jones had been able to function, but he had been listless and unhappy. Finally, he sought psychotherapy. After several sessions, the long-buried grief welled up to the surface and he was finally able to discharge it. He cried and cried until he finally cried himself out. Following this discharge of his grief, the anger emerged and that too was discharged.

In the description above, Mr. Jones's grief is said to have been repressed, stored, and finally ventilated. But if it was stored, where was it stored? Where did it go when it was discharged? What was left? These questions seem absurd, because when we ask them we realize that, unlike objects, feelings cannot be stored or discharged. The questions, which are predicated on the metaphoric way we speak about catharsis, point up the fallacy in the usual description.

Emotions are not things, but abstract labels for a series of actions and processes. Mr. Jones's "grief" is a lable for a series of actions: thinking about the loss of his wife and the prospect of being alone, crying, and remembering some of the joyful times that he shared with his wife. These actions are all part of a sequence that is expected to follow the death of someone close. If they do not occur, we assume that the natural sequence has been blocked and must be unblocked or harm will result.

If feelings are not concrete things, cannot be said to be inside or outside, and cannot be accumulated or saved up, then what is the function of cartharsis? What does it do? *Catharsis is the completion of an interrupted emotional action sequence.* It is remembering something with feeling and carrying out the expressive actions that are part of what is meant by "having feelings." We can now describe the catharsis of Mr. Jones's grief as follows. When his wife died, he avoided thinking about it and thus avoided realizing the full significance of his loss. Furthermore, by not focusing on what had happened and by holding back his tears, Mr. Jones remained preoccupied with his wife's death. "Not feeling" is a way of experiencing—of being resistant, of avoiding and denying. Since one tends to think about important events, it takes a great deal of energy to avoid thinking about them. Thus, ironically, Mr. Jones was stuck with a past he didn't want to accept. Unwilling to face the painful fact of his wife's death, he was unable to let go of the past and therefore too preoccupied to take hold of life in the present.

With the encouragement and support of his therapist, he was able to face the reality of his loss. As he remembered what happened and thought about his loss and how much he loved his wife, he experienced strong feelings. He cried, not because he was getting rid of stored feelings, but because people cry when they think about the loss of love unless they somehow defend themselves. In Mr. Jones's case, he had defended himself from crying or thinking about this wife's death until he entered therapy. The event was old. It was not the feelings, but the memory, that was stored. Feelings only seem to be stored because they are elicited as memories are recalled.

Catharsis does not mean uncovering and discharging quantities of psychic energy; it means remembering something with feeling and vigorously carrying out the bodily actions that express that feeling. Understanding catharsis in this way—as part of a natural action sequence—is an important first step in explaining how it may be therapeutic. Catharsis is useful because it helps people reevaluate early painful experiences and view them more accurately. It also helps change maladaptive habits of emotional restraint. Without facing the reality of events from the past, one cannot let go of them; without beoming more feelingful, one cannot take hold of life in the present.

VARIETIES OF FEELING-EXPRESSION—BARBARA

There are many kinds of feeling. In the case below, we will see a complete feeling-expressive sequence. In addition, there are various incomplete forms of feeling-expression: partial feelings, transitional feelings, blocked feelings, instrumental feelings, and patterned feelings. We will examine each of these in this section.

Barbara came for help as her marriage was ending. During the first six months of treatment, she explored and expressed anger toward her husband and fear of being alone. Gradually she realized that these feelings stemmed more from her early life with her parents than from her husband. About eight months into her therapy, her mother died. For several months, she explored her feelings of loss and dependency—feelings that had been prominent in her therapy prior to her mother's death.

At the start of one session during this period, Barbara came in and sat on the mat—a sign that she wanted to get right to work. She said that she had awakened that morning feeling unhappy and discontent with her life. She had gone shopping at the public market, an activity she normally enjoyed, but had been uninterested in buying food. During breakfast, her lover had said warm things to her and she had started to cry. She was clearly hurting as she retold these things. She said she missed her mother, but when she started to cry, she quickly stopped herself.

Barbara: I'm not feeling that good about myself these days. I keep wondering if you're thinking critical thoughts about me. (Pause, then somewhat angrily.) If you could just say something reassuring to me, that would help!

Therapist: What would you like to hear from me?

Barbara: That you like me, that you like working with me. (Pause.) That you think I'm handling my grief very well. (Starting to cry.) That you think I'm doing well. (Crying harder.) That I'm doing well! (Barbara has been rubbing her head with her hand. She's crying fairly hard now, but not sobbing.)

Therapist: What's your left hand doing?

Barbara: (Still rubbing her head.) It's loving me! It's saying, "I'm doing well." (Barbara cries for a minute or two and slowly stops, sits quietly for 30 seconds or so and looks up.)

Therapist: What's up?

Barbara: I distracted myself. I started thinking about junk.

Therapist: What junk?

Barbara: Oh, what I'll do when I leave here, and about your bill. It's high this month.

Therapist: (Teasingly.) Hope you're getting your money's worth.

Barbara: (Suddenly angry.) I'm not today! I ask you for some reassurance and I get shit! "Reassure yourself," you tell me. Bunch of shit! (Reaching back and hitting the mat behind her vigorously and with both arms alternately.) Goddamn it! That's not what I wanted. It's not what I wanted!

Barbara hit for a minute or two, then got swept up in her flailing at the mat with her fists, kicking her feet, and yelling. Some of her vocalizations were words ("That's *not* what I want!") and some were angry shouts and growls not formed into words. She tired physically but was still angry. She rested her arms but kicked her feet. Then she stopped moving but continued to yell, roll from side to side, and hit the mat occasionally. Her eyes were closed during most of this. Her anger no longer seemed to be focused on the therapist.

Therapist: What's going on?

Barbara: (Still angry.) That's just the way *she* was. She was there most of the time, but when I needed her most, she wasn't there. Everybody said she was so good. I couldn't criticize her. When she wasn't there, I didn't even think "Where are you?" I just tuned out and got depressed. (Speaking rapidly.) I literally didn't know what hit me. (Pause.) I know what hit me! You did! (Talking to her mother.) With your goodness and all your compassion, where were you when I came home from camp? Off at some goddamn meeting saving the world! What about me? You sent me away for the whole summer and you weren't even there when I got home! (Rising tone, very angry, hitting the mat, kicking, yelling). You weren't even there when I got home! You weren't there! Aunt Louise was there. That was supposed to make it all right. Well, it didn't! Where were you? (Now Barbara begins to cry and then sob. She continues to hit the mat, but more slowly, softly and aimlessly.) Where were you? Oh Shit!

Barbara cried for 5 to 10 minutes, saying only a few words: "Ohhh!" "I wanted you." "Where were you?" She was still lying on her back on the mat. She stopped gradually, sobbing less, crying softly. She opened her eyes, looked at her therapist, and said, "Hi." The tempo in the next exchange was much slower and quieter—the calm after the storm.

Therapist: "Hi." (Pause.)

Barbara: Jeeze. (Pause.)

Therapist: What?

Barbara: I sure was mad at her.

Therapist: Mm-hm.

Barbara: I didn't know I needed her so much . . . that I actually hurt so much about the time she wasn't there. . . . I guess the message was, "How could you find fault with your mother? Everybody knows how good she is." (Pause.) And she was, too, in lots of ways.

Therapist: If she hadn't been, you probably wouldn't miss her so much.

Barbara: Yeah. I guess so. (Starts crying again softly.) Boy, I do miss her. I can't get used to the idea that she's gone. She's just not here anymore. She's not in the hospital, she's not in Westfield, she's not in her house. She's not really in the cemetary. Just gone. (Pause. Then to the therapist.) I was pretty pissed at you for awhile! (Laughing.) Looks like you survived.

Therapist: Yeah. (Pause.) So my not giving you what you wanted brought you right back to the old days.

Barbara: Yeah, and more so probably cause you both [therapist and mother] did give me what I wanted most of the time. It's like a shock. (Pause.) Sounds like I have it in me to get very mad at people who take pretty good care of me most of the time—like you and her. That could be tough on those closest to me. Brian [Barbara's boyfriend] said something like that to me yesterday. He said most of the time I love him well, am appreciative of him, and everything, but then suddenly I'll fly off the handle and act like he was this big disappointment. (Pause.) Sounds like maybe I've got a little mother stuff with him.

Therapist: Could be. (Lightly.) Next time you're mad at him, you could explain that it's only 'cause he loves you so well that you get so mad. He's part of a very exclusive club.

Barbara: Right. "You only hurt the one you love." Lucky him!

Therapist: He is lucky. You have a lot to give.

The therapist then said that it was time to stop. They made an appointment and hugged goodbye.

This session was noteworthy for its completeness: it represented a full cycle of therapeutic work. Such a cycle sometimes is completed in a single session but more often spreads over several sessions. The following factors made this session complete:

1. Barbara was aware of, and reported, feelings she was having in her present life outside of therapy.

2. She reported and expressed thoughts and feelings about the therapist.

3. Full expression of her feelings toward the therapist brought her to early experiences in her life when she had had similar feelings.

4. She continued to express her feelings fully as her mother became the object of the feelings.

5. She had a specific memory of a time she had felt these feelings previously.

6. As she expressed her feelings, they shifted (in this case, from anger to sadness). Such a shift often occurs in a completed feeling cycle.

7. She returned her attention to the present, felt better, and had some awareness of the therapist ("Looks like you survived") and of her present real situation.

8. She applied her feeling experience to her present life outside of therapy, saw how her childhood hurt could be affecting her present relationships negatively, and looked at how she could change that.

In contrast to this example of a complete feeling-expressive cycle, the following are common sorts of expression that are not complete.

Partial Feelings

Partial feelings are extremely common and often useful. They are even evident in the complete feeling cycle described above.

For example: when Barbara started to cry and then stopped herself, or when she distracted herself by thinking about "junk," she was having partial feelings. Partial feelings may serve as transitions toward full feelings or they may block full feelings. Even seemingly vigorous feeling-expression may be a defense against some other feeling that is more difficult to accept.

Transitional feelings are one class of partial feelings; they lead to other more complete feelings. For example: Duncan frequently yawned in therapy as he started to talk about personally important matters. Soon he was feeling more fully. Then, near the end of his hour, as he stopped, the yawns would return. For him, yawning seemed to be a natural transition into and out of his feelings. Paul, however, talked and yawned all through his sessions, never getting to more complete levels of feeling-expression. For Duncan yawning was a transitional feeling. For Paul it was not.

Another sort of transitional feeling occurs in relation to sadness. For most people, full expression of sadness entails weeping, sobbing, and sometimes wailing. Few adults, however, can cry as freely as when they were children. It has been trained out of them. What is left may be a halting trickle of tears and a feeling of sadness. If the rest of the sequence follows, that soft moment is a transitional feeling. Frequently, however, the rest of the sequence is aborted. Clients may start to cry, but tense up and resist or stop breathing, interrupting the sequence. A partial feeling is "transitional" if it leads to the expression of a more complete feeling. We say a partial feeling is "blocked" if it does not lead to a more complete feeling-expression.

At other times, partial feelings result from a confluence of two or more feelings which, like cars at a busy intersection, get in each other's way. Sometimes people can fully express one feeling and then shift to another: For example, they may suddenly shift from sadness to anger, yet they experience both feelings fully. At other times, however, feelings block each other. For example, people are sometimes sad, angry, and afraid all at once. They sit all huddled up, shoulders forward, and cry with a depressed, peevish, "poor me" sound. The result is that none of the feelings—fear, sadness, or anger—is fully expressed.[1] The following example illustrates how mixed feelings can block each other.

---

[1]Partial feelings that result simply from a mixture of several feelings must be distinguished from *instrumental feelings*, which are neither expressive nor therapeutic. For a detailed discussion of the latter, see the next section of this chapter.

In his first 15 months in therapy, Chris worked well and made good progress on many of his goals. Recently, he and his therapist decided that he was still more fearful and hesitant than he would like to be. They decided to focus on this issue. Chris role-played angry and confrontive scenes in his sessions, and kept a log of his experiences of telling people things that he thought they might not like to hear. He pushed himself to be blunter in saying what he thought without the usual censoring and trying to be a "nice guy."

In one session when Chris and his therapist were discussing who was frightening to confront, they got around to what Chris might have to say to his therapist. The thrust of his complaint was familiar—that the therapist did not give him enough love and attention. Although he tried to speak forcefully, there was a pleading tone in his voice. It seemed to say, "Please give me more" rather than "Goddamn it, I'm mad that you haven't given me more!" After the therapist pointed this out, the pleading stopped and Chris *sounded* more assertive. However, he expressed his fear in his facial expression—specifically, through raised eyebrows that gave his face a questioning, deferential, fearful look. It was as though the frightened part of him had migrated from his voice to his eyebrows and was waving his eyebrows like white surrender flags. "Don't pay attention to my angry voice, I'm not really mad. Please don't get mad at me."

Seeing this, the therapist said, "Keep talking the same way, but keep your eyebrows down."

The eyebrows kept waving. Chris was only vaguely aware of when his eyebrows went up.

Therapist: All right. I have here in my desk a little biofeedback machine.
Chris: What's that?
Therapist: Scotch tape.

The therapist ran a strip of Scotch tape diagonally from above Chris's left eyebrow to his cheek and another to his nose. Since the two eyebrows had been moving up and down in unison, the therapist taped only one eye. This kept Chris's eyebrows down and made his anger more believable. In less than five minutes, however, Chris learned to raise his right eyebrow while leaving his left one taped down. His therapist then taped the right one as well, and in the next few minutes, Chris's anger became stronger and clearer. There did not seem to be any way in which Chris's fear was blocking his anger. His eyes were very intense and clearly angry. His voice broke with a little sob and then he went back to strong anger. His voice broke again.

Therapist: What's up?
Chris: I'm seeing my parents. I wish they could have given me more.

Chris cried for a few minutes, but it was almost time to stop, so the therapist did not encourage him to go on. As Chris stopped crying, they talked for a few minutes about how the session went. They agreed that anger was the hardest feeling for Chris to accept, that sadness and fear had been worked on a good deal previously, and that the focus should be kept on assertiveness outside of sessions and direct, nonfearful expression of anger in therapy sessions.

In this session, there were at least four instances in which one feeling blocked another. First, Chris's pleading tone, a partial expression of both need and fear, blocked his anger. Later, his raised eyebrows partially expressed his fear and blocked his anger. The same was true when his right eyebrow declared independence of his left and rose by itself. In the fourth case, sadness invaded his anger as he started to cry about the love he had not gotten from his parents. In this last instance, it is more difficult to decide whether the surge of sadness should be regarded as defensive—a way to avoid expressing the anger fully—or as a flowing from one feeling to another. Although the sadness sounded both real and intense, one tends to be suspicious when, as in this case, a series of defenses has already blocked the expression of an unwelcome—and, to Chris, uncommon—emotion.

In this session, we can see clearly how one feeling can be used to block another. With an experienced client like Chris, it may be wise to focus for awhile on the feeling that is most troublesome for him. Clients with less fluency in getting to and expressing their feelings will probably profit more from a laissez faire approach in which almost any feeling expression, however partial is accepted and welcomed. This is particularly true at the beginning of therapy as we see in the following example.

When Steven began therapy, he was quiet and passively angry, sitting for long periods without talking. What he did say made it clear that there was a part of him that very much wanted something better for himself. Part way through his third session, he said some particularly hopeless things about how he would not be able to change in therapy and his life would continue to be empty and pointless. Steven's therapist pointed out that they had been doing well a few minutes earlier; then suddenly Steven had lapsed into depression and hopelessness. As they talked, it developed that Steven felt let down by a therapist he had seen previously and by his parents who always seemed to be in a separate world from each other and from him. Steven said he was afraid that his present therapist would also disappoint him. The therapist told him that if he could express his anger, he would not need to be hopeless and depressed.

Steven: Stop bugging me about it. It won't make any difference.
Therapist: Yes, it will. (Silence.)

> *Therapist:* Like right now, you're having angry thoughts about me.
> *Steven:* No, I'm not. (Pause.) I wouldn't be, if you'd get off my back.
> *Therapist:* OK. So you want me to get off your back. Tell me so.
> *Steven:* (Woodenly and unconvincingly.) Get off my back.

The therapist chose not to comment on the negativism in the empty compliance, but rather, to take Steven at face value and work with the statement. With a more experienced client who clearly could do better, a more confrontive response would be appropriate.

> *Therapist:* Say it again. Let's hear the anger.
> *Steven:* (With somewhat more feeling.) Get off my back.
> *Therapist:* Good. Look at me and say it again.
> *Steven:* (Looks at therapist.) Get off my back. (Then in a conversational tone.) This won't do any good.
> *Therapist:* Express that anger and you won't have to feel helpless. This time show me real slowly with your fists where you'd like to hit me.
> *Steven:* That won't do any good.
> *Therapist:* It won't really knock me out, if that's what you mean. But it could help you feel your anger.

At this point, the therapist showed Steven how to swing very slowly with his fist and feel it land on the therapist's chin. The therapist also showed Steven how to hit the pillow hard with his fists. They worked with these motor channels and the therapist urged Steven to shout at him and look at him. They gradually arrived at the following exchange:

> *Steven:* You piss me off! I don't have to do what you say.
> *Therapist:* Try just hitting the pillow and saying "no."
> *Steven:* (Hits pillow.) No!
> *Therapist:* Good. Do it again.
> *Steven:* (Hits pillow.) No! No!
> *Therapist:* Three times without me telling you to.
> *Steven:* (Hits pillow each time.) No! No! No!

This is not the kind of self-directed work that more sophisticated or experienced clients do, but it is occasionally needed. The feelings expressed are partial feelings, and the anger being worked on is also the cause of the passive resistance. So it is a kind of bootstrap operation. Partial feelings are sometimes all that is available and so must be used.

Instrumental Feelings *and* Patterned Feelings

In contrast to the partial feelings discussed above, instrumental and patterned feelings are neither truly cathartic nor therapeutically useful. Instrumental feelings are not communicated to express something, but to get something. The expression of feeling is instrumental to the pursuit of some other goal. If someone sees a mouse and says, "Oh, the mouse scared me!", he is primarily expressing his feeling of fear. If instead he says, "I'm afraid there's a mouse in the kitchen. Would you please bring me a cup of tea?", he is using his fear to get the other person to bring him tea. While there is nothing wrong with this, it is not the healing sort of feeling-expression we have been talking about throughout this chapter. We all display emotion at times to get what we want from people. The problem with this instrumental use of feelings is that it can subvert the expressive use of feelings. Two examples of instrumental feelings in psychotherapy sessions follow:

John had read about feeling-expressive therapy; he knew what he was "supposed to feel." In his first few sessions, he pretended to feel very angry and very sad. He raged and hollered, but his feelings were not connected to the sounds he made. His motivation was not really to express his feelings, but to have the therapist approve of him.

Julia was overweight and had an agreement with her therapist to diet. Frequently, however, when her therapist asked her what she weighed, Julia put her head down and cried. When her therapist continued to press the point, Julia cried harder, or got angry, glared at the therapist, shook her fists, and said, "Stop it! Stop it!"

Julia's feelings were somewhat more connected and more real than John's, but they were also instrumental. She was crying and raging in order to get the therapist to stop confronting her about her weight. We believe that this type of feeling-expression is not helpful in creating personal change (although it may be helpful in getting other people to change *their* behavior).

The examples of John and Julia are clear-cut instances of feelings being used instrumentally rather than expressively. While not useful as feeling-expression, they are, of course, perfectly fine places to begin finding out what feelings drive John's need for acceptance or Julia's need to be filled up or armored with a layer of fat. Reality is more continuous than categorical, and useful feeling-expression often has instrumental aspects (e.g., clients are partly motivated to be "good," get A's, or prove the therapist wrong). Therapists differ with respect to their willingness to tolerate instrumental undertones in a client's feeling-expression. Regardless of where the line is drawn, we believe there are some sorts of "feeling-expression" in which the instrumental aspect is so predominant that the possibility of deriving any benefit from them has been lost and interruption is mandatory.

The second type of expression that appears to be emotive but is not useful for personal change is "patterned" feeling. This term was coined by Jackins (1965) to describe rigid, highly repetitive behavior that seems to be an endless reiteration of early family interactions; it functions as a chronic defense against a genuine, spontaneous emotional response. The expression of patterned feelings does not help people change or even feel better in more than a very transitory way.

Patterned feelings are illustrated in the following examples.

In therapy and out Doug responded angrily to a wide range of emotionally stimulating situations. Whether it was a loss of someone close to him, trouble at work, or a near accident in traffic, Doug's response was to rage and blame others. Someone was always trying to do him in and he was not going to stand for it! Superficially, this might look like feeling-expression, but it was not. It was Doug at age thirty-three imitating the father he had had when he was four. What, at four, was a reasonable effort to adapt to difficult surroundings had become a patterned, self-defeating reaction that made it hard for Doug to experience the world accurately or to respond to it flexibly. In therapy, Doug blamed and raged at his therapist. At home, his wife was the object of his tirades. His real feelings could be experienced only if he gave up that patterned anger.

Ruth was constantly afraid. She lived a constricted life with little human contact. Her job, occasional meetings with a friend, and family gatherings provided her only opportunities to be with people. Even minor efforts toward a more social way of life were soon aborted due to "fear." She had had models of fear-ridden lives in both parents. While she could sit in a therapy session and tremble and sweat with fear—and had done so for many hours—this "expression" of her fear did not help her change.

The implication of these examples is that patterned feelings are characterological defenses—pseudofeeling states embedded in a life style devoted to the acting out of a feeling. While this is often the case, it is not always so. Patterned feelings can also be less pervasive, occurring only in certain circumstances. For example, some people may smile when they are angry and have the sense that they "can't help it." The angrier they feel, the broader their smile. Other people may cry and seem to feel sad when others yell at or criticize them. Such patterned feelings are less embedded in an entire way of life than is the case with Doug and Ruth.

LETTING GO

We believe that much of what happens in good psychotherapy can be described as a paradoxical process of letting go and taking hold. In this section, we will show how the therapy process encourages the client to let go of certain beliefs and emotional baggage.

Most people have a hard time letting go of their past because they struggle to resist its influence and are reluctant to view their family history as it really was. Paradoxically, the first steps in letting go of the past involve returning to it, cognitively and emotionally.

The most obvious way to "return to the past" cognitively is simply to remember and discuss it. This occurs in most long-term reconstructive therapies. However, remembering often yields summary descriptions colored and biased by ready-made theories rather than experiential exploration of visceral attitudes and feelings. Regression may facilitate more vivid uncovering and exploration by helping clients to loosen habitual patterns of control. Regression is an important ingredient in most long-term therapies and it can be enhanced in cathartic therapy.

Several of the British analysts have written about the therapeutic value of regression. Donald Winnicott (1958) stressed the importance of giving up the "false-self system," and Harry Guntrip (1969) wrote that it is not possible to become fully adult without letting go of the "pseudoadult self." These and other writers have recognized that most of us spend a fair amount of time denying and suppressing some of our childish needs and feelings. One example is the longing for dependency which is often highlighted in the psychotherapeutic relationship. In the extreme, clients may express their longing for dependency directly or sense but reject it and behave almost belligerently independent and self-reliant. Those in the first group ask the therapist to tell them what to do and take care of them. They may ask for frequent sessions and solicit reassurance from the therapist, whom they hope will be a good, nurturing parent. Those who reject their dependency needs may inquire frequently about the therapist's feelings or health, emphasize their independence and strength, and complain that it would be better to relate more as friends than as "doctor and patient." One such counterdependent client surprised his therapist by beginning his first session with a hearty, "How ya doin', kid?"

The first step in dealing with the longing for dependency is to recognize it and the defenses against it, and to bring these to the client's attention. In feeling-expressive therapy, we help clients to acknowledge these longings, express them energetically, and use this expression as a bridge to the past. The following two examples illustrate this process with a client whose wish for dependency is relatively direct and with one who stubbornly denies these longings.

Peter, a 30-year-old businessman, came to treatment seeking relief from anxiety and loneliness. Although he held a responsible position and was nearly the same age as his therapist, he quickly began treating the therapist as a powerful authority figure. In the first and second sessions, both his dependent wishes and his defenses against them were evident at various points. Peter and his therapist agreed that this was an area of conflict for him which should be a focus of their work together. At the start of the third session, Peter spoke in a somewhat complaining tone about the burdens of his job and home life, and his wish for help. He said that he felt badly about himself for not being more competent at handling his problems without help and that he would do whatever the therapist directed him to do. "Just tell me what to do; I need some help."

Recognizing in the process as well as the content of these communications Peter's wish to be taken care of, the therapist encouraged Peter to ask for help.

> *Therapist:* Ask me to help you.
> *Peter:* Please help me! I need help.
> *Therapist:* That's right, say it again.
> *Peter:* Help me! Please! Help me!

Over a period of several minutes, Peter's voice got louder, more insistent, and then more overtly needy. Through the rest of the session, Peter continued to express his wish for help from his therapist, sometimes just talking about the kind of help he would like and other times feeling how nice that would be, or how sad or mad he was that he did not have that help. He cried freely about his wish for "parenting" but did not discuss his parents. His entire focus was on the present.

In the next session, Peter again began by asking for help and direction, and the therapist again encouraged vivid and childlike expression of these wishes. Feeling that it was time to look for antecedents, the therapist asked Peter, "Who do I remind you of?"

Peter looked puzzled and then thoughtful. "No one. My father never helped me; he wouldn't tell me anything. . . . He was never home." But as Peter talked about his father, he slowly became sad and tearful. He recalled his lonely childhood and how seldom his father had been with him when he was small. When Peter tried to change the subject his therapist kept his feet to the fire saying "Go back to how he hurt you. Tell me about him not being there."

Peter remembered a late Fall day when he had sat cold and alone in the car waiting for his father to return from "doing a couple of errands." He felt his loneliness keenly and cried hard as he recalled and relived that time. He saw himself clearly in that memory, expressed fully the feelings he had not expressed then, and was able to see how that memory and many similar experiences set the stage for his present desperate feelings of needing help.

This is a different order of experiencing from a verbal report of having been hurt as a child or a summary statement that "my father wasn't around much." Peter's expression was, in part, a preverbal communication with powerful associations to childhood. By crying, he said, in effect, "When I was a little child, I was badly hurt. When I cry, I feel like that child again, and I can remember and admit the hurt." This example from Peter's therapy shows clearly how regression, a staple of many long-term therapies aiming at basic character change, is enhanced by catharsis.

Karl, a 42-year-old college professor, came to therapy quite depressed following the breakup of a love affair. Because of the intensity of his depression, Karl recognized that he needed treatment, but because he feared his dependent feelings, it was very difficult for him to permit the therapist to assume the stance of caregiver. For example, Karl was very solicitous about the therapist's state of mind before each session. He habitually greeted her with questions such as, "And how are *you* today?" When seeing another client leave with eyes red from crying, he commented about how difficult her job must be and how he hoped she had someone to talk to. He also found it hard to engage in role-playing and other dramatic aspects of feeling-expressive therapy because of his fear of giving way to his feelings. He asked the therapist to explain her theories. When she did so, he asked many challenging and probing questions, constantly testing to see if she was intelligent, strong, and happy enough for him to risk trusting her to take care of him.

The therapist understood that all of these maneuvers reflected Karl's fear of letting anyone take care of him. One day she demonstrated this and helped Karl really to feel it in the following way: When Karl asked her how she was feeling, she said that she was certainly glad he had asked because as a matter of fact she wasn't feeling well and was glad to know that someone cared enough to ask. As she said this, she got up, motioned to Karl to sit in her seat, and took his seat. Still talking, she began a recitation of her pains and troubles, interjecting occasionally how good it was to have someone who would listen. At first, Karl warmed to the task, feeling more relaxed and comfortable asking about her problems than he did telling of his own. After a few minutes, he tired of this exercise, however (a clue that they were on the right track), and asked if they could stop.

To Karl's surprise, the therapist said, "No! Stay with it. You're always asking me how I am. I'm telling you. See what that feels like." She then continued to complain and tell stories about how difficult her life was.

As this continued, Karl came to see clearly how his taking care of others kept him from feeling his own strong needs to be cared for and he felt how empty and isolated that left him. "OK, OK, let's stop!" It was painful for Karl to experience his inability to let others care for him.

The therapist knew that this understanding was not enough. It needed to be connected with memories about how the process started. So she said, "Remember when you were little? Who made you the little man of the house? When you were scared, when you needed help, who was there for you?"

Slowly, softly, Karl began to cry. The therapist reached out and took his hand. When she did, Karl could really let himself feel that he was being cared for, and he cried hard, remembering several incidents when, as the oldest child, he was moved away from an awareness of his own needs for comforting toward a pseudoadult expression of concern for others.

With Karl, as with Peter, emotional expression aided the regression. Although each started with a different stance about dependency, they both moved forward in therapy as a result of contacting their dependency feelings through catharsis.

Letting go also means giving up control. This is an important but easily misunderstood concept. To begin with, we do not mean yelling at people any time one feels like it, sobbing in public places, hitting people, or breaking things. We do mean that in therapy it is often useful to follow the flow of feelings and give full expression to them. Perhaps a better way to think of it is letting go of the fear of losing control. A flexible control allows strong emotional expression within appropriate contexts and limits such expression where it is not appropriate. We seek to teach such control to our clients as we encourage them to let go of the rigid, fearful overcontrol that robs them of feeling and spontaneity.

One of the most bizarre forms of psychopathology, catatonic schizophrenia, is a grotesque caricature of overcontrol. More mundane and typical examples of the harmful effects of the fear of losing control include being unable to have orgasm, never being playful, and obsessive worrying.

The fear of losing control is probably based on the sense that the self is not solid, competent, and acceptable. The more profound the self-doubt, the more rigid the need for control. In feeling-expressive therapy, we do not suggest that our clients go out and wreak havoc on the world by giving free vent to all of their fantasies, impulses, and wishes. (We tried that, but received too many complaints!) Instead, we help people to discover those aspects of their personalities—impulses, wishes, and feelings—that they are afraid to express and therefore exert great energy controlling. We encourage them to acknowledge those unacceptable impulses and we teach them acceptable ways to express those feelings.

Giving up control does not follow simply from passively letting clients express themselves as they usually do. For example, helping a whiney, complaining, hypochondriacal client to let go does not mean simply encouraging him to whine and complain. Doing so would only allow the usual pattern to continue and would do nothing to help him give up control. Instead, his anger must be mobilized, usually by using more active techniques such as role-playing, exaggeration, and confrontation.

People who are stuck in the past tend to react to present situations and relationships as shadowy re-enactments of past events. For example, an employee who works diligently and waits patiently to be rewarded with raises and promotions may be behaving inappropriately. Waiting patiently and being "good" may have been an effective way to deal with parents; it is usually not an effective way to deal with employers.

People are particularly prone to confuse present and past realities in situations associated with chronic conflicts or traumatic experiences. Although conflict and trauma are two distinct concepts, they are often related. The following example illustrates how a person can react to present conflict as though it were in the past.

Sarah was a psychotherapist who, despite excellent training and potential, found that many of her patients became disenchanted and dropped out of treatment after a few weeks. Although she recognized that the problem might be related to something personal, she had very little idea of what it might be, so she sought help at the Therapy Center.

It soon became apparent that Sarah responded to the anxiety of first meeting new patients by offering enthusiastic promises about how much could be accomplished. She led her clients to expect too much too soon, and most of them became disillusioned and withdrew. Such an obvious technical error was striking in the case of someone as bright and well-trained as Sarah.

Further exploration made it clear that, on the one hand, Sarah believed that she was capable of and should produce extraordinary results while, on the other hand, she felt a deep sense of inadequacy. Put another way, she was stuck with two residuals of her past: tremendously high goals and a sense of inferiority. When she met new clients, she tried to still her own doubt and fear by promising more than she or anyone could deliver. Naturally, many were let down when treatment turned out to be longer and harder than they were first led to expect.

Sarah's dilemma is illustrative of many. She did not react to people in the present (her clients) as unique, but rather, as people from her past (her parents) who demanded much of her but rejected whatever she offered.

One useful way to look at catharsis is in learning-theory terms. We can view feeling-expression as helpful in extinguishing conditioned emotional reactions that attend situations of conflict and enhancing stimulus differentiation. Traumatic experiences are associated with anxiety and lead to avoidance. Similar experiences recapitulate these reactions and, if the original anxiety was extreme, these reactions generalize to new situations that only faintly resemble the earlier trauma. The feeling-expressive therapist helps clients to remember and describe these experiences as vividly as possible. Emotional expression clarifies the memories, which ⅁ in turn stimulate more intense emotional expression. It is as though the experiences were being relived, but without the original painful consequences. With no punishment forthcoming, emotional upset, withdrawal, and avoidance begin to abate. With repetition, the conditioned emotional reaction is extinguished and the client enjoys an enhanced ability to differentiate the present from the past.

Unhappily, without such a re-educative experience, the generalized expectancy of danger is often a self-fulfilling prophecy. Because she expected her clients to demand much from her, Sarah promised much. Because she promised much, she acted as though she would fail. Then when she did not deliver and acted like a failure, her clients felt disappointed and sought help elsewhere. By helping Sarah trace the antecedents of her reactions and feel the pain of her parents' harsh expectations, her therapist helped her to distinguish events that were truly threatening (her parents' withdrawal of love and support when she was small) from those that merely restimulated her associations to earlier upsetting experiences.

TAKING HOLD

As we let go of the automatic influence of the past—as we let go of childhood's dream of endless love, and childhood's nightmare of rejection, isolation, and death—as we clear away enough emotional frost from life's windshield to have some dim awareness of who people really are, separate from who we need them to be; and as we recover our ability to feel, what then? Then we must take hold of life in the present, dealing with people as they are, not as we want or fear them to be.

What this means for the feeling-expressive therapist is that the clarity and fresh perspective following catharsis needs to be used to think about behavior. "So your mother's ignoring you when you were little made you feel terrible. What do you need to do now when your husband ignores you?" People often see only a narrow range of possibilities available to them when dealing with painful situations. By contrast, taking hold means considering a variety of choices, trying out several, and staying relaxed enough to be able to tell which ones work. Many shuttles are necessary between feeling-expression and behavior in order to let go of the pain and constriction and take hold of new, more satisfying ways of behaving. At each step, the therapist must insist that the client examine a wide range of choices, trying them out thoughtfully and evaluating them accurately.

In addition to trying out new ways of behaving, clients must give up old, nonproductive ways. Whether these old ways are as obviously destructive as drinking too much or as subtle as blaming others for one's troubles, they serve as an easy out that tends to block more thoughtful, and ultimately, more satisfying choices.

Two primarily somatic mechanisms of cathartic therapy also potentiate taking hold of life in the present. The first, tension-reduction, may take the form of crying, laughing, or shouting angrily. The Feeling Therapy group has shown that catharsis lowers various physiological measures of tension (Karle et al., 1973; Woldenberg et al., 1976). When feelings are aroused but not expressed they may lead to increased tension but full expression of feelings seems to result in tension-reduction. Still, if catharsis only produced tension-reduction there would appear to be better means: running, playing tennis, or getting drunk. It is what happens after the tension-reduction that counts: in therapy, tension-reduction counterconditions anxiety as we saw above, and helps clients think more clearly about their experience.

The second somatic mechanism of cathartic therapy may be the single most powerful therapeutic mechanism of feeling-expressive therapy: breaking down chronic habits of emotional avoidance and suppression, and helping people become more feelingful.

Since discussions of catharsis are so deeply rooted in the concept of feelings as things that get stored up, feeling-expression is often treated as an expulsive process of getting rid of feelings. We believe, however, that the *process* of emotional expression may often be of greater value than the *content* of emotional expression. It expands our range of emotional responsivity. Most of us have overdeveloped habits of automatically suppressing, rechanneling, and limiting our emotional reactions.

By expanding our capacity to feel, we automatically make it easier to take hold of our lives. Feelings help us to experience and negotiate the world. They are a signal of our needs and impulses, and an incentive which motivates us to gratify those needs and impulses. We have a better chance of meeting our needs if we know what they are.

The infant's cry arouses strong affects in the parents; sometimes nurturing, sometimes punitive. The young child soon learns which sorts of feeling-expression will be adaptive and lead to satisfying outcomes and which will not. The blocking of some feelings and the rechanneling of others are the beginning of psychological defenses, with all their advantages and disadvantages. While control and delay often enable feelings to be channeled into appropriate outlets and wishes to be gratified, defenses that are too rigid may interfere with healthy adaptation by blunting life's enjoyment or setting the stage for explosive acting out.

SUMMARY

We live in a culture that proscribes many forms of feeling-expression and our child-rearing practices often alienate people from their feelings. Catharsis is a major tool for correcting this emotional blunting and is the completion of an interrupted emotional action sequence, not the expulsion of long-buried feelings.

Illustrative material described a full feeling-expressive cycle and differentiated this from various incomplete feeling cycles. Much of what happens in good psychotherapy can be described as a process of letting go and taking hold.

Our intention in doing feeling-expressive therapy is to help clients experience and express their feelings fully while remaining aware of the social and interpersonal restraints on emotional expression. We believe people who are aware of, and live from, their feelings are better able than others to let go of past hurts, to take hold of their present opportunities, and to interact lovingly and satisfyingly with their fellow human beings.

REFERENCES

Ayer, A. J. *Language, Truth and Logic.* New York: Dover Publications, 1946.

Breuer, J. and Freud, S. *Studies in Hysteria.* New York: Basic Books, 1957.

Guntrip, H. *Schizoid Phenomena, Object Relations and the Self.* New York: International Universities Press, 1969.

Jackins, H. *The Human Side of Human Beings.* Seattle: Rational Island, 1965.

Karle, W., Corriere, R. and Hart, J. Psychophysiological changes in abreactive therapy—Study I: Primal therapy. *Psychotherapy: Theory, Research and Practice,* 1973, *10,* 117 -122.

Patterson, C. H. *Theories of Counseling and Psychotherapy.* New York: Harper & Row, 1966.

Schafer, R. *A New Language for Psychoanalysis.* New Haven: Yale University Press, 1976.

Winnicott, D. W. Metapsychological and clinical aspects of regression within the psychoanalytic set-up. *Collected Papers.* New York: Basic Books, 1958.

Wolberg, L. B. *The Technique of Psychotherapy.* New York: Grune & Stratton, 1977.

Woldenberg, L., Karle, W., Gold, S., Corriere, R., Hart, J., and Hopper, M. Psychophysiological changes in feeling therapy, *Psychological Reports,* 1976, *39,* 1059 -1062.

2

Intense Feeling-Expression in Healing and Psychotherapy

> For it is only when the detailed circumstances of the loss and the intimate particulars of the previous relationship . . . are dwelt on in consciousness that the related emotions are not only aroused and experienced but become directed towards the persons and connected with the situations that originally aroused them.
>
> John Bowlby
> *Attachment and Loss*
> *Vol. III Loss*

Feeling is central to all human experience, and every psychotherapy treats feelings. In addition to feeling, people think and act, and no therapy can succeed without addressing all three aspects of the human personality. Most therapists place one or another of these attributes on center stage while the others play crucial supporting roles. Our concentration on feelings represents a strategic choice rather than a denial of the complexity of human nature. Analysts focus on thinking because they believe only intense concentration will reveal and uncover the meaning of early memories and thoughts. Behaviorists treat behavior directly because they think this is the most powerful way to impact the other aspects of personality. Feelings, too, are difficult to apprehend and change; for us, they provide the best leverage to change the whole (thinking, behaving, and feeling) person. What sets us apart from many other cathartic therapists, however, is that we also make a programmatic attempt to alter thinking and behaving directly.

In order to acknowledge our debt to others and to place our work in context, we shall describe the current spectrum of therapeutic approaches and then contrast our work with other recent cathartic therapies.

CURRENT VARIETIES OF PSYCHOTHERAPY

Psychotherapies are most usefully grouped under three major themes which represent the primary modes of change sought: changes in the inner person, changes in behavior, and changes in interpersonal relationships. In Table 2-1, we have grouped a sample of current approaches to psychological treatment according to this schema.

Therapies in Group I (changes in the inner person) share a tactical commitment to altering individual personalities, assuming that these inner changes will help effect subsequent changes in behavior and personal relations. People are seen as reacting to inner forces determined by past experiences of which they are, at best, only partially aware. Some of these therapies are designed to promote insight into unfathomed inner promptings and conflicts while others concentrate on emotive expression of previously constrained feelings. Behavior is understood as meaningfully related to past experiences: without insightful awareness or increased expressiveness, these experiences are liable to be unwittingly repeated.

The paradigmatic example of therapy aimed to modify inner forces by insight is psychoanalysis (Fenichel, 1945). Psychoanalysis is designed to remove amnesias and recover repressed memories—to make the unconscious conscious. The client is instructed to free associate—to speak freely all the thoughts, feelings, memories, and dreams that come to mind—while the analyst silently analyzes what is said and occasionally makes interpretive comments. Interpretation (i.e., pointing out unconscious meanings) is the decisive technique (Greenson, 1967), and resistance and transference are the primary foci.

The second subgroup of therapies designed to promote inner change concentrates more on emotional expression and less on insight. In client-centered therapy (Rogers, 1951), patients are helped to talk about their feelings by therapists who listen in an accepting, supportive manner and intervene primarily to convey empathic understanding. Other therapies in this subgroup, like Janov's primal therapy (Janov, 1970), aim at intense emotional ventilation and involve the active use of cathartic techniques to disrupt defensiveness and promote dramatic emotive expression.

Behavior Therapists (Group II) do not treat symptoms as symbols of underlying problems, but as the problems themselves (Bandura, 1969). Symptoms are understood to be involuntarily acquired and reinforced learned responses to environmental stimuli. Understanding these stimulus-response connections enables the behavior therapist to alter them by modifying the contingencies or reinforcements. Behaviorists use diverse techniques but are united by a common strategy of systematic observation of the stimuli that evoke problem behaviors and the reinforcements that maintain them.

TABLE 2-1
Types of Change Sought in Current Varieties of Psychotherapy

I. Changes in the Inner Person

A. *Intellectual Insight*		B. *Emotional Expression*	
psychoanalysis	*Freud*	vegotherapy	*Reich*
analytical psychology	*Jung*	client-centered therapy	*Rogers*
will therapy	*Rank*	gestalt therapy	*Perls*
individual psychology	*Adler*	experiential therapy	*Mahrer* *Whitaker*
character analysis	*Horney*		
ego analysis	*Klein*	experiential therapy	*Gendlin*
sector therapy	*Deutsch*		
brief psychotherapy	*Bellak*	bioenergetics	*Lowen*
direct analysis	*Rosen*	primal therapy	*Janov*
hypnoanalysis	*Wolberg*	feeling therapy	*Hart, Corriere, & Binder*
personal construct therapy	*Kelly*		
rational emotive therapy	*Ellis*	re-evaluation counseling	*Jackins*
reality therapy	*Glasser*	new identity therapy	*Casriel*
transactional analysis	*Berne*		
existential analysis	*Binswanger*	feeling-expressive therapy	*Pierce & DuBrin*
daseinanalysis	*Boss*		
logotherapy	*Frankl*		
short-term dynamic therapy	*Malan, Davanloo*		

II Changes in Behavior

A. *Classical Conditioning*		B. *Operant Conditioning*	
systematic desensitization	*Wolfe*	modeling	*Bandura*
implosive therapy	*Stampfl*	family therapy	*Patterson*
conditioned reflex therapy	Salter		
biofeedback training	*Green*		
sex therapy	Masters& Johnson		

III Changes in Interpersonal Relationships

A. *Individual*		B. *Group and Family*	
interpersonal psychiatry	*Sullivan*	group psychotherapy	*Yalom*
family therapy	*Bowen*	family therapy	*Minuchin Ackerman*
hypnotherapy	*Erikson*	psycho-drama	*Moreno*
neurolinguistic programing	*Bandler & Grinder*	strategic therapy	*Haley*

The third major group of therapies focuses on changes in interpersonal relations. Some therapists use the therapeutic relationship as a laboratory to teach clients to relate more intimately, while others instruct clients to change the way they relate to people in their environment. The former approach is illustrated by Sullivan's interpersonal psychiatry (Sullivan, 1953). The latter approach is used by Bowen (1978), who meets individually with clients and coaches them on ways to improve their family relationships.

Other interpersonal therapists meet with families and help the members understand and change their patterns of family interaction. These changes are thought to generalize to "real" life outside the group. Family therapists bring members of the family together and attempt to alter their patterns of interaction in order to resolve problems in symptomatic family members and increase the harmonious functioning of the family.

In feeling-expressive therapy, we concentrate first on promoting emotional expression, and so our work is closest to those therapies listed in group I.B. of Table 2-1. In addition, however, we explicitly promote insight, behavior change, and ehanced interpersonal relations. Unlike many cathartic therapists, we do not assume that emotional expressiveness automatically leads to changes in the other spheres. Instead, we talk with our clients about their experiences to help them see the behavioral implications of their feelings and to foster insight. We also set goals and reinforce behavioral change. Further, we meet with couples, families, and groups to encourage explicit changes in family and social relations.

HISTORY OF CATHARSIS IN BEHAVIOR CHANGE

Although they have only recently come into vogue, cathartic helping approaches have ancient origins in drama, ritual, and healing (Nichols and Zax, 1977).

The value of catharsis has been debated since the time of ancient Greece. Plato, the supreme rationalist, condemned theatrical drama because it was cathartic. By arousing the passions, he argued, catharsis undermines the state and disturbs its citizens. His pupil Aristotle (1951) argued just the opposite: theatrical catharsis does not arouse feelings, but rather, purges them and hence exerts a therapeutic influence. The dispute between these two great thinkers illustrates the opposing views about catharsis that persist even today. Does catharsis provoke or purge the passions?

In fact, the answer is "neither." Vicarious participation in someone else's activity (be they tragic heroes or football players) is not catharsis.

Catharsis is not the stimulation of feelings, but rather, the uncovering of dormant feelings, which is accomplished by relaxing psychological defenses. Nor does catharsis purge people of their feelings. Catharsis does not get rid of feelings; it allows them to be experienced and expressed.

When catharsis was used in ancient religious and magic rituals, the rationale was predicated on the Aristotelian notion that catharsis provided purgation and rebirth into a purified state. Primitive healing ceremonies were highly charged emotional events. Although possession by spirits, rather than repressed emotions, was the accepted explanation for problems in living, the implications were similar—the spirits (or feelings) must be exorcised.

Shamanism

The occult powers attributed to the shamans (the folk psychotherapists of primitive cultures) created a powerful expectation that after the sufferers expressed the strong feelings called forth, the healing rites would be successful. Furthermore, the highly ritualized and authoritative nature of the proceedings gave the afflicted permission to depart from social norms of emotional restraint. Shamans typically began the rites by performing feats of magic to demonstrate their power, enhance expectation of success, and generate an emotionally charged atmosphere. Once primed, the emotional arousal of the afflicted was further enhanced by drum-beating, chanting, and the excited shouting of community members. In addition, the afflicted often consumed intoxicating mushrooms or narcotics.

Among the most dramatic features of these healing rituals were the performances of the shamans. Bedecked in fantastic and mysterious costumes, the healers leaped about convulsively while shrieking in unintelligible "spirit language." This was understood to signify a state of ecstasy, during which the shaman journeyed to the spirit world to recover lost souls. Meanwhile, the other participants chanted, played musical instruments, and danced, provoking intense emotional reactions in the patient and audience alike. As these dramatic ritual performances climaxed, the patients experienced hysterical delerium—screaming, crying, and confessing misdeeds.

Although the shamans' concern with demonstrating their power seems quaint and outdated, it relates to an important problem for modern practitioners. We believe that it *is* important for therapists to be powerful, and to demonstrate their power by displaying understanding and an ability to help people change. The danger, however, is that the therapist's power may obscure the client's responsibility for changing. In fact, a subtle balance must be maintained in which therapists accept the need to be powerful, while at the same time encouraging clients to work hard—in and out of therapy sessions—and to take responsibility for their therapy.

Shamanistic healing rituals provided somatic-emotional catharsis through bodily movement and vigorous expressions of emotion. They also provided cognitive-emotional catharsis through remembering and "confessing" a series of distressing experiences. Often such ceremonies provided a ritualized outlet for culturally tabooed emotions. Following these dramatic outpourings of emotion, patients were given comfort and support from assembled family members as well as the shaman.

Religious Revivalism

Another example of emotionally charged rituals are religious revivals. Itinerant revival preachers traveled from town to town, speaking to large and eager crowds. As soon as the faithful were assembled and attentive, the preacher delivered blistering condemnations of evil, reviling and terrifying sinners with graphic tales of the hellfire that awaited the unrepentant. This emotional browbeating may or may not have frightened people into reforming their habits, but it certainly stimulated strong feelings. Crowds, primed in anticipation for an intensely emotional experience, got what they came for: weeping, wailing, and swooning. Although the espoused goal was conversion, emotional expression may have been the most therapeutic feature of religious revivals.

The major drawback to religious and magical rites was their infrequency, ritualization and isolation from everyday experience. Thus, the catharsis they provided was also isolated, rather than being incorporated into daily living. Although they unquestionably did a great deal of good, we think that vivid expressions of feeling are therapeutic not because they exorcise "evil spirits" or "repressed affects," but because they help people to become more feelingful, thoughtful, and active.

Hypnotherapy

Another cathartic procedure with a long history is hypnotherapy, which began with Anton Mesmer and led to Breuer and Freud's cathartic method. Hypnotism in its early guise as "animal magnetism" (Mesmer, 1779) was used to treat various neurotic ailments; its success lay in providing patients with the specialized conditions necessary to stimulate emotional catharsis. Just as priests and shamans invoked the power of demons and gods to explain their results, Mesmer and his followers invoked the occult to explain the effects of mesmerism. These supernatural explanations were effective in helping people overcome their resistance to emotional expression, but unfortunately the feelings expressed were perceived as involuntary results of the hypnotic trance rather than natural, healthy reactions. Whenever ritualized performances are seen as necessary for the display of strong feelings, the results are probably limited to what can be achieved by tension-reduction and suggestion. Treating emotions as evil spirits subject to scourging by special ceremonies is unlikely to alter habits of emotional suppression in everyday social life.

Breuer and Freud (1957) used hypnosis to help patients remember traumatic incidents and express the feelings associated with them. This "cathartic technique" marked the beginning of modern cathartic psychotherapy. In fact, the idea that neurosis results from repressed traumatic events and can be cured by remembering and discharging the associated affect still underlies most cathartic approaches to treatment.

Though many viewed Freud's cathartic technique as both a cognitive and an emotionally expressive procedure, it was always more intellectual than emotional. From the start of his clinical investigations, Freud was more interested in uncovering memories than in producing emotional discharge. In fact, his biography suggests that he himself was uneasy in the presence of strong emotional expression (Jones, 1953). Although he abandoned the cathartic technique, Freud never really was an emotivist. When he found that remembering traumatic childhood events did not produce lasting behavior change, he rejected the traumatic theory. In its place, he developed the conflict theory (Freud, 1904), which states that the key is not the uncovering of specific early experiences, but rather the recognition and expression of feelings and impulses. That is, the hidden and denied aspects of the personality must be recovered, rather than particular events from early childhood.

Pierre Janet (1925) developed a treatment for hysteria which was remarkably similar to Freud and Breuer's cathartic method, but with a greater emphasis on strong emotional expression. According to Janet, when memories of traumatic events are dissociated from consciousness, they often lead to neuroses. Resolution of the neuroses requires that the traumatic memories be uncovered. At first, Janet hypnotized patients and suggested that they forget their unpleasant experiences. When the results of this technique proved to be disappointing, he developed a cathartic procedure that he called "mental liquidation" (Janet, 1925). He believed that when an event took place which required a response, psychological tension was aroused and unresolved tensions from similar experiences were restimulated. If these emotional action tendencies were blocked, neurosis resulted. Janet believed that hypnotizing patients and encouraging expression of the repressed feelings provides not only catharsis but also reassimilation or liquidation of the traumatic memory.

During World War I, Freud's and Janet's ideas about repressed emotional memories were an important influence on those treating soldiers with traumatic war neuroses. Soldiers commonly faced terrifying battlefield experiences where tremendous feelings were aroused but could not be expressed. As a consequence, many developed acute neurotic reactions. Among the most common treatments for these war neuroses was cathartic therapy, facilitated by either hypnotism or drugs. One prominent pioneer of cathartic hypnotherapy was William Brown (1920), who believed that liberation of the terrible feelings associated with battlefield memories was the key to treating these traumatic reactions. He hypnotized his patients and told them to visualize their most horrible battlefield experiences. Once they had been given the permission and the direction to stop avoiding these memories and feelings, the patients faced them and gave full expression to their emotions. While remembering horrible battlefield experiences with hallucinatory vividness, the soldiers were seized with emotion: they wept, moaned, screamed, and thrashed about.

Repeated experiences of such highly cathartic sessions were apparently effective in resolving many severe traumatic neuroses. Descriptions of these procedures repeatedly emphasize the importance of directly and physically expressing the emotions, as opposed to simply remembering and reciting the experiences (Brown, 1920; Hordern, 1952; Shorvon and Sargant, 1947; Simmel, 1944; Watkins, 1949).

War and death are among the most profoundly emotional human experiences. It is no surprise, therefore, that war neuroses and bereavement are among the problems for which cathartic therapy is most often considered appropriate. We believe, however, that the emotions stimulated by war and death are but dramatic and powerful examples of everyday occurrences. Soldiers under fire must exert every effort to avoid the dictates of their feelings. Otherwise, they would cringe in terror or flee. Often these attempts at repression succeed through the extreme measure of dissociation, with debilitating psychological consequences. Similarly, during bereavement, people only gradually face the awful reality of their loss and aloneness (Bowlby, 1961, 1980; Kubler-Ross, 1969); and in cases of pathological mourning, people resolutely deny the fact of their loss (Freud, 1937; Gorer, 1965). As we mature into adulthood, we all suffer many losses: friends move away, family members disperse, and, perhaps most painful of all, we slowly realize that there is no one to take care of us as our parents once did. Although these losses are less dramatic and more easily ignored than death or battlefield mayhem, they also need to be mourned if we are to let go of the past and take hold of the present. For all losses—dramatic or commonplace—cathartic expression is helpful.

MODERN VARIANTS OF CATHARTIC THERAPY

Since the work of Wilhelm Reich in the 1920s, a number of clinicians and theorists have contributed to our understanding of emotion in psychotherapy. We will sketch their work briefly in this section. A more detailed treatment can be found in Nichols and Zax (1977).

Wilhelm Reich's Vegetotherapy

The pioneer and intellectual leader of modern cathartic psychotherapy was Wilhelm Reich (1949, 1960). Reich was the first to emphasize the need for sustained catharsis over a prolonged course of psychotherapy rather than singular dramatic abreactions. Recent cathartic therapists have followed Reich's emphasis on intense catharsis and borrowed some of his techniques for achieving it. Many, however, have overlooked his keen awareness of the subtleties and strenghts of psychological defenses. The key to liberating feelings, as Reich well understood, rests with understanding and slowly diminishing defensiveness.

Reich (1949) defined emotional resistances as the essential stuff of character. These resistances act as an armor that blocks feelings. According to Reich, anxiety is bound by "character armor" that protects people from painful affective internal and external stimuli. As he became increasingly concerned with character armor, Reich concentrated more on *how* his patients were saying things and less on *what* they were saying. This led him to discover how patterns of resistance involve somatic control. He found that people not only learn to avoid or "forget" certain topics, but also learn to control affect by altering their posture, tone of voice, and pacing of speech.

Fundamental to Reich's vegetotherapy was the notion that chronic muscular rigidity develops to ward off anxiety and, later, affect in general. As character armor becomes muscular armor, therapy becomes more directly concerned with chronic muscular rigidity. Although emotion is central to vegetotherapy, Reich never treated it as the only valid expression of one's humanness; vegetotherapy encompasses intellectual analysis as well as muscular massage and emotional catharsis. We too, have found that an exclusive focus on emotion may help patients to cope with temporary stress, but does little to achieve long-term change.

Reich brought a renewed respect for the body into psychotherapy, but never abandoned reason as a therapeutic tool. Although Reich himself sought to blend reason and emotion, mind and body, his influence has led to a reactive shift away from rationality in psychotherapy. The myth that surrender to feelings and passive acceptance of bodily impulses lead to happy and productive living has spawned therapies devoted to purging (as opposed to liberating) emotions.

Alexander Lowen's Bioenergetics

Bioenergetics (Lowen, 1958, 1967) contains some interesting extensions of Reich's therapeutic technique. Its most striking feature is the extensive use of physical means to reduce defensiveness and achieve catharsis. Lowen has found that the majority of people are unaware of most of the tensions in their bodies, except perhaps for headaches and lower-back pain. He has helped patients to experience their chronic stiffness and limited mobility by subjecting various muscle groups to stress. For example, he might have a patient attempt to arch his back. Most people are able to do so only to a limited extent and with considerable pain; this exercise underscores the fact that these muscles have been chronically contracted for so long that they have lost much of their elasticity. In line with his belief that the capacity for emotional expression is proportionate to the degree of muscular coordination, Lowen has developed a full repertoire of expressive movements. Like Reich, he emphasizes full and deep respiration. Bioenergetics deepens patients' breathing via various exercises designed to reduce diaphragmatic blocks. Passive positions, such as arching backwards over a chair and breathing deeply, are usually followed by active, expressive movements.

Lowen has observed that the release of unhappy feelings is usually followed by feelings of desire and affection. His analogy is that when the frozen exterior is thawed, longing for contact and warmth erupts in crying. He has stressed the therapeutic value of expressing unhappy feelings rather than merely recognizing them: "It is one thing to be able to recognize that one is sad, it is another to be able to cry" (1967, p. 236).

Stanley Keleman (1971), another neo-Reichian therapist, has concentrated on relaxing chronic muscular rigidity in order to release feelings. Keleman encourages his clients to hit, kick, scream, and ventilate their impulses. He hopes that by temporarily giving up control, people will increase their energy and open themselves to sensate experience. Keleman has described his work as "re-eroticizing" the body. He believes that there are forces of self-actualization in all of us which only need some assistance to show themslves. Thus, Keleman's approach is similar to many in the humanistic psychology tradition which aim to revitalize our animal being.

Although we agree with Lowen that character is molded by and reflected in muscular activity, we think that he overstated the case when he wrote (1967) that character is functionally identical with muscular armor. Reich's genius enabled him to see that many habitual psychic constrictions were translated into chronic muscular rigidity. His followers seem to have emphasized this aspect of his work without due recognition of the complex nature of psychological conflict.

Conflict ingrained over the course of many years cannot be dissolved simply by loosening the body and its feelings. While such loosening may stimulate latent impulses or conflicts and help people to work out more appropriate solutions, it will not eliminate the reasons for the restraint, which are embedded in day-to-day living.

Janov's Primal Therapy

The most widely known recent cathartic approach is Arthur Janov's primal therapy. Janov's theory of psychopathology (1970, 1971) is compellingly simple: there is only one cause of disorder—blocked painful emotions—and only one cure—re-experiencing these painful emotions. When a child's basic needs (i.e., food, shelter, affection, stimulation) are frustrated, the child experiences traumatic distress that Janov calls "primal pain." Since this pain is too much for a little child to bear, the child escapes it by repressing both the pain and the unmet needs. As the child grows to adulthood, both the thwarted needs and the resultant pain are kept out of awareness. Instead of feeling pain, the growing child feels only anxiety, which leads to tension-reducing rituals and the pursuit of symbolic gratification. Thus, a child whose parents gave love and affection only as rewards for accomplishments may become an adult driven to achieve. However, since the satisfaction sought is symbolic, real needs are never recognized or gratified.

Primal therapy begins with an intensive three-week period of individual daily sessions of two to three hours each. Patients are told to lie down and describe their problems. Whenever recollections evoke feelings, patients are urged to focus on them. As they become engrossed in emotion, they are told to cry out to their parents—to tell them of the terror, anger, and frustration of their childhood. A variety of other techniques are used to block emotional defensiveness, including visual imagery, neo-Reichian body work, and aggressive verbal attack. Janov discourages tension-reducing rituals such as smoking, foot-tapping, finger-drumming, or speaking in gentle tones in an effort to prevent clients from becoming too comfortable to feel. He consistently batters their defenses with direct verbal assaults. The aggressive, authoritarian quality of these attacks probably stimulates feelings iatrogenically more than it reduces defensiveness. Stuffing pillows into patients' mouths, making them gag, and yelling at them are some of the more questionable of these "busting" techniques.

Although the dangers of Janov's strong approach are relatively obvious, excessive softness may lead patients to enjoy therapy instead of changing from it. It probably is not possible to help patients explore long-avoided feelings without at least a little pushing.

Group sessions involving forty to fifty primal therapy patients and several therapists are held thrice weekly and are designed to encourage private catharsis rather than interaction. Patients enter the group room, lie down, and re-enter the world of their private feelings. After approximately two hours, they may either leave or remain to discuss childhood memories. These discussions are more monologue than dialogue, consistent with Janov's disinterest in sympathetic rapport between patients and therapists or among patients.

Janov should be credited with emphasizing intense and protracted emotional expression that goes beyond occasional breakthroughs of feeling to a genuine emotional transformation. In addition, he has developed a variety of effective emotive techniques and has pioneered expansion of the fifty-minute hour. However, we think Janov has overstated two propositions common to all cathartic therapies. The first is that all psychological disorders are based on emotional inhibition; the second is that this inhibition stems entirely from events of infancy and early childhood. While we agree that young children are especially vulnerable to the effects of emotional suppression, we disagree with Janov's relentless pursuit of material from infancy. First, it neglects important conflicts from later childhood and adolescence. Character may be molded in early childhood, but it is not fixed. Second, even though emotional suppression begins in childhood, it may be more productive to explore feelings from recent events. Remembering experiences from early childhood may produce insight, but expressing more recent and accessible feelings may better serve to promote emotional expressiveness.

We also differ with Janov's view of transference feelings: he says such feelings have no importance while we believe they have great importance. We share the view held by most therapists that relating intimately to one therapist over an extended period of time helps the client learn to corrent distortions and projections in a way that provides a model for future relationships. Janov's insistence that maladjustment stems from frustration in early childhood restricts the primal therapist's field of focus. In our opinion, the therapist who wishes to foster free and spontaneous expression of feeling should maintain an open mind about what feelings and events are most significant. Theories should leave the practitioner neither free from, nor blinded by expectations.

While we agree with Janov that rigid defenses inhibit feelings and impulses, we do not agree that the healthy personality is defense-free. Nor do we believe, as Janov does, that defenses should be breached as quickly and forcefully as possible. In feeling-expressive therapy, our goal is less to penetrate defenses than to permit and encourage patients to relax them. The former approach, like rape, may be quicker, but the latter, like seduction, is liable to produce more positive results in the long run.

Moreover, once patients have relaxed their defenses, the feelings and impulses that emerge need to be channeled selectively into appropriate forms of gratification. Janov fails to see this as a problem because he assumes that uncovering and expressing emotions automatically resolves the needs and impulses which create the emotions. However, the client, still faces the challenge of taking hold of life in the present. Without forethought, expression of impulses is likely to lead (again) to frustration.

Hart, Corriere, and Binder—Feeling Therapy

In *Going Sane: An Introduction to Feeling Therapy* (1975), Hart, Corriere, and Binder have written a thorough and useful discussion of emotional suppression and cathartic treatment. These "feeling therapists" do not try to expel feelings; instead they regard emotional ventilation as a natural consequence of relaxing defenses and as a step toward living *from* feelings, not *without,* feelings.

Emotional disordering prevents direct contact with feelings, life experiences, and other people. People who are neither in touch with, nor able to respond from, feelings are never fully aware. They may develop specific symptoms or cling to a generally dimmed life style in which they hold back feelings, avoid intimacy, and seek solace in spectator activities such as TV. Life becomes a struggle to avoid pain, not to find joy.

To open long-closed channels of feeling, the feeling therapists prescribe full awareness and direct expression of feelings. Catharsis is central to this technique; it is used to help foster "complete feelings," rather than simply to ventilate or discharge feelings. Feeling therapy promotes catharsis—and thus fuller expression of feeling—by disrupting defenses and encouraging regression.

New patients meet with individual therapists at frequent intervals for approximately four weeks. During this initial treatment, patients learn how to feel and how to counter their defenses. The feeling therapists recognize that the process of change does not begin and end at the door to the therapy room. Several types of groups are offered and patients take part in two or three concurrently. Feeling therapy requires total involvement. Patients not only enter treatment, they join a community. This total commitment to a life of giving and getting therapy is at once a great advantage and a potential weakness of feeling therapy. The careful screening, rigorous demands, and long-term commitment required of patients provide great leverage for producing profound personal change. Any self-contained institution such as a monastary, prison, or the Center for Feeling Therapy has great power to indoctrinate its members into a new and more favored life style (LeVine, 1966). For many people, however, this type of commitment is not possible. For a therapy to be useful for any significant fraction of those who seek help, it must be able to accommodate people who cannot make such a total commitment.

The strategy employed to help patients change from repressing to expressing feelings involves five steps: (1) integration—uncovering feelings in the present; (2) counteraction—becoming aware of defenses and expressing them directly; (3) abreaction—associating feelings with past events and vividly expressing those feelings; (4) proaction—alternating awareness of past and present feelings so as to disentangle them; and (5) reintegration—developing insight and beginning to live from full expression of feelings.

The feeling therapist responds almost exclusively to feeling and resistance, encouraging the former and blocking the latter. Techniques are used sparingly and seem to be designed largely to counter defenses. One noteworthy technique is that of exaggerating defenses in order to overcome them. Simply altering defenses in therapy sessions may enable patients to break through to cathartic expressions of feeling, but unless some awareness of the nature and function of the defenses is developed, they are certain to be reinstituted later. Thus, feeling therapists ask patients to intensify the expression of certain defenses in order to experience their own unique ways of holding back.

Therapeutic comments typically aim to make the client's memories vivid with feeling. For example, the therapist may say: "What was it like?"; "What is (was) happening?"; "Visualize it." As the patient begins to get in touch with feelings, the therapist helps to revive scenes from the past and encourages cathartic expression. For example, the therapist may ask the client "What do you want?" to encourage awareness of needs and feelings or instruct the patient to "call out" or "reach out" to encourage direct, full expression of feelings.

Feeling therapists are plainly, unabashedly, and stridently confrontive. They do not hesitate to come on strong; patients are permitted no refuge in dissimulation or avoidance. Those who do not abandon themselves to feeling may be told "You're just blabbering what someone else told you!" or "You're full of crap!" They claim that they are not being hard on clients but on clients defenses. The distinction—a valid one—may be easier to understand in print than in practice.

The vitality of feeling therapy is based on refined eclecticism and creative innovation. It skillfully blends theories and techniques from a number of approaches with innovations of its own. The major strategic advantages of feeling therapy stem from recognition of the need for, and the difficulty of, re-educating people to live from feelings. Feeling therapy is an intensive, multimodal, long-term process that includes direct attention to modifying behavior outside of the therapy office. With respect to intensity and duration, feeling therapy rivals, if not surpasses, psychoanalysis—long the definitive example of total therapeutic involvement.

Ironically, the feeling therapists, who espouse action and responsibility, foster a subtle passivity by claiming that feelings are sources of wisdom that must be obeyed. Our view is that feelings are made and chosen through the processes of thinking and acting. Although many feelings have the quality of an imperative, sometimes this imperative should be followed, others times not. Feelings also involve attributions that may need to be qualified or even rejected. For example, simply accepting the statement "I was an unhappy child, and my parents made me that way" is an evasion of personal responsibility.

Harvey Jackins's Re-Evaluation Counseling

Harvey Jackins, a one-time labor organizer, has spent the last twenty-five years developing and organizing re-evaluation counseling, a lay self-help group in which catharsis plays a central role (Jackins, 1962, 1965).

Jackins believes that healthy functioning becomes eroded by the repression of emotions. In his view, the natural human response to distressing events—typically seen in children—is spontaneous emotional catharsis, or "discharge." Unhappily, socialization in our culture blocks this natural process of recovery by placing taboos on the direct expression and discharge of feelings. From an early age, we hear "Big boys don't cry," "Don't feel bad," "Don't be angry," and "You didn't really want that anyway." In short, we are taught not to discharge feelings. This pattern of emotional suppression is so ingrained that we respond to it almost reflexively. If someone should cry in our presence, we become anxious and typically comfort her/him by saying, "It'll be all right. Dry your eyes" (i.e., "stop"). According to Jackins (1962), this happens because discharge is mistakenly identified with the pain that stimulates it. However, discharge is not the hurt. Tears are not grief, but the means of expressing and recovering from emotional pain.

Jackins believes that undischarged feelings interfere with clear thinking by blocking the organism's ability to learn from experience. The more repressed emotion a person has, the more he or she is likely to react nonrationally to future situations. The more similar a new situation is to an old one that caused undischarged hurt, the more likely the person is to become "restimulated." For example, a woman with unexpressed feelings of anger toward her domineering mother will behave less rationally with her mother than she would if she had discharged her anger; she will also tend to overreact to other domineering people she encounters because she will respond to these people less as new individuals and more as reminders of her mother.

The solution Jackins proposes is to learn to get in touch with and discharge repressed feelings from the past. He believes that discharge liberates energy and automatically leads to insight ("re-evaluation"). When sufficient emotional discharge takes place, the person is freed from the stultifying feelings and irrational behavior left by the distressing experiences.

In re-evaluation counseling, interpretation and analysis are eschewed in favor of listening and giving "free attention" to the client. When questions are asked, they are intended to indicate interest in the client and to bring out vivid detail about what is being said, rather than to produce explanations about why things happened as they did. However, the counselor must also be alert to defensive maneuvers ("control patterns") and counter the client's attempts to avoid experiencing feelings. The client's task is not just to talk, but to reveal and discharge emotional pain. The counselor's task is to spot and interrupt the "control patterns" that block expression.

Jackins believes that cathartic discharge alone can alter basic character structure by facilitating insight and a rational re-evaluation of living patterns. The simplicity of his theory and technique facilitates his efforts to teach members of the lay public to help each other. Jackins differs from other theorists in his faith that re-evaluation will spontaneously follow cathartic discharge without assistance from the counselor. Discharge is said to be the outward manifestation of a profound healing process that includes freshly clarified perception and, ultimately, a new, more rational understanding of experience.

Separating the experience of catharsis from attempts to achieve insight may be a productive tactic whether one believes that insight spontaneously follows catharsis or requires working through in the therapeutic relationship. It seems unlikely that one can experience catharsis and cognitive restructuring at the same time. Therefore, in our work, we often suspend attempts to understand experience until a full measure of catharsis has been achieved. Following intense discharge, the client's enhanced rationality can lead to reconceptualization. However, we believe a trained therapist faciliates this new understanding. Jackins fears that the helper will impose his or her own values and solutions on the client. While this is a valid concern, we believe the benefits of helping a client to re-evaluate painful experiences far outweigh the costs.

Jackins's theory of emotional disorder is intuitively appealing and straightforward. However, while we think that it fits the facts of experience (it is phenomenologically correct), it treats feelings as bad objects to be expelled. This notion, implicit in Jackins's writing, is effective in promoting catharsis, but becomes a handicap in working for changes in thinking and acting. While achieving catharsis is no easy matter, and we concur with Jackins as to its central importance in therapy, we find his single-minded emphasis on it too limiting. We are more eclectic than Jackins in that we use methods from several therapeutic models. We also differ in our view of what is useful about catharsis and in our preference for a more active role for the therapist in aiding the client's postcathartic re-evaluation.

Daniel Casriel's New Identity Therapy

New identity therapy (Casriel, 1972), colloquially called "scream therapy," has two particularly useful facets. First, clients are urged to make nonverbal sounds that usually build to loud screams. This process can greatly amplify genuine feeling and breach verbal defenses, although it takes on a rote, exerciselike quality when used thoughtlessly. Second, Casriel's concept of bonding goes a step beyond the physical touch and holding employed by other emotive and humanist approaches. In bonding the therapist or another client gently lays on top of the client who is working, thus providing safety and support. The client holds on and calls out to parents or simply screams in a wordless expression of feeling. Although strange to imagine from a written account this technique can be a very powerful cathartic tool. Like Reich and Lowen, Casriel sees people as frightened of their own joyful, sexual, and needy feelings. His bonding technique can help clients to deal with these fears.[1]

FEELING-EXPRESSIVE THERAPY

Feeling-expressive therapy is part of a long tradition of catharsis in healing and therapy. Like other cathartic therapists, we strive to liberate people who have chosen defensive security at the expense of satisfaction and zest. People go to great lengths to avoid feeling pain and fear, often suffering more from their efforts to avoid feeling than they would from the feeling itself. Unfortunately, these efforts to avoid pain have a high cost—remaining stunted and cut off from the full experiencing of life.

[1]For a more detailed treatment of the history and modern varieties of catharsis in psychotherapy see Nichols and Zax, *Catharsis in Psychotherapy* (1977).

Symptoms are not caused by what people feel, but by what they will not let themselves feel. These blunted feelings interfere with clear thinking and inhibit action.

Like the other cathartic therapies we have discussed, feeling-expressive therapy is designed to break the cycle of suppression, confusion, and inaction by promoting catharsis through sustained concentration on feelings and defenses. However, we differ from the other approaches in two major respects. First, we do not view catharsis as a means of ridding people of stored up feelings, but rather, as a vehicle for relaxing defenses so that clients can become more feelingful. Second, although we concentrate on catharsis, we also work directly on insight and behavior change.

Feeling-expressive therapy comprises five integrated components: intense expression of feelings, goal-directed behavioral change, peer-counseling, intrapsychically focused group therapy, and a philosophy of development we call "letting go and taking hold."[2]

Intense Feeling-Expression

7

Vigorous and sustained expression of feelings is the hallmark of feeling-expressive therapy. We begin by focusing on the feelings described by our clients: we track them, amplify them, and try to understand how they effect behavior. "Accepting feelings"—a cliché in psychotherapy—is not enough. Mere description of feelings is not therapeutic; full expression is.

"Peter left last night, and I feel sad" may sound like an expression of feeling, but in fact it is little more than a signal that feelings are taking place. The sadness is only vaguely apprehended and, without active intervention of the therapist, the client's experience of the feeling will remain incomplete. We have devised a number of techniques to help clients express their feelings fully. In the process, they learn to overcome resistances and inhibition. In the above example, we would ask the person to give vigorous expression to the feeling of sadness, which might lead to crying, sobbing, and/or shouting "Don't go! Please don't leave me." It is hard to predict the exact path the feelings will follow, but we believe it is critical to help the client amplify and fully express the feelings that emerge.

In seeking full expression of strong feelings, it is not enough to simply make the client more aware of pain. People often stop expressing feelings when they become too immersed in what is hurting them. They need to feel safe in their relationship with the therapist if they are to discharge

[2]See Chapter 1 for a detailed discussion of this philosophy.

their feelings. The feeling-expressive therapist therefore monitors both the experience of pain and the sense of safety, keeping these in balance so that the client may continue expressing feelings. In Scheff's description (1981) of the client as a "participant observer," he differentiates overdistanced and underdistanced emotion from the preferred "esthetic distance" at which the client can sense both pain and safety and thus give vent to full feeling-expression.

Goal-Directed Behavioral Change

Our emphasis on behavioral change has two distinct sources. One is our commitment to helping people change. We help clients set and define goals early in treatment and then use them for direction during the course of therapy. We make it clear that we do not simply offer friendship, dependency, or emotional "fireworks." Rather, we offer a serious, arduous method for achieving specified behavioral change that encompasses both symptom relief and personality change.

Our second reason for emphasizing behavioral change stems from our interest in feelings. Emotional change and behavioral change often occur together and reinforce each other. We know that if a person fully expresses anger (feeling), he or she will be less inclined to act irritably toward others (behavior). This feeling-to-behavior connection is widely acknowledged. On the other hand if a person determines to act thoughtfully and kindly toward others (behavior), there will be emotional sequelae such as feelings of anger or fear. In this case, the irritable behavior is defensive; thus, when the client gives it up, the blocked feelings emerge. Although this behavior-to-feeling connection is less widely appreciated than its converse, it has important implications for the treatment of various disorders—particularly those with an addictive component, such as overeating, compulsive working, or substance abuse. The behavior-to-feeling connection is also important, for example, in treating couples who repeatedly use the same patterned behavior to avoid intimacy.

Peer-Counseling

Peer-counseling is a therapy-like process in which two clients meet together and take turns being client and counselor. At first, the counselor remains passive, mainly listening. As trust develops, however, the pair may agree to be somewhat more active in making therapeutic interventions with each other. Peer-counseling offers additional therapy hours, teaches clients to use feeling-expression for their continuing development after formal therapy has ended, and reinforces clients' personal responsibility for change.

Clients are invited to use space at the Center without charge for peer-counseling during evening and weekend hours when it is not needed for therapy. The combination of peer-counseling, workshops and groups creates a considerable sense of community among participating clients. We believe this sense of community is useful and supportive, especially to isolated and socially cautious clients, who can practice new ways of approaching people in a safe environment.

Clients also learn firsthand about resistance and transference phenomena while acting as peer-counselors. Then, when they themselves experience similar feelings toward their therapist they can more readily see the resistant and tranferential aspects of them. Similarly when they come to a choice point in a therapy session where a riskier direction is also the more rewarding one, they are more likely to choose that course if they have peer-counseled. In fact, people seem to be better clients if they also spend some time being counselors. Because the opposite is also true, all the therapists at the Center also peer-counsel regularly.

Intrapsychically Focused Group Therapy

The fourth characteristic of feeling-expressive therapy is the intrapsychic focus of our group work. The focus on group process that is common to other approaches (Yalom, 1970) is de-emphasized in our work. Although group members interact supportively and occasionally confrontively, they concentrate primarily on their own feelings and behavior. While one member is talking, other members often simply listen, although at times, they may role-play, give encouragement, or help in some other way. Although we occasionally ask clients to examine their interactions with other group members or to give feedback to others, these activities are not emphasized.

An example of our intrapsychic emphasis is the way group members deal with anger toward each other. They typically state the feeling and may even shout at the group member they are angry at, but then, as the anger flows, the focus changes to significant figures in the client's life. Initially, these may be current figures—wife, friend, or child—but, with exploration, figures from the past often emerge as the source of these angry feelings.

In general then, feeling-expressive therapy groups provide a supportive setting in which members can express their own feelings and make plans to change their behavior. They are encouraged in this process by seeing and helping others do the same. A strong bond of compassion and understanding often develops through this sharing—a sense of being members of a community of people working together on similar problems.

Letting Go and Taking Hold

Our philosophy of development, "letting go and taking hold," provides a framework that informs our overall therapeutic strategy and many of our specific interventions. The goal of therapy is to help people let go of whatever has been holding them back and take hold of their lives. This usually means letting go of magical beliefs of being saved or rescued by strong, parent figures and taking hold of one's own responsibility for life.

Our clients spend many therapy hours recovering childhood memories and expressing the feelings attached to them. Clients often look at old family pictures, interview family members, and do whatever they can to reacquaint themselves with their beginnings. They cry about the loss of the people who once cared for them. The purpose of this process is to let go of the old relationships and dependencies, of the child-parent relationship. Sometimes, when living parents are amenable, a new adult relationship can be formed between client and parent. Ideally, the client lets go of regret, dependency, and blame, and takes hold of her/his own self-responsible, present-focused, energetic, joyful life. People often hold themselves back from fully participating in the present because of hurts received long ago. Letting go and taking hold means letting go of these fears based on early hurts and taking hold of the people, experiences, and events in the present which give life meaning and satisfaction.

The concept of letting go and taking hold provides a consistent direction for therapeutic interventions. For example, if adult clients feel sad or angry about the way their parents are treating them in the present, we may begin by urging them to connect those feelings to experiences from the past. This involves an exploration of memories and a vigorous expression of old hurts. Following this catharsis, however, we will remind the clients that their parents are no longer going to take care of them. We stress that it is time for them to let go of their parents as caretakers and instead take responsibility for their own lives. Crying about the past is encouraged; blaming people from the past is discouraged. We ask clients to express their anger and sadness directly, and we remind them that in the present they are on their own. When they first become aware of how they were hurt as children, the urge to blame is strong. Having a value scheme like the one we are describing helps us walk the fine line that allows people to express their childlike hurt vigorously, yet discourage them from blaming their parents or others for their present difficulties. Our implicit message is: "Feel free to express fully to us the pain that you felt growing up. You can expect comfort, support, and acceptance. But know that in the present, you are responsible for your own life—for making it good or letting it founder." This point of view helps us to be both caring and confrontive in work with our clients.

SUMMARY

All psychotherapies can be classified in terms of the type of change they seek to promote: Changes in the inner person, in behavior and in interpersonal relationships. Catharsis has long been a part of the healer's armamentarium from the earliest shamans, through religious revivalism and Mesmer to the current group of therapies which use feeling-expression. Among the contemporary approaches, we looked at Reich's and Lowen's body therapies, at Janov's primal therapy and the feeling therapy of Hart, Corriere and Binder, and at Jackins' reevaluation counseling and Casriel's new identity therapy.

Finally we described feeling-expressive therapy in terms of its five components: intense expression of feelings, goal directed behavioral change, peer counseling, intrapsychically focused group therapy and a philosophical emphasis on letting go and taking hold.

REFERENCES

Aristotle. *The art of poetry*. New York: Odyssey Press, 1951.

Bandura, A. *Principles of behavior modification*. New York: Holt, Rinehart, & Winston, 1969.

Bowen, M. *Family therapy in clinical practice*. New York: Aronson, 1978.

Bowlby, J. Processes of mourning. *Internat. J. Psycho-Anal.*, 1961, 42: 317–40.

Bowlby, J. *Attachment and Loss Vol III Loss*. New York: Basic Books, 1980.

Breuer, J. & Freud, S. *Studies in hysteria*. New York: Basic Books, 1957.

Brown, W. The revival of emotional memories and its therapeutic value. *British Journal of medical Psychology*, 1920, *1*, 16–19.

Casriel, D. *A scream away from happiness*. New York: Grosset & Dunlap, 1972.

Fenichel, O. *The psychoanalytic theory of neurosis*. New York: Norton, 1945.

Freud, S. Freud's psychoanalytic method (1904). *In therapy and technique*. New York: Collier Books, 1963.

Freud, S. Mourning and melancholia. *Standard edition of the complete psychological works of Sigmund Freud*, 243–58. London: Hogarth Press, 1937.

Gorer, G. *Death, grief and mourning in contemporary Britain*. London: Cresset Press, 1965.

Greenson, R.R. *The technique and practice of psychoanalysis, Vol. I.* New York: International Universities Press, 1967.

Hart, J., Corriere, R., & Binder, J. *Going sane: An introduction to feeling therapy*. New York: Jason Aronson, 1975.

Hordern, A. The response of the neurotic personality to abreaction. *Journal of Mental Science*, 1952, *98*, 630–39.

Jackins, H. *Elementary counselor's manual*. Seattle: Rational Island Publishers, 1962.

Jackins, H. *The human side of human beings*. Seattle: Rational Island Publishers, 1965.

Janet, P. *Psychological healing: A historical and clinical study. Vols. I & II*. New York: Macmillan, 1925.

Janov, A. *The anatomy of mental illness*. New York: G.P. Putnam's Sons, 1971.

Janov, A. *The primal scream*. New York: Dell, 1970.

Jones, E. *The life and work of Sigmund Freud (Vol. I)*. New York: Basic Books, 1953.

Keleman, S. *Sexuality, self & survival*. San Francisco: Lodestar Press, 1971.

Kubler-Ross, E. *On death and dying*. New York: Macmillan, 1969.

LeVine, R.A. American college experience as a socialization process. In T.M. Newcomb and E.K. Wilson (Eds.) *College Peer Groups*, Chicago: Aldine, 1966.

Lowen, A. *Physical dynamics of character structure*. New York: Grune & Stratton, 1958.

Lowen, A. *The betrayal of the body*. New York: Macmillan, 1967.

Mesmer, F.A. *Memoirs sur la decouverte du magnetisme animal*. Paris: Didot, 1779.

Nichols, M.P. & Zax, M. *Catharsis in psychotherapy*. New York: Gardner Press, 1977.

Reich, W. *Character-analysis*. New York: Noonday Press, 1960.

Reich, W. *Selected Writings*. New York: Noonday Press, 1949.

Rogers, C.R. *Client-centered therapy*. Boston: Houghton, 1951.

Scheff, T.J. The distancing of emotion in psychotherapy. *Psychotherapy: Theory, Research and Practice*, 1981, *18*, 46–53.

Shorvon, H.J. & Sargant, M.B. Excitatory abreaction: with special reference to its mechanism and the use of ether. *Journal of Mental Science*, 1947, *93*, 709–32.

Simmel, E. War neurosis. In S. Lorand (Ed.) *Psychoanalysis today*. New York: International University Press, 1944, 227–48.

Sullivan, H.S. *The interpersonal theory of psychiatry*. New York: Norton, 1953.

Watkins, J.G. *Hypnotherapy of war neuroses*. New York: Ronald Press, 1949, 244–45.

Yalom, I.D. *The theory and practice of group psychotherapy*. New York: Basic Books, 1970.

3

Therapeutic Techniques

> "The eventual independence of the patient is our ultimate object . . ."
> Sigmund Freud
> *The Dynamics of the Transference*

We view techniques as *methods* used to reach *objectives*. Although there are an infinite number of techniques, all can be organized according to the method used and the objective sought. The five objectives and twelve methods presented here categorize most of the techniques used in feeling-expressive therapy. The objectives spring fairly readily from our understanding of the tasks of therapy. The methods, however, could be categorized in various ways. In choosing our twelve categories, we tried to avoid being either too broad or too narrow in scope. We deliberately chose to make the categories meaningful rather than logically tight. Some categories, for example, are defined by therapist behavior (prescriptions), and some by client behavior (kinesics). Suggestions are involved in several of the techniques (focusing, attention to breathing, prescriptions) and there is some overlap between categories (e.g. coaching and teaching). They are intended as a conceptual aid not as a thorough system for categorizing interventions.

**Table 3-1
Objectives and Methods
of Feeling-Expressive
Therapy**

Methods	Objectives				
	1. Understand Client's History and Current Life Situation	2. Counter Defenses	3. Facilitate Expression of Feelings	4. Integrate Feeling and Meaning	5. Change Behavior
1. Statements of Support and Encouragement					
2. Giving Permission and Coaching					
3. Focusing					
4. Role-Playing					
5. Humor					
6. Kinesics					
7. Touch					
8. Attention to Breathing					
9. Prescriptions					
10. Questions for Information					
11. Confrontations and Interpretations					
12. Teaching					

OBJECTIVES

1. Understand client's history and current life situation.
2. Counter defenses.
3. Facilitate expression of feelings.
4. Integrate feeling and meaning.
5. Change behavior.

First, it is necessary to understand the client's situation in terms of the past, the present, and future plans. The therapist may ask "Who are you?"; "How do you want to change?"; "What's been going on lately?" As client and therapist work together to liberate feelings, it becomes necessary to counter defenses. If that goes well, the feelings are experienced and expressed fully. Then comes a quieter time of relating the feelings to the past and the present, and discovering meaning and connections. Finally, this new understanding is related to the client's current life situation and client and therapist work out a strategy for rational living. Let us examine each objective more closely.

Understand client's history and current life situation

Understanding the client's history and current life situation is essential in order to assess needs and to plan a strategy for treatment. Before the therapist can assess the nature and extent of the client's pathology, she/he must learn about the client's present living situation, family history, interpersonal history, and work and school history. Previous therapy contacts and the reason for seeking help at this time also should be discussed.

Typically, this objective is the easiest to achieve, although the client's early childhood history may be inaccessible at the beginning of treatment. Most clients like to share their past and present life events with an interested listener. As clients talk, both the unhappiness that brought them in and the latent emotion in the material being discussed will tend to move them toward expression of feelings. The therapist who wishes to encourage this kind of openness for future work must allow some such expression. Yet the objective of information-gathering must be kept in mind and more history taken when the emotion subsides.

We use the first session to find out what motivated the client to seek help, and to gather whatever history and current life information seem appropriate. We also promote feeling-expression as a kind of socialization device that says, "This is what we do here." Sometimes, this stimulates a brief discussion of what therapy is about. Questions such as "How will this (expression of feelings) help me?" often mask other concerns. Behind the question may be the unstated fear of "losing control." By inquiring into such concerns, the therapist may uncover and be able to address important resistances to feeling. The therapist may need to explain briefly what she/he is seeking to accomplish by promoting catharsis. Without some idea of why expressing feelings is helpful, clients are liable to avoid doing so and to feel embarrassed or upset if their defenses are breached. By explaining the procedure and dealing openly with conscious resistances at the outset, the therapist can form an alliance with the client as active participant rather than resistant or passive opponent from whom emotions are wrenched.

The second session is focused on finding out specifically how the client would like to change. We also regularly explore several areas of living (e.g., sex, work) to find out how much satisfaction the client derives from them. In the course of these inquiries, we find out more about the client's life situation and history. After the second session, information-gathering usually diminishes in importance and other objectives become more salient. Each person's therapy has its own rhythm, however, and sometimes quite late in the course of therapy a critical piece of history emerges from repression or the shadows of "inattention."

The therapist's own intuitive curiosity, which often operates outside of the therapist's conscious awareness, can be a very acute sensor and important guide for information-gathering. A single timely question may lead to the uncovering of important information. Since curiosity can also be prompted by the therapist's countertransference, self-awareness and self-monitoring are required to be sure that the question is in the client's interest. However, we believe that therapists are more likely to err in not following their curiosity enough than in following it too much.

Although we believe that it is absolutely necessary to find out a good deal about the client's past and present life, we do not take a formal history, as we find that structure too rigid and distancing. Such procedures tend to take on a life of their own and distract the therapist's attention from the critical first steps of forming a trusting relationship with the client. For the same reason, we do not advocate taking written notes during the session.

Counter Defenses

Countering defenses is decisive to the success of any therapy and is among the most challenging aspects of feeling-expressive therapy. It requires persistence, caring, cleverness, patience, memory, and courage to help a client to give up defenses against the full expression of feelings and recognize the impulses behind them. "Impulse" here means a tendency to express a particular emotion, think a particular thought, or behave in a particular way. "Defense" refers to a competing tendency to inhibit that feeling, thought, or behavior. Ideally, the therapist forms an alliance (Greenson, 1965) with the part of the client that seeks positive change and together they work toward overcoming the defense against that change. It is here that hard judgments must be made. Which impulses are to be supported and which defenses opposed by the therapist-client coalition? Will the client or the therapist bear major responsibility? How is one method chosen over another? When is silence indicated and when should some more active method be used?

Which defenses should be countered?

The therapist must counter whatever defenses get in the way of the client's ability to reach the agreed-upon goals. Suppose that a client had a goal of being less depressed. Anger, loss, and low self-esteem are usually involved in depression. Therefore, the therapist would induce expression of anger and sadness associated with the client's loss. Any defenses inhibiting such expression would be countered. For example, the client might state that she could not be angry at her father because he had suffered a lot and always had done the best he could. This thought, rational though it might sound, would be serving a defensive purpose at that point and the therapist would need to counter it in order to facilitate the expression of anger.

In addition, high priority must be given to countering defenses that (1) are so pervasive as to be mobilized in response to virtually every feeling-expression or (2) threaten the therapeutic relationship itself. An example of the first is hypomanic "speeding": the client talks so fast and keeps so busy that no real contact can be established, and no feeling can be focused on for a meaningful period of time. An example of the second sort of defense is a continual tentativeness about engaging in therapy. The client who is always deciding whether or not to be in therapy is, in effect, not in therapy. Another example is the client who has unexpressed anger at the therapist. Addressing these two sorts of defenses early in therapy and whenever they reappear is absolutely essential. Otherwise, the work will either end entirely or be reduced to a meaningless exercise.

A useful rule of thumb is to *encourage the expression of the most basic or primary feeling presently available.* For example, a person may be angry about how he has been shut out and excluded, but thinking about expressing his anger may make him fearful. The therapist may encourage the client to express fear first in order to facilitate the expression of anger. The danger is that "expressing" fear can itself become a defense against anger. An important part of this rule of thumb is the phrase "presently available." The therapist may know that saying goodbye to a parent will eventually include some angry feelings. Yet if there is no evidence that the client is close to feeling angry, then that feeling is not available and it would be useless or even harmful to force its expression. So the therapist tries to facilitate the expression of the least derived feeling that *is* presently available.

Ideally, a client's focus proceeds from derived impulses to more basic ones and from current life figures to early ones. Unfortunately, things are seldom that simple because people often get stuck at one level of feeling. Today's fresh emotion can become tomorrow's emotionless rehash. Today's insight may be tomorrow's defense. When these things happen, we know that fear, the need for the therapist's approval, or some other resistant process has interfered with the smooth flow of feelings. To interrupt that process and continue to uncover feelings, the therapist must be alert and persistent. Clients never like to be interrupted when they are being resistant; they like it even less when they have been trying to please. So courage and firmness are needed as well as perceptiveness.

How can we know when apparent feeling-expression, self-exploration, and cooperation have in fact become defensive and retrogressive? Usually, the therapist's clinical sensitivity allows her/him to make such discriminations. For times when this intuitive process does not work, here are some guideposts.

One is the therapist's boredom or sleepiness. When this feeling is present, the therapist should ask: (1) "Is this client or this content conflict-laden for me?" and (2) "Am I short of sleep?" If there are no apparent countertransference or reality-based reasons for the sleepiness, then it may be that a defensive process is operating in the client. People are inherently interesting. If they become boring, they probably are not talking in a feelingful way about what is really on their mind.

A second guidepost that is harder to pinpoint might be called "the sights and sounds of progress." A client who is working effectively usually moves at a moderate pace from topic to topic and from one emphasis to another. In contrast, clients sometimes rush breathlessly from area to area, apparently too enchanted with what is just around the bend to stop long anywhere. In fact, since it is fear, rather than enthusiasm, that sets the frantic pace, not much gets done. In other cases, the same fear can keep clients focused for weeks on the same person, memory, or life dilemma. Unlike the breathless pace, which is easily seen as defensive, the stuck pace is more difficult to identify. There are times when it is productive to linger on a particular episode or issue. However, when feelings are scarce or seem labored, when no new ways of viewing the issue emerge, or when no new behavioral changes occur, we can safely assume that the client is stuck.

Another test of the quality of therapeutic work is variety of content. Therapy sessions should be concerned with the client's past, the present, and the therapy relationship (Menninger, 1958). If one of these areas of the therapeutic triad has not been discussed recently, a defensive process may be operating and the avoided area should be probed.

Finally, when a client is working well, voice tone and pace should differ throughout a session. The best test of this is to listen to a tape of a session, skipping around and playing brief segments from different parts of the hour. If each section sounds the same, there is a defensive process at work.

Good therapy is real, alive, and flowing. When an alert therapist and a cooperative client follow the thread between thoughts and feelings, there is a connected unfolding that both recognize as "good work."

Who is responsible for opposing the defenses?

The responsibility is shared, of course, but each member of the therapeutic alliance has unique responsibilities. The client's primary responsibilities are to (1) be present, (2) say whatever comes to mind, and (3) try what the therapist suggests. The primary responsibilities of the therapist are to (1) track the client's feelings empathically, (2) make continuous assessments of the moment-to-moment status of the client's feelings and defenses, (3) intervene to oppose defenses and promote expression of feelings, and (4) connect these molecular events with an overall view of the client's difficulties, personality style, and therapeutic objectives.

We believe that common metaphors for the therapist as teacher, guru, doctor, or guide tend to portray the client in too passive a light. The term "consultant" seems more accurate. The client wants to change and hires a consultant to help. Although this metaphor portrays the relationship as cooler than it really is, it places the initiative and strategic control with the client, where they belong.

At times, of course, the therapist is directive, making suggestions, pushing the client to look at something, and setting ground rules for the therapeutic interaction. However, the therapist's activity is always designed as a tactic to further the client's strategic goals. Similarly, a client's feelings of dependency on the therapist do not alter the fact that the client is the initiator of the therapy, the person who seeks change, and the employer of the therapist-as-consultant.

How is one method chosen over another?

The choice of a particular method is usually intuitive. It may be affected by how well a particular tactic worked previously and/or by its suitability for a given content, feeling, or defense. Also, therapists have personal styles that affect how they choose methods. Some favor gentle coaxing while others are more challenging and confrontive. Ideally, therapists should have a wide variety of methods available to suit any situation and not be so constrained by personal limitations that only a narrow band of methods are available to them. Frequently, surprise is an important element. The defense is attacked from a different direction or with different weapons than the client expects.

When is silence the best method?

Silence is frequently the perfect "method." It puts the responsibility for action squarely on the client. It also is a surprise if the therapist has used a series of active methods to which the client has responded passively. Silence is particularly useful when the client is being resistant and inactive. It clearly conveys that the next move is the client's and it does not suggest what that move should be. Thus, the client is the sole author of what she/he does and will have a harder time disowning responsibility than would be the case otherwise.

Facilitate Expression of Feelings

This objective is the essence of feeling-expressive therapy. It is the primary vehicle of our work and the main reason for countering defenses. When the client is feeling safe and defenses have been successfully countered, feelings bubble forth and seek expression with a surprising force. If the therapist stays with the client, the expression of feelings reaches a very intense level.

The potential for intense feeling-expression is present in all of us. When people first see others sobbing loudly for half an hour or pounding and shouting furiously at maximum volume, they are often startled and uneasy. Many wonder whether it is an "act" or a response to the demand characteristics of the situation. In fact, people who express their feelings so intensely in therapy usually have recovered that ability during therapy (an ability we all had as young children) and they experience such expressions as very real and helpful. There is also a sense of choice. Clients seldom feel that they *have* to express their feelings at a given time. Although their feelings are real, they choose when and how fully to express them.

We do not maintain that all feelings have to be expressed at full volume or that people who express themselves quietly do not change. We do believe that it is useful to have access to a full range of emotional responses, including noisy and intense ones. Most people live their lives within a severely restricted and somewhat unreal range of emotional expression. People who demand attention with histrionic displays of emotion are no less limited than those who respond in a subdued and restrained way to all of life's delights and hurts. We try to help people recover the ability they had as children for real, full-spectrum feeling-expression.

The goal, then, is to help the client express feelings as fully as possible in a real way that leads to insight and behavior change. In general, the therapist pursues this goal by (1) continuing to work effectively against defenses as feeling-expression unfolds, (2) being in intimate contact with the client, (3) choosing appropriate methods, and (4) not being afraid or upset by strong feelings.

Integrate Feeling and Meaning

When feelings are fully expressed, clients frequently begin to think about their implications: "As a kid, nobody told me what was happening and here I am as an adult always asking questions"; "It makes me so mad that my father controlled me all the time—but that doesn't mean that I have to argue with every boss and cop I run across." Often these insights help clients to differentiate past realities from present ones. Frequently, they allow clients to make finer distinctions between people and events than they previously could. Present situations are responded to for what they are, rather than as shadowy reproductions of painful early experiences. The power and clarity of these postcathartic insights are often quite impressive.

At other times, however, such insight does not occur spontaneously. Some clients get lost in the feelings and are unable to see how they relate to issues of daily living. Others seem to make poor connections and draw unwise conclusions about what the feelings mean or what changes in behavior they imply. At these times, the therapist needs to intervene.

If a client simply avoids thinking about the implications of newly discovered feelings, the therapist can gently urge that this be done or can suggest some possible meanings and implications. In some cases, the therapist may need to be more forceful and suggest tasks for the client to try outside the sessions: "It was very costly for you to be close to people when you were small. This week push yourself to be close to Kevin even though it scares you. Find out through that experiment whether intimacy needs to be as costly as it was when you were a child." Such suggestions use insight to link feelings to new behavior. As we mentioned in Chapter 2, feelings are not objects that need to be expelled, but rather, important guides and motivators toward more satisfying living.

When a client draws erroneous conclusions, the therapist is obliged to intervene firmly. The therapist has helped to engender an altered state that may lead the client to beliefs or action sequences that are clearly inappropriate. Clients occasionally say things such as, "After all that crap my mother gave me, I think I'll go over this afternoon and tell her off"; "I've been taking care of people all my life. I'm gonna leave and let my wife take care of the kids." At such times, the therapist needs to help the client separate therapeutic work on feelings from real-life action.

The impulsive statements above have a shoot-from-the-hip quality that can be quite harmful. Feeling-action connections are neurotic as often as they are healthy. A healthy feeling-thinking-action connection should have a less hectic pacing. Ironically, the wrong movement from feeling to behavior can initiate a backlash of self-reproach or anger from others that confirms the clinet's earlier fear of expressing feelings or changing behavior. At times, the therapist simply needs to restrain the client from taking some ill-considered action. At other times, it may be necessary to confront the client with her/his inferences and show how the very defense that is supposedly being attacked is in fact operating in the client's formulation of the situation and of what should be done.

Change Behavior

We believe that when feelings are expressed fully, they lead to new ways of viewing both self and world; these new cognitive constructions then lead to changed, more satisfying behavior. However, this process does not happen automatically. We have found it helpful to review goals with clients every six months or so. This provides a structure in which client and therapist can look together at the amount of success they are achieving in reaching agreed-upon goals. Less formally, we often simply remind clients what they came for and ask them what they are doing in their life outside therapy to achieve these goals.

We have found that in trying to be forceful about behavioral results, we have, at times, become shortsighted, spending too much time examining specific interactions and exhorting clients to try harder and too little time exploring feelings and meanings. In general, however, like most therapists, we pay too little attention to behavioral results rather than too much.

Part of the problem is that the therapeutic process encourages regression and dependency. Since being taken care of feels good, clients have some motivation to stay in therapy by resisting change. Persistent attention to behavioral change conveys our unwillingness simply to provide "purchased friendship" (Schofield, 1964). The client's progress toward change can be used as a way of assessing the degree to which dependent gratification—rather than personal change—is the motivation for therapy.

METHODS

Before turning to the specific methods used to reach the objectives discussed above, we must first try to describe some metatechniques that guide the use of specific techniques.

First, we pay a lot of attention to feelings. This may sound obvious and simple-minded, but it is surprisingly difficult to make this point clearly. The problem is that all therapists pay attention to feelings and we pay attention to other things besides feelings. Yet, there is a qualitative difference in our approach. The most obvious ways we pay attention to feelings (e.g., having clients hit pillows) are in many ways the most trivial. The most important ones are harder to see. Basically, they involve matters of philosophy and strategic choice.

In an emotive approach, more attention is paid to expressions of feeling—even covert or subtle ones—and less attention is thus available for other potentially useful channels. We feel this tradeoff is worthwhile. Since we use more of our attention to listen to feelings, we have less available for other good purposes such as listening for subtle references to the therapist (Langs, 1982) or noticing whether imagery is visual or auditory (Grinder and Bandler, 1981). Each therapist chooses areas to highlight and lets others go. Obviously, feelings are not all we notice, but, relative to other therapists, we notice them more.

We try to make it safe for clients to feel by setting a tone that helps them feel safe enough to show their feelings. This, too, may seem obvious or commonplace, but in fact it is a point of controversy. Many therapists are careful not to encourage dependency. They do little to help, support, or care for the client, instead presenting themselves as strictly neutral. These therapists are concerned that more nurturant behavior would be a disservice to the client as it would encourage harmful, unrealistic dependency (Brenner, 1976). Others, including some psychoanalysts, see value in being somewhat more responsive and friendly (Stone, 1961).

We believe that if clients are to share deep feelings from childhood, with their attendant sense of vulnerability, considerable warmth and support from the therapist are indicated. We believe that such a warm, active relationship forms the best basis for vigorous confrontation of defenses. Clients can only hear and use interruptions of their defensive ways after a basic sense of personal respect and warmth has been established. We cannot *make* clients trust us or feel safe, but we can set a tone that makes it more likely for trust and safety to develop. We believe the most successful interventions occur in a relationship that is somewhat warmer and more supportive than the psychoanalytic model of "neutrality."

There is probably some increase in dependent behavior in response to our warm, active approach, but we accept this as a reasonable cost for the benefits mentioned above. In addition, the working through of these dependent feelings during treatment provides the client with a classic opportunity to complete unresolved issues with parents.

Our warm, active therapeutic approach and careful focus on feelings—at times, at the expense of other areas—are the two basic meta-techniques that underlie all of our specific methods. We believe that all therapists—whether or not they are aware of it—make choices in these two areas and that each choice has positive and negative consequences. These are the choices which seem to us to have the best ratio of cost to reward. Let us now look at the twelve specific methods we use to reach the five objectives discussed above.

Statements of Support and Encouragement

It would be hard to imagine a therapeutic system that did not use this method in some form. The therapist's willingness to listen and care is conveyed with a look, a gesture, or a word that says, in effect, "I've been there, too. I know how you feel." This helps clients to overcome the fear of being judged or ignored so that they can share their story or feelings without fear of censure. Of course, there are times when reassurance is withheld so that clients can fully experience feelings of aloneness or self-condemnation. But without some support, the progress of the session would frequently be slowed by the client's fear and uncertainty. Examples of statements of support and empathy are:

Sounds like you had a terrible time.

That's terrific!

It sounds like you are able to give your son better parenting than you got. Good for you.

You're really being tough on yourself today!

Good session

Stay with it. You can do it.

The best response is the one that springs fresh and new from the therapist's genuine feelings for the client. Sometimes it will be a touch, a smile, or a reference to some similar event in the client's life: "Is that like when your brother bought you the kite?" Other times it simply may convey encouragement—"Say more"—or empathy—"Sounds scary"; "You must have wanted to smack him." Empathy is also conveyed through other methods—for instance, sensitive role-playing on the part of the therapist and taking client's point of view. In that sense, the methods overlap to some extent.

However the message is given, the kernel of it is that the therapist understands and stands by the client. It says, "Okay so far. Keep going. I'm with you."

Giving Permission and Coaching

Clients often need little more than permission in order to experience their emotions. People frequently begin to have feelings as they talk about important events, but through long-standing habit they hold their feelings in. In many cases, they will feel more if the therapist simply says: "You look sad. Stay with it"; or "Sounds like that makes you angry. Say it again, louder." These statements, which invite the client to express feelings more fully, frequently precede feeling-expressive episodes. Many clients hold their feelings in for no more complicated reason than that they have not been reassured that expressing them is okay.

The therapist sometimes gives permission authoritatively, saying, in effect: "You've been told not to cry or be angry, but that advice has hurt you. It's really good to show your feelings, especially in here." At other times, the therapist is more nurturant: "Telling you to leave must have hurt you a lot. I can see the hurt in your eyes. Why don't you try to hold onto me? Maybe that will give you the safety you need to let yourself cry." The therapist also gives permission by saying such things as: "I can see how that would make you mad"; "Just because you're frightened doesn't mean you're a baby"; "I think there's more sadness in there. Stay with it." Simple statements like these can markedly increase the level and intensity of clients' feeling-expression. Giving clients the permission to feel is probably the most direct way to encourage catharsis.

Coaching is closely related to permission-giving. It involves urging clients toward feeling-expression, often by giving them strategies for gaining access to feelings or circumventing defenses. This may involve telling clients to hit a pillow, showing them how to hit it, or telling them to keep hitting it when they feel like stopping. If a client is unsure whether she/he feels angry or sad, the therapist may say: "Let out a loud sound. Let out several. You'll hear the feeling in it." Other coaching suggestions are: "Try closing your eyes"; "Just let the sobs out—don't try to stop them"; "Hold on tighter."

Permission-giving and coaching are used mostly to counter defenses and facilitate feeling-expression. Permission-giving invites clients to express their feelings while coaching combines specific-skills training with encouragement toward fuller feeling-expression.

Focusing

Focusing alters clients' awareness—what they are aware of and how they are aware of it. Although focusing can be used in the service of any of the five objectives, it is used most often and most productively to counter defenses and facilitate expression of feeling.

For example, as clients talk, certain affectively charged words stand out. Asking the client to focus on these phrases by repeating them is a simple way to increase the client's feeling response to them. The most effective phrases are pithy and pregnant with conflict or pain: "It's not fair!"; "I'll never see him again"; "Who will help me?"; "Don't leave me!"; "I hate him." Even well-chosen phrases may need to be repeated several times for the feelings to reach full strength.

Visual imagery is another useful focusing technique, as is illustrated in the following example:

> That scene you mentioned of your mother on the back porch . . . close your eyes and see that. . . . Visualize it clearly. . . . See the details. See where she's sitting. . . . See her dress. . . . Now look at her face. See it clearly. . . . What expression does she have? Now, imagine her opening her mouth and starting to talk. What does she say to you?

Other focusing techniques call attention to a particular feeling or painful event:

> So you're pretty aware of how angry that made you. But I also see some sadness in your eyes. Can you feel that, too—how it hurt you?

> That story you just told me had a part you skipped over quickly. Tell me more about the part where she said she didn't need you any more.

Finally, some focusing techniques draw attention to previously unnoticed physical sensations:

> Notice your body. What sensations are you aware of? What seems to be happening in your stomach? Your heart? Are your hands warm or cold, damp or dry?

In each of these examples, the therapist suggests that the client direct her/his attention so as to become conscious of certain thoughts.

Properly used, focusing works both to circumvent defensiveness and to expand awareness. The power of focusing derives largely from the power of the attentional process itself. Of the millions of bits of sensory data coming to us each moment, we choose to attend to only a few. We pattern them and perceive them in ways that are meaningful to us. In so doing, we exert enormous control over our *perceptual* environment even though we have much less control over our *sensory* environment. At a more general level, we can look at our lives—our friends, values, work, history—and can construe these in innumerable and highly varying ways. We can choose to see the cup half empty or half full; we can make of the ambiguous pluses and minuses of our social network almost any picture, of loyalty or desertion, of joy or pain, that we choose to. To a great extent, the attentional process shapes these attributions. Which interactions do we choose to remember and which do we forget? Which do we emphasize and which do we let pass? Since directing our awareness helps to determine our perceptual environment and the meaning we make of our lives, focusing is clearly a powerful tool for modifying the client's consciousness.

Sometimes, no matter how hard they try, clients are unable to remember details of early events. Focusing can be very helpful in such cases. The therapist asks the client to make up a story about what *could have* happened. These stories often bring up important feelings or even help the client to remember what *actually* happened.

In using focusing, it is important to remember that people vary with respect to which sensory modalities are most alive for them (Bandler and Grinder, 1982). Some visualize fluently but cannot imagine sounds, smells, or touch. For others, the auditory channel is the clearest and most available modality. Focusing is most useful when the therapist works with the sensory system with which the client feels most comfortable. At times, clients look past a particular focusing exercise to what they believe the therapist is trying to achieve. This, of course, keeps them from focusing. For example, a young client had been grieving the loss of his father for several weeks. The therapist suggested that he picture his father at a time when they had felt close to each other, adding, "See what thoughts come to mind and what you would like to say to him." The client said he did not feel close to his sad feelings that day and did not think he could cry. The therapist replied, "I'm not asking you to cry. I'm just asking you to picture your father and talk to him. Try that and see what happens."

In this example, the therapist may, in fact, have expected tears to emerge, but she did not say, "Cry." She said, "Turn your attention to this memory and open yourself to whatever thoughts come up." She knew that this might lead to expression of feelings, but all she asked the client to do was to attend to those images and share the resulting thoughts. Such an exercise is most likely to be of help if the client can simply focus attention as suggested without being distracted by performance concerns.

Focusing also occurs without the use of active techniques such as dialogue and imagery. When a therapist asks about one detail and not another, or chooses to understand an interaction in a particular light, she/he is making a choice that focuses the client's attention in a particular way.

Role-Playing

Like focusing, role-playing is designed to counter defenses and promote the expression of feelings (objectives 2 and 3). In role-playing, memories and fantasies are acted out rather than discussed. Action is the vehicle
for intensifying emotional impact. Role-playing promotes spontaneity and
enlivens sessions with emotional action and interaction. Furthermore,
because realistic constraints are absent, clients can say and feel what they
could not or would not previously. In this way, role-playing not only
increases the level of feeling but also enables clients to experiment with
a variety of new ways of behaving.

There is considerable variety in how roles are played. Clients can play
themselves or someone else. The roles may be played realistically or in
terms of how clients see them or would like them to be. The therapist
may or may not play a role and, at times, may role-play alone. If therapy
is conducted in a group, there may be several players. The cast of characters also may be expanded by using pillows or chairs as dummy persons.

Role-playing is sometimes used as practice for real life; in such cases,
the client tests out a new skill. However, we generally use role-playing
to aid feeling-expression rather than as a rehearsal for real-life behavior.
Role-playing may be used to discover something, such as what the client
is really afraid of or wants, or what happened between the client and
someone else. Or, the goal may be simply to foster feeling-expression. At
times, the basic script and outline of the drama are predicated on what
has already been said; at other times, the unfolding drama takes surprising
directions. At times, the therapist may closely follow the client's directions
for a particular scene; at other times, the therapist may find it useful to
improvise dialogue. The degree and nature of structuring also vary considerably. The therapist and client may spend much time discussing and
setting up a dramatic situation. More frequently, roles develop spontaneously and occasionally the therapist may slip into role-playing without
any prior discussion. The therapist simply begins to talk and act like
someone in the client's history who is relevant to what is going on in the
client's present work.

The following two examples illustrate different ways in which role-
playing can be used.

Sam came in angry about a conversation that he had had with his wife
that morning. After a few minutes, the therapist felt that she knew roughly
how the argument had gone and she began to play the wife's role, saying
things that the client had indicated and adding what she guessed had made
him the angriest. The therapist offered Sam a pillow so that, in addition
to speaking angrily, he could express his feelings motorically as well. As
Sam's anger began to fade, the therapist tried out other phrases to see if

she could rekindle his fury. Later, the therapist stood at a distance from Sam and invited him to swing and kick at her while she responded in a complementary way, as though she were being hit and kicked.

In this example, the therapist simply played the role of someone that Sam was angry with in order to help him increase his feeling and expression of anger.

Judy, a 31-year-old single woman, described a recent visit to her parents, emphasizing how disappointed she had been when she realized that her parents were too troubled and weak ever to take care of her the way she wanted. She focused particularly on her father. After awhile, the therapist asked her if it would be helpful for him to play the role of her father. She said it would, and they agreed on some things that should be said. The dialogue went as follows.

Judy: (Angrily.) I've been here for three days and you haven't asked me one thing about myself.

Therapist: (Meekly.) I guess that's because I've had so much on my mind. My back's been bothering me.

Judy: (Angrily.) Oh, you and your back, you and your worries, you've always got some excuse. Goddamn you! Where were you? Where were you this weekend? Where were you when I was growing up?

Therapist: (Burdened.) I guess I have been quite a disappointment to you. I'm sorry.

Judy: The hell you're sorry. If you were sorry, you'd have been different. You're not sorry, you're just a selfish shit!

Therapist: I'm sorry. I don't ever seem to know what to do.

Things continued in this vein, with Judy hitting the pillow and yelling at her father. Then the therapist moved to an even more exaggerated portrayal of the father, hunching his shoulders forward, looking up at her fearfully, and emphasizing his inadequacy. After a few minutes, the therapist sensed a shift in Judy's feelings, as she finished one of her angry tirades by saying, "It could have been so different." The therapist responded by sitting up and looking at her warmly, smiling confidently, and saying, "It not only could have been, sweetheart, it's going to be." She gave him a startled look and asked, "What do you mean?"

Therapist: (Still portraying relaxed, calm strength.) What I mean is that what you've been saying is right, that you deserve more, and that I'm going to give you more.

Judy: (Somewhat confused and suspicious.) What do you mean you're going to give me more? I've heard that before.

Therapist: What I mean is that right now I'm going to get up, go into the kitchen, and start cooking you some chicken tetrazzini, just like I did when you were in the fourth grade and your mom went to the hospital (one of Judy's few positive memories of being taken care of by her father). And while I'm making it, I want you to sit at the kitchen table and tell me what you've been doing for the last six months and what it's been like for you.

Judy burst into tears, reached out to the therapist, and held onto him, putting her head on his shoulder as she cried. The therapist continued to play the role of the good father whom Judy had been missing. Each time her sobs subsided, he said another sentence or two.

Therapist: It will be just like it was then. We'll go out riding together. . . . (More sobs.) I'll tell you some corny jokes. . . . (More sobs.) And I'll hold you and take care of you and not let anything happen to my little girl.

After about ten minutes of this, Judy straightened up, blew her nose, and said sadly, "That's not really going to happen." The therapist nodded agreement and asked Judy if she was ready to say goodbye to the good daddy she had always longed for. Judy closed her eyes and pictured that father. As she said goodbye, she cried hard, sometimes screaming out her goodbyes; sometimes pleading, "No, don't leave me!"; and sometimes just sobbing. The therapist was mostly quiet now, letting Judy continue with her feelings on her own. She sobbed almost until the end of the session, at which point she and the therapist briefly reviewed what had happened.

In this example, the therapist alternated between realistic and fantasied portrayals of the father, using cues from Judy and his own intuitive sense of what would evoke the strongest emotion.

There is no formula for determining which type of role-playing to use and when to use it. These decisions spring from knowledge of the client, overall therapeutic strategy, and the therapist's own empathic response. Moreover, in deciding which type of role-playing to use, the therapist should take into account the level of feeling-expression manifested by the client in each session.

One type of role-playing that we have found useful is Albert and Diane Pesso's "psycho-motor therapy" (Pesso, 1972). In this system, role-playing is highly structured and the therapist is careful to behave exactly as the client prescribes. A distinction is made between the client's real and ideal parents, and the therapist carefully announces which role she/he is taking. For example:

Therapist: What would you like your ideal father to say?
Client: I want him to tell me that I'm the apple of his eye.
Therapist: I'm not Bill anymore; I'm your ideal father. You're the apple of my eye.
Client: And I want to hear that I'm your favorite son.
Therapist: You're my favorite son.

In this system, whose complexity is beyond the scope of this discussion, it is assumed that the client must be responsible for saying exactly what she/he wants to hear and the therapist must repeat it exactly. This is done because meanings and feelings frequently attach to particular words and phrases that have strong associations for the client. For instance, in the above example, the phrase "apple of my eye" may mean something much more or quite different to the client than "my wonderful child" or "someone I love very much."

One advantage of this type of role-playing is that the transference becomes clear and explicit. The therapist can play an ideal, all-giving role separate from her/himself as therapist. Although this method can be somewhat stilted, it has enough value to warrant greater attention than it has received thus far.

Humor

The healing, restorative, and perspective-giving powers of laughter are well known (Cousins, 1976; Smith, 1975). A word or phrase suddenly recasts how we view something, assumptions collide, a new facet or perspective surprises us, and we laugh. Humor is particularly useful in a cathartic approach because it both stimulates and gives partial expression to unconscious feelings and impulses. By doing so in a disguised way, it can sometimes circumvent a client's defenses, allowing expression of wishes or feelings that would otherwise remain hidden.

A joke, situation, or comment is funny to the degree that there is a sudden, skillful shift of the audience's expectation, or set, and to the degree that the audience is aroused (Schacter, 1965). A standard technique in horror movies is to scare the audience with pictures of death and dismemberment and then have some apparently frightening stimulus turn out to be harmless. A wave of laughter and relief flows through the theatre. Arousal is high and the shift of set releases the laughter. Similarly, with clients there are times when anxiety is so high that virtually any comment will bring a laugh. At such times, especially when attention is focused on a conflictual area, any comment that shifts the client's perspective—that suddenly lightens or relieves anxiety—is experienced as funny. At times like these, the therapist does not have to be Woody Allen to induce peals of laughter. Once an anxious client starts laughing, even raising an eyebrow, shaking a finger, or repeating a word may be enough to prolong the laughter for several minutes.

The example below illustrates several methods for inducing laughter. Although the feared impulses are sexual, they could as easily be aggressive or dependent.

Helen, a young woman who had never been very close to her father, was expecting a visit from him and was anxious about how it would go. She had recently been exploring her sexual feelings toward him and early memories of glimpsing his penis. After spending some time on other feelings about his visit, she turned her attention to the sexual impulses and fears that his impending visit had elicited.

Helen: I just remembered that I saw his cock. Remember? I told you about that. That just flashed through my head. Oh, shit. He had shorts on, he was walking through the kitchen to the bathroom. You know, he had boxer shorts on with a fly in the front (laughs) and I saw. . . .

Carl: Right through the fly? What did you see?

Helen: Yeah. It was open. I saw his cock hanging down and his balls and a lot of hair and stuff.

Carl: Was it teeny?

Helen: (Laughs.) No, it wasn't teeny! It was big and threatening! Kind of dark and scary and hairy and yuck.

Carl: Scary and hairy and yuck! (Both laugh.) You know he'll have it with him when he comes on Sunday.

Helen: Oh c'mon!

Here Carl simultaneously raised Helen's anxiety by confronting her with her father's (and her own) sexuality and helped her to discharge it through humor. Specifically, he did this by the use of opposites ("Was it teeny?") and by moving to a lighter level ("Scary and hairy and yuck!" recalls Dorothy's way of dealing with her fear on the yellow brick road—"Lions and tigers and bears, oh my!"). This is similar to focusing a client on her anger and then suggesting that she discharge it by hitting and shouting, or talking to a client about what makes her sad and then helping her to cry. Anxiety has less clear pathways for discharge. Shivering, yawning, and laughing are three possible pathways. In the following dialogue, Carl tries to help Helen discharge her anxiety through laughter.

Carl: He'll have it with him when he parks in the driveway and walks into good old 205 Sycamore.

Helen: (Tentatively.) Yeah. I know.

Carl: He will. If he sits on the couch, it'll be right there on the couch.

Helen: (Laughing.) I'm getting an upset stomach.

Carl: If he goes to your toilet, it'll be right there on your toilet.

Helen: (Laughing.) Oh come on!

Carl: If he takes a bath, it'll be right there, floating in your bathtub.

Helen: (Laughing hard.) That's my father you're talking about!

Carl: I know it. When you wash your bathtub out later and there's some pubic hair, it'll be his. (Helen laughs hard.) You know that?

Helen: Oh dear!

Carl: You said you're gonna have people over to meet him? Is that right?

Helen: Yeah.

Carl: I can see it. All evening you'll be obsessed with his cock. "My father's cock, my father's cock. It's right here in the room with us!" (Helen laughs.) You'll say, "Do you want a COCKtail?" and then you'll say to yourself, "Oh my God, did I say that too loud?"

Helen: (Laughing.) C'mon, saying that could make me do it. I could just say, "Get it over with Dad! Show us all your cock!" (Laughs hard.)

Near the end of the sequence, Carl and Helen used another common device—exaggeration. They exaggerated both Helen's worried obsession with her father's penis and the extent of her unruly impulses. These exaggerations elicited laughter by saying, in effect, "It's not *that* bad." They were thus instrumental in helping Helen to discharge her anxiety and in giving her an increased sense of perspective and ability to cope.

One aspect of the therapist's task in such a situation deserves special comment—the extent to which the therapist must respond quickly to feedback from the client. Certain things Carl said worked well (like talking about her father's penis as a separate entity) and he stayed with and elaborated on those themes. Others did not seem especially useful and were quickly abandoned. The therapist has no way of knowing *a priori* which comments will seem funny and which will not. The therapist must watch the client's responses carefully and shape comments toward themes that are eliciting the most laughter.

In the situations we have discussed so far, humor is used to elicit vigorous and sustained laughter in order to counter embarrassment, shyness, or anxiety. The laughter is a form of discharge, a channel for feeling-expression. In other instances, humor is used more cognitively. The reaction sought is a smile or a short burst of laughter and the goal is not to produce discharge but to alter the client's perspective.

Another way laughter can be used therapeutically is through mimicry. Defenses are rigid, predictable, and stereotyped. When a client begins a victim routine or pompous lecturing, it is easy for the therapist to mimic and exaggerate that behavior. Typically, at such times, clients are not consciously aware of what they are doing; when presented with an exaggerated mirroring of themselves, they are likely to laugh and change (the better response) or to get angry at the therapist for making fun of them (also a potentially useful response). The latter response is useful as long as the client does not act on the anger by leaving the session. There is usually some part of the client that recognizes the truth in the exaggeration and welcomes the interruption of the defense.

The danger with mimicry is that the therapist's angry countertransference easily can be expressed in sarcasm under the guise of therapeutic helpfulness (Kubie, 1971, Rosenheim, 1974). If the therapist even wonders whether angry countertransference is causing the choice of technique, mimicry and other abrasive methods should not be used. *Primo non nocere* (first, do no harm) is especially important here. Another caveat about humor is that, like any device, it can also function as a resistance, keeping something more real and useful from happening (Rosenheim, 1974). The therapist needs to evaluate this possibility before deciding whether or not to encourage laughter at any particular point.

A final benefit in the use of humor is the opportunity it gives for human contact. When two people share a laugh, there is a moment when their eyes meet in a brief triumph over anxiety. In that moment, role distinctions fade and a bond is formed out of their similarity and their joint membership in the human race.

Kinesics

The way people hold theselves, the way they move, and their facial expressions reveal a great deal about their feelings, level of tension, self-regard, and defenses. These cues also say a lot about how clients want to deal with others. In addition to providing information, kinesics is an excellent system through which to effect changes in what the client is feeling and how the feeling is being expressed. Table 3-2 presents some of the ways feelings can be expressed fully and how they can be blocked or partially expressed. The therapist's job is to move clients from blocked and partial expressions to more complete expressions of feelings. The therapist can use kinesic interventions to accomplish this change. One such intervention is a form of focusing:

> Notice this behavior. Notice how your hand is clenched. What does it want to do?

> When I came into the waiting room to start our session, you remained sitting. What are you saying to me through that?

> You're closing your eyes so tightly. What do you want to be sure not to see?

Simply calling the client's attention to the behavior can lead to fuller expression of feelings and greater self-awareness.

At other times, a more active intervention is needed. This may take the form of direct contradiction, i.e., asking the client to assume a posture, movement, or facial expression opposite to that being shown. A client who enters the office with hunched shoulders, a tentative step, and a please-don't-hit-me look on his face might be asked to come in again with an exaggerated tough-guy swagger, jutting chin, and a nobody-gives-me-shit look on his face. He may laugh so hard that he will have to try several times before he is successful. The laughter itself is helpful. It can be thought of as the sound of an old self-concept changing. The client is expressing his fear and joy at seeing himself in a new way. Alternatively,

Table 3-2
Nonverbal Expressions of Four Feeling States

EXPRESSION

FEELING	Blocked/Partial Expression	Full Expression
Sadness/pain	Slumped shoulders, seeping tears, pained facial expression, "hangdog" look, slowed movement, red eyes, quiet sighing.	Sobbing, loud crying, screaming, writhing, shouting. In general, a faster tempo.
Anger	Quiet seething, turning away, not answering, tight lips, jutting jaw, "chip-on-the-shoulder" attitude. Eyelids narrowed, eyes turned up or away.	Angry shouting, pounding, kicking, growling. Fluent phrases and sentences of anger and condemnation, warm sweating, biting.
Fear	Hunched shoulders, quiet talking, raised eyebrows, obsequious facial expression, inhibited or jerky movement, cold sweating.	Strong trembling and shaking, warm sweating.
Joy	Attenuated facial expression. (Occasionally old symptoms and worrying are resorted to if joy has been proscribed by parents or if loss of caring is feared to accompany loss of symptom.)	Head held high; smiling; relaxed, light, flowing movement; laughter; trembling.

he can actually adopt part of the new aggressive role to express a part of his hitherto denied potential. He may also begin to feel and express anger. His real anger may flow into the empty shell of the role he is asked to play.

Other examples of direct contradiction are asking a frowning person to smile; asking a tight, rigid person to walk and sit in a relaxed, finger-snapping way; or suggesting that a withdrawn person move in and express eagerness for closeness through posture, movement, and facial expression. In each case, the immediate goal is to interrupt a defense that is being expressed kinesically by prescribing an opposite kinesic. This often increases the client's feeling-expression and expands her/his behavioral repertoire.

Another intervention against a partial or blocked feeling-expression uses paradox (Haley, 1973). The therapist asks the client to exaggerate the kinesic she/he is already doing. A depressed, slouching, slow-moving client may be asked to hold her head even further down, furrow her brow still more deeply, and "please try to slow down and not jump around so much." Again, the aim is to break up a rigid defensive posture. The exact feeling-expression that is produced is of secondary importance. Whether it be laughter, rage, trembling, or tears, it will be more real, less stereotyped, and closer to the client's feelings than what was occurring previously.

Another aspect of kinesics is the client's nonverbal behavior that is "aimed" specifically at the therapist—e.g., how far away the client sits; whether the client's legs are crossed; whether the client makes eye contact; whether the client's hug is warm or cool, strong or weak, tense or relaxed. These and many similar kinesic communications have long been described and discussed in books on psychotherapy. What may be somewhat different in our approach is our active entry into the field of "prescribed kinesics." For example, we may offer one of the following prescriptions. "Move in a little and uncross your legs." "What happens if you sit up straight?" "Don't just sneer like that. Bring your face right up next to mine and stick your tongue out." Each of these interventions is designed to counter a defense that is both kinesic and interpersonal. They seek to move the client closer to feeling-expression.

Touch

While no longer as stringently proscribed as it once was, physical contact between client and therapist continues to be a controversial issue (Cowen, Weissberg and Lotyezewski, 1982, 1983). There are claims and counterclaims about its benefits (Aguilera, 1967; Pattison, 1973) and costs (Holroyd and Brodsky, 1980). Our own clinical experience, which has involved a great deal of touching, has shown that while there are a few clients for whom physical contact is so anxiety-provoking that it is contraindicated, most seem to benefit from it.

Touch can be used both diagnostically and therapeutically. Touching the client can provide information about the level and site of anxiety. Tense muscles in the jaw or back of the neck convey information. So do sweaty palms, cold hands, or warm, flushed skin. Similarly, how the client responds to the therapist's touch—e.g., with jumpiness, by moving away, or by moving closer—conveys information. There are an amazing variety of hugs, and each carries information about both the client's momentary state and habitual style.

In addition to learning about the client through touch, the therapist can use this method to intervene in many useful ways. Touch can provide a very powerful statement of empathy and support. Sometimes a client tells a painful story but does not cry. Then the therapist touches the client's arm and the tears begin to flow. The touch conveys support and caring, which make it safe enough for the client to cry.

Touch also can be part of role-playing. For instance, a client may remember her father grabbing her arm very hard when he was angry. In role-playing the situation, the therapist does likewise, not hurting the client but recreating the father's tight grip. Another client may remember a hand laid softly on his forehead when he had a headache. Again, the therapist uses touch to vivify the memory.

Perhaps the most important way we use touch is in holding clients. The expression of both fear and sadness is greatly facilitated by close, warm body contact. Again and again, clients who are not expressing their feelings fully begin to do so when they are held. The use of holding is one of the obvious ways in which feeling-expressive therapy differs from more traditional approaches. It is also one of the most controversial. We find that initially many clients are frightened by holding and find it awkward or embarrassing. Some never do feel comfortable enough to be held, but most quickly learn to accept the support and nurturance and let go of any romantic or sexual connotations holding may have had for them. We find that when we approach holding in a casual, matter-of-fact way, clients can do so as well and do not experience it as sexual. Needless to say, we are careful not to behave in a seductive or exploitative way ourselves and we often explicitly reassure clients that there will be no sexual involvement. As mentioned, there are a few clients (mostly males with male therapists) who never become comfortable with being held and, of course, we do not insist on holding anyone. Some clients begin to feel comfortable with holding only after they have attended a workshop in which they have seen other people holding each other.

Different ways of holding are used to further different objectives. When clients seek to express feelings of loss, neediness, or sadness, we often have them sit next to us on the mat, facing us, and hold them with their chests against ours and their heads on our shoulders. This warm, comforting position can give even a large client the sense of being small and cared for. When clients want to express fear, however, we are more apt to have them sit between our legs, facing away from us, with our arms around their abdomens. This position seems to provide the right kind of support to facilitate the shaking and shivering that discharges fear.

When the therapist is comfortable with holding and confident about the value and appropriateness of holding she/he can give a very reassuring message to the client: "you are safe here with me to let go and feel and

I will not take advantage of your vulnerability."

There are also times when clients need someone or something to push against. The therapist may block a doorway, challenging the client to push and struggle in order to win passage through the door. The therapist may hold a pillow for the client to hit or push. The therapist may push the client into a corner, encouraging her/him to push back. Endless variations are possible. What links these particular techniques is a sort of role-playing in which the therapist offers the client some circumscribed situation in which the direct physical expression of self-assertion or anger is permitted and safe.

Finally, touch can be used as an intervention against chronic muscular tensions, rigidities, and habits. This approach, which is dealt with extensively in bioenergetics (Lowen, 1975), is used sparingly in feeling-expressive therapy. Nevertheless, there are times when such interventions are critically important. The therapist may press her/his thumbs gently against the tensed masseter muscles in the client's jaw or smooth the frontalis muscles holding the client's forehead and eyebrows in a fixed frown. Similarly, the therapist can move against chronic muscular "expressions" of anger in the stiff neck and held-back head, the jutting jaw and tight-lipped mouth. These postures convey a sense of anger, but are not true expressions of anger. They can continue for years without giving relief. Interventions against this blocked anger should be gentle, helping the client to let go of the anger by relaxing. A gentle downward pressure on the lower lip invites the client to open the mouth and give voice to the feeling that previously has been "shut up" inside.

The major tools needed for these physical interventions are sharp observation, curiosity, and a willingness to experiment. "I wonder why she's arching her back that way." "He holds his chest like a drill instructor. Wonder what would happen if I pushed on it." "It must hurt to hold her face like that. What if I stroke those overworked muscles?" Thoughts like these, followed by reasonable and sensitive touching, can lead to productive interventions.

Attention to Breathing

Breathing is a semiautomatic, life-sustaining function that can go on indefinitely without awareness. Yet, when we attend to it, we can observe wide variations in how it occurs. For a person in good health, these variations are closely tied to both chronic and intermittent emotional factors. This makes breathing a useful clue to what clients are feeling, how these feelings are held back from full expression, and what sort of intervention could be useful. When someone alters his or her rate of breathing, an immediate change in feeling tone follows which can facilitate the expression of strong feelings.

If a slow, steady deep-breathing pattern is taken as the standard for a resting person, many deviations are possible. Some of these are simply the accompaniments of a feeling state that is already being expressed, such as the rapid breathing associated with fear or the gasping breathing that is part of sobbing. Normally, these deviations need no attention. They are not blocking expression of feeling. Other breathing patterns, however, function defensively. Stifled sighs are often heard from depressed people. These are breaths where the intake is greater than normal and the expiration begins as a sigh and then is caught and stopped, so that the rest of the expiration is controlled and slow. A complete sigh can feel good and promote relaxation when one is depressed or feeling pressured. Perhaps there is a subliminal sense that breathing has been shallow and the sigh is an attempt to change that by taking a very deep breath. Yet, somehow that process often gets interrupted. A useful intervention is to point out the stillborn sigh and ask the client for a full one. It usually takes insistent urging to get the client to sigh deeply. When the sigh does occur, it functions as a sort of self-administered confrontation. The client usually cannot hear her/his own full sigh without hearing the statement "I'm really sad!" or "I'm going too fast; I need to stop." These self-perceptions often move people toward fuller expression.

Another significant deviation from normal respiration is shallow, rapid breathing that uses only a small part of the lungs' capacity. Various interventions can be useful, including simply asking the client to breathe deeply and to exhale vigorously. At times, it is helpful to aid this process by pressing down on the client's chest or abdomen with exhalation and then releasing the pressure with inhalation, simultaneously suggesting that the client take a deep breath. This is the most straightforward and simple procedure. If the client continues the shallow breathing and will not breathe more deeply, it may be useful to ask the client to breathe even more shallowly and slowly. When the client develops a strong sense of needing air, she/he will then take a deep breath. It is also useful to ask the client what will happen if she/he breathes deeply. What bad things might happen? What good things might happen? Usually, however, when breathing is deepened, bound-up feelings surface, making speculations unnecessary.

When a client is on her back on the mat most obstructions in breathing can easily be seen by the observant therapist. Laying a hand gently on the abdomen and asking the client to breathe into the hand will stimulate deeper breathing and tend to open up the chest area to whatever feelings are being blocked by the obstructed breathing. We find that a soft and gentle "please, just breathe into my hand", is all that is needed to encourage most clients to breathe deeply.

Shallow breathing is often accompanied by rapid speech and a rapid, almost gasping, sudden intake of breath, as if the client were hurried or fearful of being interrupted. Again, it is sometimes useful to manipulate chest or abdomen to increase depth of breathing or simply to point out what the client is doing and ask her/him to slow down or stop speaking, and to breathe deeply and slowly. Frequently,. when this is done, the client feels fear. In fact, any pressured, hectic, hypomanic behavior is likely to be associated with suppressed fear.

Two other related breathing patterns also function as defenses. One is choking and stoppages in the throat that sound as though there is a closing off of the air flow. In the related phenomenon of gasping, the person appears to be getting a good deal of air, but seems to need more. In the latter case, there is a subjective feeling that insufficient air is getting in; in the former case, the way of breathing and sound suggest that the entrance and exit of the air are being interfered with somewhere in the throat. In both cases, it is often useful to intervene by (more symbolically than really) interfering with the client's air supply. The therapist may gently cover the client's mouth or put a hand to the client's throat in a way that suggests strangulation. The air supply is not really interfered with in either case, but the suggestion of such interference can often bring out the fear or anger underlying the gasping or chocking breathing pattern.

Some useful interventions prompted by breathing patterns are not related to respiration. For example, the therapist can respond to the gasping breather by saying, "It sounds like you're not getting enough." The client can then explore the idea of "not getting enough" in other life situations.

Another interesting breathing interference to watch for is the use of only the chest or only the abdomen for breathing. People frequently breath from only one of these areas without ever noticing it. However, when the therapist calls attention to it and asks the client to breathe deeply with both the chest and abdomen, one part of this breathing apparatus is apt to stay immobile. Again, the therapist can intervene by using touch or by asking the client to breath fully from the entire chest and abdomen. As the previously immobilized area begins to move, feelings that have been held back may begin to be felt. Deep breathing has a disorienting effect that can help people uncover strong, preverbal feelings. Frequently there is a nameless terror that may be connected to early fears. Feelings of dependency may also emerge. The client may become aware of longing, fear of being close, or fear of being abandoned. These feelings are often a surprise to the client, as they have emerged in consciousness without passing through the usual verbal/rational filters. Although the strength and inexplicable origin of these feelings often frighten clients, this is a useful method of gaining access to feelings.

Prescriptions

Most of us subscribe to a kind of "inside-out" paradigm in which inner states are seen as leading to behavior. For example, the inner experience of hunger leads to eating or looking for food, sadness leads to crying, and the expectation of defeat leads to a lackluster and defeatist performance. In a case of shyness and social isolation, an insight-oriented therapist would work on the inner states of fear and self-consciousness, believing that the client could become more gregarious only after those states had been changed. A behaviorist in the classical Pavlovian tradition would also focus on the internal state, seeking to substitute relaxation for tension as the response to a social stimulus. A behaviorist in the operant, Skinnerian tradition, however, would look at the behavior and seek to change it by changing the reward structure that had been maintaining it; there would be little interest in the inner states, which would be viewed as concomitants, rather than causes, of the behavior.

In our approach, we alternate between changing feelings to change behavior and changing behavior to change feelings. We spend a lot of time on inner states, exploring them and facilitating their expression. There are times, however, when we prescribe a particular behavior as the most effective way of changing both an inner state and behavior. The following example illustrates such a prescription.

Ben had a rigid and unrealistically negative view of himself and his life. His style was to present himself as troubled, unhappy, and intense. In fact, he had a great deal going for him in his life. One day, following Ben's usual litany of gloom and doom, the therapist sought to change this behavior by offering a prescription:

Therapist: Tell me about the good things in your life.
Ben: (Pause.) I feel like smashing you!

Just thinking about complying with the prescription tended to break up the defense and resulted in anger. The anger was explored for awhile. The therapist rekindled it when necessary by asking again for Ben to tell him good things about his life. After 10 or 15 minutes, the anger subsided and the therapist asked Ben if he was ready to say goodbye to his negativity. He said that he was and he spent the rest of the session alternately raging and crying about losing a familiar way of presenting himself. He was also saying goodbye to the father who taught him to be that way. At the end of the session, he was more positive in his feelings about himself and more optimistic about his life.

Our general scheme in cases such as Ben's is to prescribe a behavior that opposes a defense. Two consequences tend to follow: (1) the defense is attacked and (2) new, more satisfying behavior is initiated. Either of these results may be primary at any given time. In Ben's case, the statement "Tell me something good about your life" was intended primarily to aid the expression of feelings and to attack the depressive defense against positive feelings. However, a prescription given at the end of the session may be intended primarily to establish more productive behavior: "Do three things each day this week that make you feel good about yourself." This struggle to establish more productive behavior may well result in the client coming to the next session ready to work on the feelings that came up as she/he carried out the prescription.

The following are examples of prescriptions.

Give away $25.00 this week.

Make contact with at least four people each day, two of whom must be men.

Ask your wife out to dinner this week without the children.

Look through your old family photo album and see what thoughts and feelings emerge.

Lose three pounds by next week.

These prescriptions are intended to help clients actually change behavior that they see as unchangeable. Doing so will also elicit feelings. We may, for example, ask a meek, shy person to strut around and "act big." Or we may ask a compulsive, hard-working client to sit back and relax while work piles up on her desk.

There are times, especially in work with couples, when we prescribe roles, role changes, and role reversals. Couples frequently get into habitual roles. One is bossy and one is resentful. One worries about money and one spends it. One always initiates sex. One wants to be "close" and the other is always "busy" or "tired." All of these roles are rigidities that impoverish the life of the couple. Ideally, a couple switches roles, taking turns in the big-little, warm-cold, active-passive roles. Prescribing role reversals to a couple stuck in a certain pattern is often useful. We may tell the husband who is always making sexual advances and double-entendre jokes to stop doing so—to say nothing about sex and to go along with only mild interest if his wife initiates sex. The wife is told to imitate his usual behavior, e.g., suggesting sex or grabbing his butt as he walks by. These prescriptions can be slanted toward a fairly straightforward trying out of opposite roles or toward a more droll exaggeration of each other's roles which serves as a confrontation technique (Do I really act *that* way?") and can produce peals of laughter. The prescribed behavior can be done during the therapy session or at home.

Prescriptions are important because they keep the client's goals in view and tie the therapy session to everyday living. This is particularly important in a therapy that is cathartic and phenomenological. The therapist seeks to take the client's perspective, to spend some time seeing the world from the viewpoint of the client, especially the client-as-child. The therapist frequently encourages the client to take the latter viewpoint and to be aware of how that child hurt. This viewpoint is not inherently mawkish, accusatory, or self-pitying, but it can generate to such if the self-world balance is not maintained.

The setting of cathartic therapy is by design somewhat unreal. In order to make it safe for clients to experience long-avoided feelings, we insulate them from potentially negative feedback and we encourage them to speak their childlike wishes clearly and without fear of reproach. Although this artificial climate created to promote catharsis and regression is useful, it must also be balanced by efforts to transfer changes initiated in therapy sessions to life outside the consulting room. For example, the needy child must exchange goods with others, recognize their rights and legitimate demands, and come to terms with their limitations and foibles. The therapist should always maintain this perspective; the client should have it at the end of a session and preferably at the beginning as well.

Prescriptions are useful in helping to present clients with some real-world demands that they must face and manage. At the same time, feelings generated in the process can be worked on in the therapy session.

Questions for Information

This method is simply a way for the therapist to find out needed information such as: "How many siblings do you have?"; "What thought did you have just then when you started to cry?"; "How much do you drink?" The therapist may need hundreds of such pieces of information in order to pursue therapeutic objectives discussed earlier.

The use of questions early in therapy in history-gathering is too well-known to warrant discussion here. What needs emphasis is the importance of ongoing information-gathering about the client's present life as therapy proceeds. Much information is gathered serendipitously as other work is done. There are times, however, when a therapist suddenly realizes that she/he knows very little about some phase of a client's life. The therapy may have focused recently on early family life, with little said about the client's current family situation, sex life, or career. The therapist may notice that the client looks thinner or is often dirty and unshaven. It is surprising how often people hide their little islands of craziness. For example, "having sex" can mean many things, only one of which is intercourse. It is important to know what is really happening, and the therapist's embarrassment is no excuse for not asking specific questions.

Lack of money is often used as a "realistic" excuse for why clients "can't" go out and make friends. One young woman claimed she could not afford to go out much. After some questioning she revealed that besides her job, she also had $50,000 in savings. Why couldn't she use some of that to help improve her social life? "So I'll at least have some money when I'm old and alone." The neurotic circularity of her thinking was quickly pointed out and discussed once her true financial situation was known. Fortunately, clients are usually uncomfortable enough about these secrets to drop occasional hints. Like the child in "The Emperor's New Clothes," the therapist who can see through the pretense, can ask the obvious questions and the secret will unfold. There is probably some tendency for therapists who are less active to collect more information and for more active therapists, including cathartic therapists, to collect less. Collecting data is not enough in itself; nor is promoting catharsis. We aim to collect enough information to see the client's life in context and, as much as possible, to make that information-gathering an integral part of the therapy process.

Confrontation and Interpretation

Confrontation and interpretation are used in most forms of psychotherapy. While they play a less central role in feeling-expressive therapy than in psychoanalytically oriented therapies, they are nevertheless crucial tools for us. Confrontation is the presentation to the client of discrepant facts with an implied demand to explain or resolve the discrepancy. An interpretation is a statement that aims to relate discrepant facts and give them new meaning. Interpretation applies theory to behavior.

Many interpretations fit one of these three forms:

1. These events in your past are shaping your behavior in the present. (e.g., "Your father's brutality toward you makes you unrealistically fearful of your husband.")

2. This behavior is a symbolic acting out of that need. (e.g., "Spending all that money is a way of saying 'Give me more'.")

3. This feeling could be masking that feeling. (e.g., "You start to get

angry and then you cry. Aren't you really more angry than sad?")

Other examples of interpretations are:

You said that neither your wife nor your father would let you breathe. Maybe some of your anger toward your wife really belongs with your dad.

"Let me see if I've got this straight. You want me to take the side that says 'Don't move. Stay here.' and then you want to argue with me about that. It'll feel better if you can get that internal struggle of yours to be a fight between you and me. Your mom did that with you but I think I'll stay out of your civil wars."

Your messiness and your forgetfulness say to people around you, "Take care of me. Be my mother."

Interpretation involves attribution of causality and hence is more cognitive than other methods. The client makes many connections quite spontaneously during or after feelings are expressed. Often, these connections are correct, moving, and simply stated. At such times, the therapist should stay out of the way and let the client keep working. Such interpretations are often "deep" in that they contain material of which people are often unaware. Early childhood memories are connected to present conflicts or stresses with clear understandings of such issues as dependency, competition, and fear of reprisal. The statements are simple, direct, and feelingful without the labored complexity interpretations sometimes have.

At other times, the therapist must enter more actively into the process of making interpretations. This is done if the client seems reluctant to move to the phase of integrating and thinking about the feelings that have been expressed. Sometimes clients go off in fruitless directions, drawing inappropriate lessons from their experience. When this happens, it is important to intervene and offer a more useful interpretation. Even at such times, however, it is best if the therapist can connect an interpretation to what the client already has said: "You mentioned being afraid. That sounds right! I think one of the things you're afraid of is how people will respond when they find out how angry you are."

Examples of confrontations are: "You say you're angry, but you're smiling"; "You say you want to change, but you don't do the homework we agreed on." Not all confrontations are aggressive. Some go like this: "You say you can't love anybody, yet you take care of your kids, you have a good relationship with your sister, and three years after your divorce, your ex-husband still calls and wants to talk. You must be giving these people something that makes them want more."

Confrontations are used extensively in helping clients to be honest and genuine. In order to get along, we have all learned to go along. We pretend to be good when we are afraid, sad when we are angry, or angry when we are sad. In feeling-expressive therapy, clients sometimes pretend to have feelings when they do not or when their real feelings are different from the ones they are woodenly trying to express. The therapist has to rely on intuition to determine whether the expression is connected to a feeling. When the expression does not seem real, the therapist confronts the client: "You're yelling and pounding, but I don't feel *you* behind it. Are you really angry right now?" Whether this is done gently or bluntly, there is a risk involved. It can feel very painful when the therapist challenges the client's presentation. Since the client is in a trusting, reliant relationship with the therapist, there is the danger of coercive and paternalistic intimidation in such confrontations (e.g., "I know and you don't"). Therapists must be guided by self-trust on the one hand and humility on the other. They must continue to examine their own feelings to keep their perceptions of clients as free from distortion as possible.

Despite these dangers and the need for caution, confrontation and interpretation remain powerful and useful interventions. In confrontation, which is both painful and useful, the client hears from another how she/he is coming across and what inconsistencies or unreal aspects are present. Interpretations can tie together and make meaningful various previously disparate experiences or events.

Teaching

The more experience we gain, the more we appreciate the value of teaching as a therapeutic tool. Although there are some connections and understandings that only have meaning when clients experience them directly, there are others that can be taught. An example of the former is the way the client's feelings of extreme love or hate for the therapist illuminate the client's early relationships with parents. This phenomenon can be described, but it only has therapeutic value when the client experiences it personally. An example of the latter—those connections that can be taught—is the relationship of anger to depression. The therapist can tell a client that expressing anger fully will tend to alleviate depression while suppressing angry feelings will tend to strengthen depression. For this information to be useful it is not necessary for the client to discover it personally, only to act on it by expressing her/his anger.

There are subtler sorts of teaching: for example, we explain how the adaptations clients made as children to their families are contributing to their current troubles. We also teach clients what behaviors and attitudes are most likely to produce catharsis in the session.

Sometimes teaching approaches confrontation, such as when we tell people who are financially dependent that it will be hard for them to feel strong and competent if they do not contribute significantly to their own support.

Oftentimes we provide experiences that do the teaching. For example, after one therapist had repeatedly pointed out a client's oppositional behavior without the client understanding it, the therapist noticed that the client was sitting on his left leg and nervously holding the toes of his left foot. The therapist said, "I'll bet, for example, that if I said it was good that you were holding your toes and that you should be sure to keep holding onto them. . . . (at this point, the client let go of his toes and moved his foot out from under his leg) that you'd stop doing it!" Both laughed, especially the client, who suddenly realized what he was doing. He saw his oppositional behavior with immediacy and clarity, and went on to modify it.

Perhaps the most important things we teach are the assumptions we make about the therapeutic process. We give new clients material to read about feeling-expressive therapy and, as the therapy progresses, we teach them ways of feeling and of using feelings to create a more satisfying life.

Some examples of teaching are:

> It's important to separate your work in here from your life outside. Here you can beat them up and say whatever you want. Out there you may need to tone it down or pick your battles carefully. If you wish, we can talk about what you are really going to do in your life, but that's separate from the work you do here to express your anger.

> You're trying too hard to feel something. Just tell me what's up. The feelings will come.

> The pain you are feeling about Jerry letting you down must be coming from somewhere else. The depth of your hurt couldn't be generated by someone you've known for two months. He's got to be reminding you of someone else.

In these and other ways, we accelerate the process by educating clients about certain aspects of how the therapeutic process works and how they work. While there are many things that cannot be taught in this straightforward way, we are increasingly realizing that there are also many that can be.

SUMMARY

In this chapter, we classified techniques by the objective of the intervention and the method used. We suggested that any technique can be understood as a method used to reach an objective. We described five objectives:

1. Understand the client's history and current life situation.
2. Counter defenses.
3. Facilitate expression of feelings.
4. Integrate feelings and understanding.
5. Change behavior.

We then examined twelve methods used to implement these objectives:

1. Statements of support and encouragement.
2. Giving permission and coaching.
3. Focusing.
4. Role-playing.
5. Humor.
6. Kinesics.
7. Touch.
8. Attention to breathing.
9. Prescriptions.
10. Questions for information.
11. Confrontation and interpretation.
12. Teaching.

We pointed out that while theoretically any method can be applied to any objective, in practice, some methods are more closely related to one objective than another.

A final reminder: all these techniques are useful only when they are part of a coherent strategy based on a clear understanding of the client's personality, defenses, and goals.

REFERENCES

Aguilera, D. Relationship between physical contact and verbal interaction between nurses and patients. *Journal of Psychiatric Nursing*, 1967, *5*, 5-21.

Bandler, R. and Grinder, J. *Reframing: Neuro-linguistic Programing and the Transformation of Meaning.* Moab, Utah: Real People Press, 1982.

Brenner, C. *Psychoanalytic Technique and Psychic Conflict.* New York: International Universities Press, 1976.

Cousins, N. Anatomy of an illness as perceived by the patient. *New England Journal of Medicine*, 1976, *295*, 1458-1463.

Cowen, E. L., Weissberg, R. P. and Lotyczewski, B. S. Physical contact in helping interactions with young children. *Journal of Consulting and Clinical Psychology*, 1982, *50*, 219-225.

Cowen, E.L., Weissberg, R.P. and Lotyezewski, BS. Physical contract in interactions between clinicians and young children. Journal of Consulting and Clinical Psychology, 1983, 51, 132-138.

Greenson, R. R. The working alliance and the transference neurosis. *Psychoanalytic Quarterly*, 1965, *34*, 155-181.

Grinder, J. and Bandler, R. *Trance-formations: Neuro-linguistic Programing and the Structure of Hypnosis*, Moab, Utah: Real People Press, 1981.

Haley, J. *Uncommon Therapy*. New York: Norton, 1973.

Kolroyd, J. C. and Brodsky, A. Does touching patients lead to sexual intercourse? *Professional Psychology*, 1980, *11*, 807-811.

Kubie, L.S. The destructive potential of humor in psychotherapy. *American Journal of Psychiatry*, 1971, 127:7, 861-866.

Langs, R. *Psychotherapy: A Basic Text*. New York: Jason Aronson, 1982.

Lowen, A. *Bioenergetics*. New York: Coward, McCann and Geoghagan, 1975.

Menninger, K. *Theory of Psychoanalytic Technique*. New York: Basic Books, 1958.

Pattison, J. E. Effects of touch on self-exploration and the therapeutic relationship. *Journal of Consulting and Clinical Psychology*, 1973, *40*, 170-175.

Pesso, A. *Experience in Action*. New York: New York University Press, 1973.

Rosenheim, E. Humor in psychotherapy: an interactive experience. *American Journal of Psychotherapy*, 1974, 28(4) 584-591.

Schacter, S. A cognitive-physiological view of emotion. In Klineberg, O. and Christie, R. (eds.) *Perspectives in Social Psychology*. New York: Holt Rinehart and Winston, 1965.

Schofield, W. *Psychotherapy: The Purchase of Friendship*. Englewood Cliffs, New Jersey: Prentice-Hall, 1964.

Smith, A. *Powers of Mind*. New York: Random House, 1975.

Stone, L. *Psychoanalytic Situation*. New York: International Universities Press, 1961.

Part II
CLINICAL ISSUES

4

The Beginning
Phase—Michael's Story

"It makes me want to *scream*, the ridiculous disporportion of my guilt!
May I? Will that shake them up too much out in the waiting room?
Because that's maybe what I need most of all, to howl, a pure howl,
without any more words between me and it! . . .
Aaaaaaaaaaaaaaaaaaaaaaaaaaaaaaaaaaaaaaaaaaaaaaaaaaaaaaaaaaaaaaaaaa
aaaaaaaaaaaaaaaaaaaaaaaaaaaaaaaaaaaaaaaaaaaaaaaaaaaaaaaaaaaaaaaaaa
aaaaaaaaaaaaaaaaaaaaaaaaaaaaaaaaaaaaaaaaaaaaaaaaaaaaaaaaaaaaaaaahh
hhhhhhhhhhhhhhh!!!"
                            PUNCH LINE
"So," said the doctor. "Now vee may perhaps to begin. Yes?"
                                            Philip Roth
                                            Portnoy's Complaint

The beginning phase of treatment is primarily a time for the client to
become engaged with the therapist and the therapeutic enterprise. The
client tells the therapist what is wrong and comes to share, if not all, at
least a major portion of the therapist's vision of how therapy will help.
As they get to know each other, they decide if and how they can work
well together.

TASKS OF THE BEGINNING PHASE

Clients typically come to therapy without a clear understanding of
what is involved or how therapy can help. For instance, they often believe
that having someone nonjudgmental to talk things over with, or that
having someone on their side, is the major benefit of therapy. Although
we believe these things are helpful, we do not think they are the main
avenues for change. Rather, we think the main therapeutic agents are:
(1) a relationship that can be examined openly and (2) full expression of
feelings that are insightfully linked from present to past and lead to new
behavior targeted toward stated therapeutic goals. The content of this

89

belief system is discussed elsewhere. The point here is that if clients can experience the usefulness of this view early in their therapy, they will be much more committed to the process than if they believe they come primarily for encouragement or a sympathetic ear. Once clients share this vision of their therapy, we say they "have the big picture" and we feel that a major task of the first phase has been accomplished.

Acculturation

In a sense, beginning therapy is a process of acculturation in which the client takes on some beliefs, values, and language regarding psychopathology, therapy, and the mechanisms of personal change. The therapist has to learn what concerns the client and reframe these concerns so that the client can see how working in the therapist's mode of therapy can help the client to stop being troubled and to feel better.

Since, for many clients, the therapist's assumptions will at first appear to be wrong, irrelevant, or dangerous, this acculturation process is seldom smooth. The therapist cannot simply tell the client, for example, that early family history is important. Rather, the therapist must help create an experience for the client that will make the connection intuitively clear.

Information Exchange

The other major task of the beginning phase is sharing information. More information is exchanged during this stage than during any other; without such an exchange, none of the acculturation and engagement with the therapy process could occur. We see this information exchange as falling into four broad areas that may be outlined as follows:

I.   The therapist needs to find out:
  A. What is the immediate cause of the client seeking treatment?
  B. What are the more chronic issues and symptoms for which the client seeks help?
  C. What are the client's goals for treatment?
  D. What is the client's history and present situation in regard to family, friends, school and work, sex and intimacy?
  E. How mature and effective is the client at managing her/his life successfully?
  F. What are the client's achievements and deficits with regard to sex and intimacy, dependence/independence, caregiving, aggression, and assertion?
  G. To what extent is the client able to contact her/his feelings?

H. How does the client relate to the therapist? specifically:
   1. Does there seem to be a basis for establishing a cooperative relationship?
   2. Is the client well-motivated for therapy, and able and willing to make the necessary commitment of time and money?
   3. Has the client had therapy before? If so, how did it go? When did it end? On whose terms? Did the client flee therapy when things got tough?

II. The client needs to find out:
   A. Are the levels of competence, interest, respect, and empathy displayed by the therapist such that the client can reasonably expect success?
   B. Does feeling-expressive therapy seem believable and potentially useful to the client?
   C. Is the investment of time and money required appropriate to the client's motivation, pain, and wish for change?
   D. Does the therapist seem reasonably hopeful of success?

III. The therapist needs to teach the client how to work therapeutically, which entails:
   A. Teaching the client the basic concepts of feeling-expressive therapy.
   B. Teaching the client how to contact and fully express feelings.
   C. Communicating to the client the importance of transference feelings and of expressing both negative and positive feelings.
   D. Making interventions, seeing how they are used, and discussing the client's response with the client.

IV. Therapist and client must agree on a contract for working together, which includes:
   A. Frequency and time of meetings.
   B. Fee.
   C. Goals to be worked on.
   D. Agreement about approximate length of treatment.
   E. Division of labor (e.g., who will start the session, who will take the initiative for various tasks).

We will discuss each of these areas briefly and then illustrate them with a clinical example.

The therapist needs to find out

The therapist's data collecting begins in the waiting room. Having seen hundreds of clients wait for their first appointment, we have implicit norms regarding typical behavior. We know what behavior the waiting-room setting tends to elicit from people. At times, a new client behaves in a manner at variance with those norms and we notice it. Perhaps this client is more anxious, more placating, or more reserved than most. Some clients make a comment in their greeting that, in effect, begins the session; e.g., "Is this coffee for anybody or just for the big shots who work here?" Even less colorful opening lines and waiting-room behaviors have meaning that begins the process of finding out about the client.

To begin the actual interview, we usually ask: "What brings you in?"; "How can I help you?"; or some similar open-ended question. The client then tells her/his story about what is painful and why therapy is sought at this time. Looking back at these opening statements after the client is well-known to the therapist, it is often surprising to see how fully areas of conflict, defensive styles, and ways of relating to the therapist are foreshadowed in these first responses. People usually come to their first session full of thoughts and feelings about what they want from therapy, who they are, and how they want to change. Their opening statements usually carry a lot of information and are worth attending to very carefully. Sometimes most of the meaning is clear to both client and therapist. An example would be a statement that says, in effect, "The failure of my marriage is painful and has raised questions for me about what it was in me that contributed to that failure. I want to become a person who can have a satisfying and lasting relationship." This is a straightforward statement and, although other issues may emerge, it provides client and therapist with a reasonable basis for working together.

Other equally meaningful opening statements are less transparent, for example:

> *Client*: Well, here I am with not much to say. (Laughs.)
> *Therapist*: What brings you in?
> *Client*: Not much.

Although this client went on to tell about a lot of hurt in her life and clearly felt both sad and angry at different points in the interview, she used hypomanic defenses to keep from feeling very much and cancelled her next appointment. It was clear during the interview that she had a lot to say and that the correct answer to "What brings you in?" was "Much," rather than "Not much." Nevertheless, the first two sentences conveyed important data about her defensiveness which were confirmed in the rest of the interview and in her cancelling the next appointment. They provided evidence that her wish for help was mixed with significant resistance. This client's opening statement probably meant something quite different to the therapist than it did to the client. For the client, it might have meant little—a commercial before the news, or small talk before they "really began"—while for the alert therapist it was an ominous statement of the strength of the defense vis-à-vis the wish to change.

Another example is the following exchange:

Therapist: "What brings you here?"
Client: "My wife told me to come."

The passivity and anger in such a response are worth noting but, again, the client is unlikely to see the significance of such a way of beginning without being shown it.

Each client begins therapy with a story to tell. It usually involves a statement about pain, previous efforts to alleviate the pain, important people in the client's life and how she/he came to seek therapy. The client's story may be brief or may take up most of the session. At points where it is repetitious or boring, the therapist serves the client by interrupting. At points where the therapist's curiosity is piqued, it is usually well to follow its urgings. If the therapist is skillful and the client reasonably cooperative and articulate, there should be time in the first session for the story and the collection of at least some information about:

1. The immediate reason for seeking treatment and whether therapy has been sought previously.

2. Symptoms and goals for treatment.

3. The client's current life circumstances—job, friends, family situation, etc.

4. The client's early life (sketchy and only as it relates to the current difficulty).

5. How the client relates to the therapist.

6. What feelings are salient and how available they are for expression.

Collecting this information is less difficult than it sounds because a good deal of it will be presented as part of the story. We do not believe that an information-centered interview with numerous questions and answers is necessary or desirable. The necessary information can be gained within a therapeutically oriented interview in which the client talks about what comes to mind and the therapist occasionally suggests a direction or asks a question.

In the second session, we conduct a more structured interview in which we establish and record the client's goals for therapy. When clients are in considerable pain, it is hard for them to formulate goals more specific than "I want to stop hurting." We find it helpful, however, to push clients to be clear and specific about how they want to change. Such goals have several purposes:

1. They are markers that, later on, allow client and therapist to determine the amount and type of progress they have achieved.

2. They can be used to keep therapy focused on change so that therapy does not become an end in itself.

3. They can be used to remind a resistant client that it is the client who seeks change rather than the therapist who seeks to impose change.

In the second session, we also go over a number of areas of the client's life (work, sex, etc.) to determine how much satisfaction the client experiences in each area. This is primarily useful as a bench mark against which to measure progress. Occasionally, however, problems that previously escaped notice are uncovered in this way.

The client needs to find out

The most significant thing the client needs to decide in the first session is whether to return for a second session. The "fit" between client and therapist is part of what determines whether the client returns. If the client senses the therapist as similar, "simpathico," and empathic, there is a greater likelihood of a return engagement. Also the client's judgments about the therapist's competence, presence, and respect for her/him affect the client's decision. In addition, the client is influenced by the balance of forces of resistance and fear, on the one hand, and a wish to make the venture successful, on the other.

Although some clients are so distressed and preoccupied that they are virtually unaware of the therapist, more often we are surprised at the wealth of detail and the accuracy of insight carried away from the first session by clients and later shared with us. While actively talking, telling a story, sharing pain, and seeking help, the client simultaneously observes and evaluates the therapist, the room, the active, participating aspect of her/his own self, and even how that participating self is being affected by and is affecting the therapist.

Clients seem to return to therapy when they feel appropriately challenged. If the therapist is too aggressive in confronting the client, is hostile, or implies that nothing about the client's present life is okay, the client is unlikely to return. Even if the confrontations are accurate and not hostile, they can be too much too soon and scare the client away. On the other hand, too little confrontation can leave the client feeling empty, flat, and unchallenged—neither understood nor cared about. The therapist must be confrontive enough to "hook" the client yet gentle enough to help the client feel safe.

Finally, the client must evaluate feeling-expressive therapy and decide whether that approach is personally suitable. Feeling-expressive therapy is an active, vigorous method that frequently is confrontive and "upsetting." It is intended to promote basic personal change rather than to serve primarily as a palliative or support. The client must decide whether this therapy matches her/his goals and whether the cost in time, money, and energy seems reasonable.

These judgments about fit, competence, level of challenge, and appropriateness of feeling-expressive therapy are the client's to make. If the therapist is too involved with the client's decision about continuing, the therapist cannot attend fully to her/his own task.

The therapist needs to teach the client how to work therapeutically

Any therapy has theoretical assumptions and methods of working which must be learned by the neophyte client. This is perhaps even more true of feeling-expressive therapy because several of our beliefs and practices run counter to widely help cultural norms. Our encouragement of full feeling-expression and our use of touch are two such practices. Clients must be taught to attend to small feeling cues that they habitually screen out. The fundamental distinction between full feeling-expression in therapy sessions and inappropriate acting out of feelings outside of therapy needs to be taught and underscored. Clients need to learn to take the part of the child they once were and be empathic with that child without blaming their present-day parents for hurting them. These are but a few of the lessons that must be gradually communicated to the client during the beginning stage of therapy.

Therapist and client must agree on a contract

At the most basic level, they must agree about frequency, time of meetings and fee. They also should have at least an implicit agreement about how cancellations and payments will be handled and who will be responsible for what. There can be considerable variations among clients, even with the same therapist, as to the subtleties of who initiates, who responds, and who feels most responsible for how the session goes. Some clients are not able to use therapy time productively on their own initiative, so the therapist has to give more structure and take more initiative than would otherwise be the case. The therapist's difficult job is to be certain that these variations in style of working with different clients do not arise from the therapist's neurotic attachment to the clients' rewards and punishments. Rather, these individual variations should derive from a thoughtful assessment of each client's abilities and disabilities in relation to the tasks of therapy. We try to facilitate the process of education, mutual exploration, and contract-formation at the beginning of therapy by giving clients a brochure that describes the Therapy Center and our approach to therapy.

The content of the agreement we make with clients might be stated as follows: Plan to meet weekly in individual therapy for 50 minutes. We are willing to help you work on symptoms, but we prefer to work on longer-range character change. For symptom change, assume two months to a year. For character change, assume two years or more. After starting in individual therapy, plan later to be in a group, to peer-counsel, and to attend workshops. Pay your bill the month you receive it. Take responsibility for saying what is on your mind and what you want to work on, and for doing homework. Expect to express your feelings fully. It is a skill that can be learned. Be willing to try new behaviors, even (especially) those that do not feel "right." Try looking at your past behavior in a no-fault, deterministic way that emphasizes your having done the best you could given the circumstances. Try looking at your present behavior as modifiable by your present feeling, thinking, and willing.

Stating these usually unstated assumptions means losing subtlety and shading. In actual practice, a different, more intricate communication occurs. Nevertheless, these statements do convey the skeleton of our communication to clients and they form the foundation of the contract we arrive at with clients.

Let us now look at an individual client's beginning phase of treatment and see how the engagement with therapy and the exchange of information occur.

MICHAEL'S STORY

Michael's therapy at the Center began when he called for an appointment. He had been referred specifically to Stan, one of the therapists at the Center. In the brief conversation to set up an appointment, Michael mentioned that he was depressed, that he had been working with another therapist, and that he had discontinued because he felt "we weren't getting anywhere." He also said, "There's a lot going on in my life these days and most of it is bad. I want to get hold of it." Michael accepted the first appointment time Stan offered him and they said goodbye.

After the call, Stan reflected on what he had heard: a man in early middle age with a strong, "take charge" tone in his voice, perhaps somewhat driven. Most notable was the fact of discontinuing with his former therapist. Stan knew that he would spend some time in the first session finding out about that relationship and what went wrong with it. He was also curious about the suggestion that a number of things were all going wrong at once. He set himself the goal of trying to find the most critical area of conflict. Finally, Stan was pleased that they had so easily found a time to meet. He felt it spoke well for Michael's cooperativeness and seriousness of purpose.

Session #1

When Stan met Michael in the waiting room, he saw a good-looking, well-dressed man of medium build who looked to be in his mid forties. He appeared somewhat tired and haggard. When they sat down in the office, Michael began without so much as a "What brings you in?" from Stan.

Michael: (Looking around the office.) This place is different.

Stan: From what?

Michael: Well I spent the last few months working with William Turner and it just wasn't going anywhere. And I talked to June about it.

Stan: June's your wife?

Michael: Yeah. And she's been working with Jim Grossman for several years and I've met with him a couple of times and I like his style and I feel good with him, but I think what was happening with Turner was I was just intellectual-izing—just dealing with things in a very nice, rational, controlled, detached way and uh . . . I need help.

Stan: And your experience . . . your experience with Jim was that he was more . . .

Michael: Open, yeah, I have a good, warm feeling about him and . . . I don't have that feeling about Turner. He's very detached from me and . . . which I guess he has to be. . . .

Stan: Mm-hmm. . . .

Michael: You know I've talked to him about that. I've said "I'm angry at you for . . . you know . . . just . . . you've got this 50 minutes or 45 minutes or whatever and at the end of that you just move on to the next patient and that's . . . that's it.

Stan: You'd like more from him . . . somehow.

Michael: Yeah. Except I also recognize that I . . . I've got to deal with my own problems. . . . I mean, I can't expect other people to solve them for me. So . . . there's a limit to how much he can do. And I called him up and I said I just . . . I think we ought to suspend this . . . I'm going to try something else.

Stan: Mm-hmm. OK, and you got in touch with me cause Jim suggested it?

Michael: Yeah.

Stan: OK . . . so . . . What's—

Michael: What's the problem? I guess I would categorize it as a really severe depression. I've always been a very confident . . . outgoing . . . energetic kind of person. And since the beginning of around . . . well around July 4th, I've been on a slow decline.

Michael went on to describe his loss of confidence, said his relationship with his wife was "at an all-time low," that he was not able to work effectively, that his relationship with his parents was poor and trouble-some, and that he was not sleeping well. The verbatim section of the interview given above lasted only two and a half minutes, yet it was full of information about Michael. We see here:

1. Michael's anger and disappointment about "Turner." The critical description of him as "dealing with things in a very nice, rational, con-trolled, detached way" is very similar to descriptions we hear later of his father and contrasts with his much more positive view of "Jim," about whom he has a "good, warm feeling". In the first two minutes, Michael made clear in his feelings toward these men, the importance of the warm-cold and giving-withholding dimensions in his perception and evaluation of people. The related conflict between wanting to be taken care of and knowing "I've got to deal with my own problems" is something we will see again in relation to both his wife and his parents.

2. Despite rejecting his first therapist as an intellectualizer, Michael said of his difficulty, "I would categorize it as a really severe depression." However much he may rail against his therapist's (and his father's) ways, they are also his ways. He has a right to have help changing that distancing style but he let us know right at the beginning that it *is* his style.

3. There was a somewhat egocentric failure to take the role of the other in his early reference to June without any explanation of who she was. In that behavior, Michael made an implicit statement that others should work hard to understand him rather than that he should work hard to be understood.

4. Finally, Michael's decision to leave his first therapist was noteworthy, although its meaning was not clear. It might have meant that he ran from the appropriate and necessary deprivation of therapeutic work and sought only, or mainly, nurturance. Or it might have meant that he was a thoughtful consumer who believed he could do better for himself elsewhere. There is subsequent evidence for both these possibilities. The best guess would seem to be that both motivations were operating. However, the first has more implications for treatment. The danger in this sort of situation is that the therapist's narcissism will blind him to the important transference statement present in the change from one therapist to another.

During most of this session, Michael told his story while Stan listened, asked questions, and sought to increase Michael's awareness of his feelings. Stan did not seek to promote feeling-expression. He found out during the session that Michael was 43, had been married 15 years, was the father of four children, and was a physician/teacher at a medical school. Outgoing, competitive, and not especially introspective, he came primarily for help with depression, a condition he had had for about 10 months. In essence, Michael's story was that 10 months earlier he had had an angry confrontation with his parents. Also, at about that time, his wife had started back to work. She had been financially and psychologically dependent on him previously, but was now less so. This was a loss for Michael. Sex, never an outstanding part of their relationship, had become infrequent, cold, and unfulfilling. Michael's parents were critical of June and June was critical of them. Michael felt caught in the middle and paralyzed. He was angry at all three for giving him so little. Michael's depression was primarily noticeable to him as a decreased self-confidence, a loss of his usual assertiveness, and a tendency to put off going to work. He had some early-morning awakening, but in other respects his sleep, appetite, and bowel functions were normal. He reported having thought of suicide, but had not spent much time with that idea or made any specific plans. Stan decided that while Michael clearly needed help, there was no immediate threat to life. The plan was to treat him using only psychotherapy and to focus fairly soon on vigorous expression of anger. This is usually a fast and effective way of treating depression. Stan planned to keep an eye on Michael's depression and reconsider medication if it did not improve within a month or two.

About 10 minutes into the session, Michael felt sad for a moment. His therapist took the opportunity to focus Michael's attention on that feeling—not so much to express it at that moment as to get familiar with what a sad feeling feels like. The sadness came over Michael as he talked about his wife:

Michael: She's grown over the years to the point where she's now able to handle things completely on her own and . . . what's that with me. And I . . . I uh. . . .

Stan: You sad right now?

Michael: Am I sad? Yes, . . . I . . . I'm really . . . I guess I would describe myself as being desperate. All the support systems I had seem to have evaporated. Oh . . . June and I talked about what . . .

As Michael began to feel sad his words became garbled ("what's that with me."). In the next sentence he sounded sad at first ("Am I sad? Yes"), but quickly moved back to a more defended posture. By the time he got to "support systems" he was feeling very little. Stan interrupted him in midsentence.

Stan: So let me just. . . . I want to understand what happened. As you said that she didn't need you anymore, you felt sad?

Michael: Well, yeah. I guess so. You know I'm having a hard time identifying how I feel about things.

Stan: Well, did you feel like you could cry?

Michael: (Pause.) Not really, because this goes back to the whole notion of in . . . of control and of my trying to keep all my feelings in check.

During the pause, Michael again seemed to feel some sadness. Then he kept his feelings in check by talking about his tendency to keep his feelings in check!

Stan: OK. So you have this sort of automatic control thing you do to actually keep from crying.

Michael: Yeah.

Stan: But do you know what I mean . . . the feeling of "It feels like I could cry?"

Michael: Yeah.

Stan: And did you feel that then?

Michael: Yeah. . . . Yeah, I did. . . . I felt sad. I don't want to lose her.

Michael looked and sounded sad at this point, but then he started talking about how he had always gotten satisfaction from having people rely on him and he lost the feeling. At this point, Stan reverted to a more passive listening mode.

A contact had been made, a struggle joined. The first session, however, is not a good time for a major battle. By conveying a keen interest in feelings, the therapist let Michael know something about the therapy he was beginning—part of the acculturation process mentioned earlier. Michael had some moments of getting to know his feelings better, and Stan gathered some data about the strength and nature of Michael's defenses against feeling.

About halfway through the session, Michael told Stan how he used to take care of his wife and be strong. Now that he was feeling down, she was not reciprocating. She was being grouchy.

Stan: A grouchy momma. At least you were a good daddy when you took care of her.
Michael: (Laughing.) I was. I *was* a good daddy. I'd give her medicine when she was sick and take care of her. (Still laughing.) I was a good daddy and she's being a grouchy momma. It's not fair.

The best word for the tone in the last sentence ("It's not fair") is probably "peeved." There was clearly anger in it, expressed in a tone of irritation. Eventually there is deep rage to be felt and fully expressed, but in this exchange the anger was only partially expressed. It was present as irritation or annoyance which we will continue to hear as a leitmotif throughout Michael's beginning sessions. The words that express the tone best are "It's not fair".

Michael's ability to be light about his being a good daddy and to laugh a little at his wish for a good momma is an encouraging sign of his ability to step out of his usual set and see things from a different perspective.

A few minutes later, Michael said his folks would like him to visit them in Florida and leave June and the children home. Moments before he had said that June was ungiving sexually.

Stan: It must be hard at times to resist those siren calls from your mother.
Michael: Yeah. She could make my breakfast for me. I cook a lot of the meals at home.
Stan: That could be nice for the kid in you to be taken care of like that.
Michael: Yeah. Sometimes I'd like to go lay all this on her. Tell her how bad things are, but I couldn't 'cause they already don't like June.
Stan: You don't get any sex from June—you might as well go to your mother. Of course, you wouldn't get any sex from her either, but at least you'd get breakfast!

Michael did not respond to the light tone here, but continued to say, in effect, "How come I'm such a good guy and yet neither my parents nor my wife appreciates me and gives me what I want?" As the session neared its end, Stan made several statements to the effect that Michael was causing himself pain by being so attached to his parents' approval and disapproval. His responses to these statements were remarkably consistent. Whether he said "Yes. They are very bad", or "I'd like to be close to them", he made it clear that letting his parents alone was not an alternative he seriously entertained.

As the session ended, Stan told Michael what the fee was and gave him a brochure describing the Center. They set a time to meet again and as they got up to go Stan said, "I'll give you a hug before you leave." As they hugged, Michael began to shake. Stan noticed and commented on it: "Got the shakes there, huh?" Michael said "yes" and stared to cry. He added, "I've always been so strong. I don't want June to leave. I'm scared of losing her." Stan and Michael stood hugging for perhaps a minute. Then Michael moved away and said, "Boy that surprised me." Stan replied, "Me, too. Guess you just needed a little safety to feel that hurt." They talked for a minute and then said goodbye.

The hugging and tears at the end of the session deserve some comment. We think touch and hugging are useful for most clients, although we do not typically hug clients in the first session. Perhaps Stan saw something in Michael—some openness or wish for closeness—that he responded to in initiating the hug. Some combination of surprise and reassurance let Michael cry then rather than earlier. Stan felt both pleased that Michael was that open to his feelings and also somewhat alerted. In a man as unaccustomed to crying as Michael was, tears might signal depression rather than openness to feelings. Stan took that as another bit of data indicating that Michael's depression should be addressed soon and primarily through the expression of anger.

Session #2

The second session is usually the time for agreeing on specific goals for the treatment. Stan came to the second session knowing that Michael would want help with his depression; he also assumed that Michael would need help in clarifying how he wanted to change in other respects. Stan could see that Michael was quite dependent on both his parents and his wife and tended to focus on their failings as the cause of his discontent. His main way of trying to earn the love he wanted was to be good, helpful, and strong. When he did not get the love he sought he became resentful. Stan wanted Michael to see these things and have a goal of changing them. He realized, though, that unless Michael fully understood the connection between his dependency and his unhappiness, making such change a formal goal of treatment would do no good. Therefore, Stan entered this session with a plan both to make an agreement about goals and to help Michael see some of the connections between his underlying character structure and the development of the symptom of depression.

When the actual session began, however, Stan's agenda got delayed. As they sat down, Stan asked Michael what thoughts he had about the last session. Michael responded by talking at length about the issues dealt with in the first session. He said he was angry at his parents, especially his father, for being cold and distant. He talked of being pulled between parents and wife, and gave more details about the distance that had developed between him and his wife. Frequently interspersed was the charge of unfairness: "I take care of everybody and no one takes care of me."

Michael mentioned that he was concerned about work, but that did not seem as focal as his other concerns. Stan's comments were aimed mainly at helping Michael to get past a recitation of how he was being treated badly to an expression of real anger. This was only partially successful. After about 25 minutes, Stan suggested they move on to the main agenda for the meeting—agreement on goals.

The goals agreed upon were:

1. Regain confidence and assertiveness. Be less depressed.

2. Have more frequent and more enjoyable sexual relations.

3. Feel more resolved with parents. Be more adult and more self-sufficient.

4. Have a closer relationship with June. Spend more evenings together.

The goals were specified so that most had countable and publicly observable referrents. This is often difficult to do but worth working at because goals stated more vaguely make later assessment of progress difficult and subject to the mood of the client or therapist.

Goals 1, 2, and 4 came quite spontaneously from Michael. The third goal most clearly bore the imprint of Stan's thinking and was elicited as follows:

Stan: I've heard a lot about your folks. It's hard to believe you wouldn't have some goals about your feelings toward them.

Michael: Yeah. Ah . . . I'd like to have a good relationship with 'em but . . . uh . . . I'm not willing to have it really on their terms. I'd like for them to be able to express their feelings with me more openly.

Stan: So that's a goal you have for *them*; to express their feelings more openly. We're talking about *you*. How you'd like to be different.

Michael: I'd like to get out from under their thumb. Be . . . uh . . . more of an adult, more self-sufficient.

This exchange expresses the heart of the alloplastic/autoplastic issue. We all would prefer to change our environment rather than ourselves.

Michael stated that wish very clearly, but then backed off when confronted with the illogic of his *parents'* acting differently because *he* was in therapy. His last sentence, however, had a noticeably more depressed tone than his earlier one with its hope for an alloplastic solution. Also, despite further questions from the therapist to clarify how Michael wanted to change, clarity was not forthcoming. To think clearly about that would mean letting go of his parents as parents—a course he was not yet ready to take. The best that could be hoped for at this early stage was intellectual acceptance of the need to let go. Really letting go is the work of therapy.

The remainder of session two was spent in going over the Personal Satisfaction Form.[1] In general, Michael reported low levels of satisfaction in most areas of his life. In talking about wanting to be close to people, Michael said, quite insightfully, "I'm really torn. I want contact, but I'm a little jumpy." Finally, near the end of the session, he shared some of his reactions to the therapist and the Center. He said that the informal atmosphere both pleased and frightened him. Stan looked at these reactions with him and said it was important to keep sharing such thoughts. As we will see in the next section this is an issue with which Michael has not finished. It is the issue with which he starts the next session.

Session #3

If the first session is the time the client tells her/his story and the second session is the time for setting goals, then the third session frequently is the time for doing the first sustained work on feeling-expression. Feelings often are expressed in the first two sessions, but they usually are not pursued. Feelings arise as the client talks and the therapist may push some (as Stan did in the first session) either to test defenses or to communicate an interest in feelings. However, typically there is no sustained attention given to feeling-expression until the third session.

Stan entered the third session wanting to get Michael to move on his feelings but well aware of how he scooted away from them in the first sessions.

While Michael was in the waiting room, he heard a client screaming in another office and he mentioned this to Stan as soon as they sat down. Stan used this issue as an opportunity to do some teaching.

Michael: I don't know if it's a tape recorder or if she's actually here . . . this woman who was screaming at the back of the house?
Stan: She's actually here. (Stan waits for Michael's reaction.)
Michael: That really bothers me. Because I've never done anything like that myself.
Stan: (Lightly.) Today could be the day!

Michael: I've never. I've always. . . .

Stan: Today could be the day, Michael!

Michael: Been controlled. (Laughs.)

Stan: What do you think about the possibility?

Michael: Scares me.

Stan: (Indicating understanding.) Uh-huh.

Michael: 'Cause I pride myself on being in control. That's an important phrase for me.

Stan: Mm-hmm.

Michael: And I'm not in control of my life right now. Don't like that at all.

Stan: Uh-huh. And that woman *was* in control.

Michael: That's hard for me to believe.

Stan: Uh-huh.

Michael: It really is. . . .

Stan: Yeah . . . if *you* were sounding like that *you* wouldn't be in control?

Michael: Not by my standards.

Stan: Yeah . . . well, she's in control in the sense that if I walked in and said, "Excuse me, there's a fire, we need to go outside," she would dry her eyes and go outside. And at the end of the session, routinely the therapist will say, "It's time for us to stop," and within a few minutes she'll be . . . maybe puffy-eyed. . . .

Michael: Uh-huh.

Stan: She will feel different than she did before, but she'll be able to go back to a state that's functional. You understand what I mean?

Michael: Uh-huh.

Stan: And then she'll come in next week and she'll say, "Let me see. What's on my mind? This is on my mind. I felt this way," and perhaps she'll work herself back to feelings similar to those she felt this afternoon.
In other words, I'm saying it's a skill you learn—to both function in the world and be in control as you understand it, and also to let yourself feel and express those feelings strongly.

Michael: Yeah.

Stan: It's a high quality of control to be able to let yourself feel at the right time and to let yourself stop feeling enough to function at the right time.

Michael: Mm-hmm. . . . Right now I have everything all bottled up. Big cork jammed down on top of the bottle.

This important information exchange is characteristic of the beginning stage of therapy. Stan was teaching Michael that he could learn the skill of feeling-expression and that he then could choose to express his feelings fully, partially, or not at all depending on current circumstances. Michael's comment that if *he* were making that sort of sound *he* would be out of control was probably true for him at that moment. Michael's history of "bottling up" feelings meant that when he does express his feelings, he is more likely to express them inappropriately. He is likely to experience his feelings as being caused by people or events ("She made me angry") rather than his own internal processes. He is also apt to act in an all-or-none way, either denying that he is angry or being furious. After he has had more experience with feelings, he will take more responsibility for them and his response capability will be more flexible (less/more, rather than off/on).

At the point where Stan said, "that woman was in control," he chose to spend some time teaching rather than seeking direct feeling-expression. He remembered, however that he made that choice and that he might want to return later to that fork in the road and pursue the more directly feelingful possibility.

The conversation about expression and control continued for awhile and then turned to Michael's concerns about his inability to work efficiently and his dissatisfaction with his parents and his wife. He said he and his wife "had sex last night, but it sure wasn't making love." He described it as cold and perfunctory.

Stan: So you're hurting right now.
Michael: Yeah.
Stan: And somewhere in you there are some sounds like you heard coming out of the back office. (Stan returns to Michael's opening comment.)
Michael: Mm-hmm.
Stan: Can you make a sound like that now? (Pause.)
Michael: Runs against m. . . . (Embarrassed laughter.) It runs against my nature to do it.
Stan: Uh-huh.
Michael: I mean I . . . I . . . I'm embarrassed to do that. (Laughs.)
Stan: Sure. I understand that you've had years of training about being tactful.
Michael: Yes. Tactful. That's the word. Keep everything smooth!

Michael had used the word "tactful" several times in earlier sessions to describe his family members and their values. Stan purposely used that word to pace Michael and to show empathy for, and presence with, him. Michael responded strongly and well. Having successfully paced Michael, Stan led now and Michael followed. Stan suggested that they move to the mat and that Michael remove his shoes. Michael complied and removed his tie as well. His words conveyed some caution, but his other behavior showed good movement in the direction Stan had suggested.

Stan: So now let's. . . . Can we get you to take your shoes off?
Michael: Sure.
Stan: And why don't we move over here on the mat, which is where I usually go to work more intensively on feelings. Find a way that is comfortable for you there. . . .
Michael: This is different than what I'm used to.
Stan: That's the reason you came here, isn't it?
Michael: Because I wasn't getting anywhere.
Stan: So I recognize that it is hard to just let out a sound and start doing something new. But one of the ways to do things that are new is just to start.

What did you hear when you were listening to that woman in the back?

Michael: I couldn't really hear what she was saying. I think she was talking about or at somebody who wasn't there.

Stan: Mm-hmm.

Michael: I couldn't get the words.

Stan: And what kind of a feeling would you say she was having?

Michael: Very angry. She was in a rage.

Stan: Anger. Are you angry?

Michael: Yeah. But I don't want to hurt these people. They're important to me.

Stan: Who?

Michael: June and my parents. And I can't get angry openly at work.

Stan: This may be the only place you have a chance to do that.

Michael: That's right.

Stan: On the one hand, it feels kind of strange and new. On the other hand, this may be a terrific opportunity for you. . . . So in any way that feels even a little like you . . . kind of a magnified version of you . . . express it. Let me tell you some of the possibilities.

At this point, Stan describes and demonstrates use of the plastic bat, the pillows, and the mats as motoric channels for expressing anger.

Stan: Now the other thing you have is your voice. Sometimes its nice to say "You bastard!" and sometimes it feels better just to let out a sound—"Uhh!", "Ohh!", or whatever your sound is. So let it go, whatever you're mad at.

Michael: I'm mad at June. Sometimes . . . I'd almost like to do violence to her sometimes.

Stan: Mm-hmm. . . . So in an imaginary way do violence to her here.

Michael, who was sitting on the mat and leaning against the wall, began to reach back with his fists and forearms, hitting a second heavy mat on the wall. He hit it tentatively and without speaking.

Stan: Open your mouth and let out some sound.

Michael: (Hitting.) Uh! Uh! Uh!

Michael hit and shouted simultaneously perhaps a dozen times. His voice was relatively loud, but there was a sudden stop to each "uh" that held back some of the feeling. Relatively little real feeling was being expressed at this point. Michael was trying out something new and was not yet comfortable enough with it to use it as a channel for expression.

Stan: Were you picturing June as you were hitting?

Michael: What I think is game-playing on the sex issue.

Stan: Mm-hmm. Anything particular she did last night?

Michael then described how their sex had felt to him the previous night. The essence of it was that he experienced his wife as cold, mechanical, and very distant from him. Near the end of this description, he began to talk in meliorist terms about how he might have been able to make it better if he had done such and such. Stan suggested that that discussion be put off for another time and that Michael stay with his anger. Stan wanted to keep Michael focused on expressing his anger. Also, he saw Michael as too angry at present to carry out any useful new behavior with his wife without subverting it. The next 20 minutes or so of the session focused on Michael's anger toward his wife. Stan urged him to hit and shout, and occasionally role-played June, repeating some of her most angering statements. He also coached Michael, saying things such as, 'Listen to that cold angry voice. You gonna take that? Smash her!" A couple of times, Michael began to sound more sad or needy than angry. When this happened and he was asked how he felt, he sometimes said "sad" or "hurt," but then he went on to talk about other provocative things his wife had done, thus returning to his anger.

The content of "Michael's Complaint" was that he had done this and that good thing for his wife, yet she reciprocated by leaving him emotionally and not taking care of him. There was a whiny, complaining tone to this which Stan knew came from Michael's fear of his anger. Stan's goal was to help Michael express his anger fully and directly. Clear, full expression of anger can help people change. Whining and complaining cannot.

Partway through this segment of the session, Stan sensed that Michael had reached a moderate level of feeling-expression, but did not seem to be progressing to deeper feelings.

Stan: Now there's something I don't understand. When you were hitting that thing before you looked really *pissed! Really pissed*! Am I right?

Michael: (Laughing.) Yeah.

Stan: But what I hear from you now is much lower key. There are these data that tend to suggest she's not being very good to you, yet in fairness to her, it should be said—etc., etc.

Michael: Yeah.

Stan: So let's take words away from you. Let's say that words are so much a part of the balance thing that they get in your way. So hit and scream if you want, but don't say any words. Go ahead.

Michael hit hard at the mat on the wall. He gradually increased the strength of his hitting and the volume of his shouting. His anger was strong and believable. Every minute or so, however, he stopped.

Michael: Uh! Uh! Uh! Uh! Uh!

(Pause.)

Uh! Uh! Uh! Uh! Uh!

Uh! Uh! Uh!UHH!! UHH!!

(Pause.)

> *Stan:* Now when you stop like that, is there a sense of running out of anger or is it more you run out of air and strength?
> *Michael:* Air and strength.
> *Stan:* So, uh . . . push yourself as much as you can. Use good judgment. Don't overdo but push yourself longer if you feel you can.

Michael then hit and shouted much longer and more strongly than he had before. As he was getting his breath afterwards, he said he had clearly visualized his wife lying in bed with her back turned to him. This powerful image focused much of his anger about not being cared for. It came to him very clearly when he was hitting and he used it subsequently to get back to his anger.

Near the end of the session, Stan said he was pleased with how willing Michael had been to try out new ways of expressing his feelings. Michael said, "Well that's cause I hate where I am and I spent two months with Turner going nowhere." With considerable energy, he talked about how stuffy and intellectualizing his first therapist had been. With very little encouragement, he started to yell about how little he had gotten from him. Interestingly he said that at one point he nearly had struck his therapist. This is an example of the all-or-nothing, bottled-up quality of his feelings mentioned earlier. While he was expressing anger at Dr. Turner, his therapist mentioned some ways that he seemed to be experiencing Dr. Turner as similar to his father. With hardly a missed beat, he went on to his father, yelling at him and hitting the mat vigorously. He was at least as angry at this point as he had been earlier at his wife.

Stan was pleased that Michael was expressing his feelings so fully but saw that their time was nearly gone. About ten minutes before they were to end, Stan interrupted Michael to tell him that they would need to stop soon. Michael said a few more angry things about his father and then they talked some about what had happened in the session. Stan mentioned the importance of separating therapeutic expression of anger from acting out angrily and inappropriately outside of therapy. He did this partly because of the enthusiasm with which Michael had taken up the expression of anger in the session and partly because Michael had said things in earlier sessions that made Stan uncertain as to whether he understood this important distinction. Satisfied that Michael understood this concept, Stan ended the session and they bid each other goodbye.

This session showed some movement from the beginning phase to the middle phase of therapy. Those parts of the session in which Michael was taught to express his feelings belonged to the beginning phase. Stan was teaching him how to express his feelings more fully, and Michael was sharing things in his history that made that difficult. However, the parts where Michael expressed enough real feeling to derive therapeutic benefit belonged to the middle phase, conceptually speaking, even though they occurred in the third session. Thus, there was already a dovetailing of phases. This session was partly beginning phase and partly middle phase.

Session #4

In this session, Michael focused on his relationship with June and began to express feelings clearly and well. Yet, there was something vaguely disquieting about it. Perhaps it was Michael's reluctance to face himself squarely and accept responsibility for changing. There was a somewhat self-satisfied sense that he had been good and was annoyed that his wife was acting up. The paradoxical but logically consistent framework that Stan was using and wanted to convey to Michael went something like this: "You are here because some parts of *your* life are unsatisfactory and *you* want to change some aspect of *you*. One way we seek this change is by helping you to express your feelings—feelings that may have as their object people in your life, such as your wife. The purpose of expressing your feelings, however, is to change *you*, not your wife. You yell at her here so that *your* mind will be clearer, not so that *she* will change."

Parts of this session threw doubt on the completeness with which Michael subscribed to this point of view. One occurred early in the session when he spoke, somewhat grudgingly, about some useful changes he and June had made in their way of relating to each other.

Stan: Sounds nice.
Michael: Yeah, it was. But to contrast with that, the next day she bugged out on me.
Stan: It's hard to stay with the good stuff, huh?
Michael: What do you mean?
Stan: You've told me about some nice moments you had Wednesday night. But when I try to get you to stand by that, you scoot back to how she was bad on Thursday.
Michael: Yeah.
Stan: Wanting things to be *great* could keep things from being *good*.

They worked for a few minutes with Michael's difficulty in saying simply, "This about June is good." It was as though the need to say "Yeah, but this part is bad" had a life of its own. It recurred seemingly unbidden, like a conversational tic. In hindsight, it probably would have been well to stay with this direction, but, through some combination of Michael's resistance and Stan's inattention, this rich lode was abandoned and Michael got back to being angry at his wife. Here was a case where a feeling had become a defense. Even though the anger was full and sounded real, it served to keep Michael away from the more frightening path—being open toward, and appreciative of his wife.

Near the middle of the session, issues of sexism and sex roles were broached regarding career conflicts and who was to have major responsibility for the children. Michael said the children often complained about their mother not being there when they came home from school or went to bed. The therapist suggested that they might be expressing Michael's wish. Michael agreed that this could be so. They talked some about what it was like with June working and about how Michael's feelings about that could conflict with his thoughts and beliefs.

Near the end of the session, after this rational conversation, Michael said he thought he would stop at home on his way to work to make sure June had gotten up! This slipping back into childish and pseudoparental ways was what gave this session an unsettling feeling. It seemed hard for Michael to settle down with the idea that *he* had to change.

At the end of the session, Stan had two salient thoughts. One was that next time he would interrupt Michael's blaming and complaints, and instead focus him on his own responsibility for having his life feel good to him. The other was that Michael had said very little about his childhood. Most of what he had said about his parents concerned relatively recent interactions with them. Stan was perplexed that he had let so much time go by without focusing their attention on Michael's experiences of himself as a child. He knew there must be something in Michael that said "stay away from that area." Stan determined to explore Michael's childhood next session, knowing that there would almost certainly be a struggle.

This failure to discuss early childhood experiences is the clearest way in which Michael's therapy is atypical. Most new clients talk about their family history much earlier. Stan knew that Michael would never become fully engaged in the therapeutic process until he experienced the connection between early family history and current life problems. He wanted to make sure that Michael had such an experience next time.

Session #5

The first exchange after the initial "hello" set the tone for the meeting. Stan daparted from his typical unstructured opening. He wanted to find out about Michael's early history and, more important, he wanted Michael to experience the significance of it.

Stan: I realize that we have talked very little so far about your early life.
Michael: Well, I have some vivid memories about that and that's relevant because my father called me last night and—

Note that Michael started to talk about his *present* relationship with his parents rather than his childhood. After a couple of sentences, Stan interrupted and said:

> *Stan*: Tell me what it was like growing up with those parents of yours.
> *Michael*: All right. Let me jump around a little bit. When I was 18—
> *Stan*: Why don't you jump around from before you were 12?

Stan would have preferred to get Michael talking about the years before six, but started later as a sort of compromise, hoping gradually to lead Michael farther back in time. Michael responded with recollections from the time period specified, but they were fact-filled and feeling-free. It was clear that Michael was actively avoiding a feeling connection with his childhood. There was probably something in the vulnerability of those early times that he found very threatening. His recollections also kept shifting away from his parents and toward his peers. Stan kept pushing the defense.

> *Stan*: You know something interesting?
> *Michael*: What?
> *Stan*: I'm not hearing a word about your mother or father. . . . You're telling me about kids your own age and about school, but I haven't heard a word about your father. . . . Isn't that interesting?
> *Michael*: Yeah.
> *Stan*: So push yourself to talk about him. What was he like?
> *Michael*: My father wasn't around much.

Michael talked with somewhat more feeling about his busy, often absent father. There was a touch of the "unfair" tone mentioned earlier and a surprising story about how Michael's father would chase him when he was angry and not be able to catch him. When asked about his mother, Michael said she had been present more than his father. But he added:

> *Michael*: She would get frustrated with us because we were growing so fast. We were physically strong and we could outpower her and the discipline function would be referred to our father.
> *Stan*: Who wasn't able to catch you.
> *Michael*: Mm-hmm.
> *Stan*: So those are necessarily memories from when you were older. You spent some time in your life being totally dependent on your parents.
> *Michael*: Mm-hmm.
> *Stan*: When you couldn't possibly outpower your mother or run faster than your father.
> *Michael*: True. Yeah.
> *Stan*: You don't have so many memories of that.
> *Michael*: No. I don't. I remember being a Cub Scout and liking that.

Stan kept trying to push Michael back in time and toward a sense of being helpless and dependent. It looked as though that experience was the one Michael was most resistent to experiencing.

> *Stan*: Tell me, "Once upon a time I was very little."
> *Michael*: Once upon a time I was very little (Laughs.) What else? What comes after that? (Laughs.) I think I was born full grown!

Michael's laugh conveyed a sense of giddy fear in facing his dependency and vulnerability.

> *Stan*: Must have been tough on your mother.
> *Michael*: Yeah.
> *Stan*: Did you have a tie on when you were born?
> *Michael*: I think so. Yeah. (Laughs.)

Here the strain of the battle showed in Stan's responses, which were somewhat angry and cool. For a moment, he lost the firm, caring pursuit he had been undertaking and took on a bantering style somewhat similar to Michael's. Stan's next comment was said more compassionately. He seemed to be back on the track.

> *Stan*: I'm going to take that statement seriously. I'm going to believe they didn't give you much space to be a kid.

Michael heard this but still could not quite get past "It's unfair" to a sense of compassion for the little boy in him who had been treated coolly and pushed to perform. The session continued as a seesaw battle in which Michael sought to maintain his cool, distant, grown-up stance while Stan tried to get him to feel his childhood hurt. The following example is illustrative of numerous similar exchanges. Michael was saying how, as the oldest child, he had borne the brunt of parental expectations. His brows were knitting together with hard work and responsibility. To break up this defense, Stan interrupted as follows:

> *Stan*: Say, "I was a needy little fella."
> *Michael*: I was a needy little fella. (Pause, then a laugh.) I can't imagine myself little. (Giddy laugh.) It's been so long . . . feels like the dark ages . . . 40 years ago. . . . (Then much softer.) But I was there once.
> *Stan*: (Softly.) You sure were.
> *Michael*: I do remember one time when my mother was warm and caring for me. I cut my chin falling off my bike and went home crying. And my mother took good care of me.
> *Stan*: What'd she do?
> *Michael*: Oh, she washed it, and patted it gently, and reassured me. . . . So that was good. . . . Then she took me to the doctor . . . and together they took care of my hurt (Michael begins to cry quietly) and nobody said to me that was a dumb thing to do or . . . why did you do that. (Still crying softly.) They were good to me.

Stan: Did she sit with you?
Michael: Mm-hmm. And she was there when the doctor sewed it up.

All this was said slowly, tearfully, and with feeling. Quite suddenly, the tone changed. The next sentence had a totally different sound—the "unfair" tone.

Michael: But I remember her giving more attention to my little sister. And the reson was, she was sick all the time, so she got most of the attention.

At the end of this exchange, Michael got scared and went back to his familiar complaining defense. Prior to that, though, he had become very open and feelingful. Stan's pursuit was finally successful and Michael did his part by keeping his feeling going for a considerable period of time. A whole cycle of feelings moving from defensive to open and back to defensive again was repeated at least ten times in this session. There was a tendency for the later cycles to have a larger proportion of feeling time than the earlier cycles, but the change was subtle.

Near the end of the session, Michael realized that he loved and held his children more warmly than his parents had loved and held him. This perspective helped him to feel that if he had had himself for a child, he would have been more loving and present than his parents had been with him. This realization brought about more compassion and less complaining than had been present earlier.

This session was part beginning phase and part middle phase. There was information exchanged: Michael talked about his childhood, and his therapist taught him how to work and helped him to have a lively experience of his past. There was also middle-phase work: the repeated attacks on the same defense, the working through of insights, and the invitations to feel, offered and reoffered.

As he grew up, Michael fashioned for himself the best way of being that he could, given his experiences, his reinforcement history, and the coping devices that were available to him. He sought help from Stan because the old ways no longer worked for him. His striving, his wish to control, his perfectionism, and his resentful sense of unfairness had gotten him a lot and cost him a lot. He had clung to them for decades and was not about to give them up just because Stan asked him to. This session gave some sense of how firmly he held onto them and also how much he wanted something better for himself.

Session #6

This session is a companion piece to session #5. The same theme recurs: Michael's attempt to contact his childhood neediness and hurt and to feel himself wanting his mother. In this session, however, Michael seemed much more able to "take the trip." He was more calm, he more readily let himself feel soft, and he cooperated more fully with his therapist's suggestions. Most of the session was middle phase so only the beginning-phase parts are described here.

Near the start of the session, Michael said that things were going better at home and that he felt less depressed and more able to work. Indeed, he seemed better—neither as depressed nor as hypomanic as he had been in earlier sessions. Stan knew, however, that Michael's resistance and practical, nonreflective nature could carry him out of therapy as his depressive symptoms eased. He gave Michael a perspective on the process of change in therapy which distinguished symptom alleviation from basic personality change and he urged Michael to work for personality change.

During this session, Michael worked on his childhood memories of his mother, calling out to her while Stan held him and expressing his anger and hurt at her distance and separateness from him. The only beginning-phase transactions were those in which Stan taught Michael aspects of working: how to call out to his mother using only nonverbal sounds, and how to be held by the therapist to facilitate a sense of safety and closeness. As mentioned earlier, Michael felt remarkably safer and was much more in touch with feelings than in the previous session.

SUMMARY

In this chapter, we have looked at the beginning phase of therapy both in general and in particular. Michael's story illustrates the acculturation process that characterizes the beginning phase. Michael was taught to express his feelings more openly, to blame and complain less, and to be more open to his needy feelings. He was given some ways of viewing feeling-expression as distinct from social arguing or complaining and was reintroduced to his childhood. Conversely, Michael also put his own imprint on the therapy process and insisted that Stan adopt and adjust to *his* style in some ways. For example, he delayed the examination of childhood issues for several sessions, brought a lot of energy to the process, and was slower to cry hard than most clients. Stan had to fit his process to Michael's style, and Michael changed some ways of viewing his life in response to Stan's interventions.

We heard Stan find out who Michael was with respect to personal style, history, family, and work. Meanwhile, Michael did his own investigating and comparison shopping, comparing Stan to Dr. Turner, and asking Stan about the decor of his office and the strange sounds coming from other offices. These were ways that Michael found out what he needed to know about Stan and the Center.

Stan taught Michael how to work and look at his behavior and feelings in a way that would facilitate progress. Finally, during their first few sessions, Stan and Michael came to a common understanding about the fee, the meeting time, the treatment goals, and how they would work together.

¹See Chapter 10.

5

The Middle Phase— Joan's Story

> Midway along the journey of our life
> I . . . found myself within a gloomy wood.
> So hard it is its aspects to describe,
> This savage, harsh and fearsome wilderness,
> That fear rekindles with the memory . . .
> Yet to recall the good that came of it
> I shall set forth all else I there beheld.
>
> Dante
> *The Inferno*

With these words, Dante begins *The Inferno*. We are reminded of them because the middle phase of therapy can also be a "gloomy wood," "fearsome" and hard to describe. Yet, as was the case with Dante's vision, good comes of the effort to describe it.

Imagine a park with walls around it and only two places to enter and leave. If snow fell overnight, by the end of the next day, there would be well-traveled and fairly predictable sets of footprints where people entered and left the park, but all sorts of random wanderings within the park. Describing the beginning and ending phases of therapy is like describing footprints near the gates—the paths in and out. Describing the middle phase of therapy is like trying to find order and lawfulness in all the meandering footprints between the entrance and exit.

TASKS OF THE MIDDLE PHASE

For clients who pursue the full course of therapy, the middle phase is usually a good deal more than the middle third. The first five sessions may be spent in the beginning phase and the last five primarily on termination. All the rest, perhaps 30 to 100 or more sessions, fall into the middle phase. By the time the middle phase begins, the therapist has a good idea of who the client is and what the main issues are, and client and therapist have agreed on goals for the treatment.

Working Through

One of the hallmarks of the middle phase is the leisurely and repeated working through of conflict areas, feelings, memories, and ways of behaving. There is enough time and safety to approach each major issue in several different ways. The following example illustrates middle-phase working through of dependency feelings.

Peter was the youngest of five children and the only son. His somewhat overprotective mother and older sisters took care of him and also controlled him. His father was loving but was gone much of the time. When Peter sought help at age 30, he had already left home at 16, left graduate school without finishing, left several jobs, and left his wife. He had begun to see a destructive pattern in his leaving people and situations. During the middle phase of Peter's therapy, this issue was explored in many different ways. The focus moved from person to person, from feeling to feeling, from past to present and back again, and from the relationship with the therapist to outside figures in Peter's life. In such a therapeutic "dance," there are only so many steps. Eventually, the same steps will be repeated, yet each repetition is somewhat different. Peter's growing awareness allowed him to return to old territory with a deeper, clearer vision. The process of working through is thus more like a spiral that a circle.

Peter focused first on his former wife and expressed anger that she was so controlling, always telling him what to do and how to do it. He was angry and defiant, shouting, "Fuck you! You're not going to tell me what to do!" This led to the expression of similar feelings toward bosses, teachers, his older sisters, and his mother.

At first, he stoutly disclaimed any feelings of anger toward his therapist, saying that she was just the opposite of all the others—fair, flexible, and not at all controlling. Eventually, however, when the therapist confronted him for paying his bills late, he was able to contact his angry, rebellious feelings toward her as well.

Slowly, Peter began to sense the needy, dependent feelings behind his defiance. At first, recognizing these feelings made him laugh explosively. It was a surprise to him to feel that he really wanted love and caring from the people whom he had fought with and resisted for so long. As he felt his need more strongly, he cried out, sobbed, and raged. What he had wanted as a child had only been available to him at the unacceptable cost of letting go of his autonomy. He alternately felt his need, and his fury at not having his need fulfilled.

Many subsequent sessions focused on Peter's feelings toward his therapist. Love and longing alternated with fear and anger about being controlled. Peter and his therapist also looked at how he was dealing with people in his current life. Together they considered how he could handle those times when his conflict about dependency was restimulated.

When Peter and his therapist began termination, the dependency issue surfaced again as Peter struggled with yet another separation. However, this time Peter's dependency was dealt with as a feeling to be expressed rather than acted out.

This example shows how a nuclear conflict appears throughout the middle phase in various guises. It needs to be examined in relation to the therapist, early life figures, and current life figures. It must be considered as impulse ("Love me!") and as defense ("Who needs you?"). Finally, more adaptive behavior must be developed for meeting this need appropriately.

Exploring Feelings toward the therapist

One of the main tasks of the middle phase is exploring the client's feelings toward the therapist. These feelings are fluid, constantly moving and shifting, changing in tone and intensity. They need to be uncovered and expressed for several reasons. First, feelings of which the client is not fully aware are likely to be acted on impulsively, as in stubborn resistance or premature termination. When the client is persistently encouraged to express these feelings, they are much less likely to result in intransigence or flight from therapy. Second, expressing feelings toward the therapist creates an *in vivo* experiment that allows the client to see that angry feelings do not destroy the therapist and that loving feelings need not be acted on sexually. It is very important for clients to learn that feelings *may* be linked to behavior but *need not* be. The ability to disengage feeling from action and choose whether or not to act on feelings is liberating and makes expressing feelings much easier.

The third and most important reason for looking at the client's feelings toward the therapist is that the client's unfinished business with parents and early caregivers can be worked through in the relationship with the therapist. Not all of the client's feelings toward the therapist are transference; some feelings arise from the real relationship. However, when the nature or intensity of a feeling is not explicable as a response to the actual characteristics of the therapist, then transference is involved and an excellent therapeutic opportunity is at hand. At such times, a door to the client's archaic past opens; if client and therapist go through it, they will have an unusually clear glimpse of the client's experience of early caregivers. Is the therapist inappropriately seen as disappointed, devouring, or demanding? If so, then the client probably experienced mother or father in these ways. Transference feelings are not a reliable guide for knowing what the client's parents were actually like, but they are a good indication of how the client experienced them.

Discovering feelings about the therapist and then encouraging their full expression is one of the main tasks of therapy, especially the middle phase, when the climate of safety is usually at its maximum. The relationship has been well established and is not yet threatened with dissolution. One of the most difficult aspects of this task is conveying to the client the idea that sharing these feelings with the therapist is both important and safe. The same childlike part of the client that generates transference feelings also exaggerates their capacity to affect others in general and to cause the therapist's destruction in particular. This kind of magical thinking is commonly seen in clients' unwillingness to express warm feelings toward someone they are angry at, even if that person is far away, because they do not want "to give him the satisfaction." Similarly, it is frightening to share angry feelings or destructive fantasies with a therapist one depends on and needs. Clients fear that the expression of such feelings or fantasies could hurt, alienate, or even destroy the therapist.

A fourth reason for examining the client's relationship with the therapist is that these feelings also illuminate current relationships outside of therapy. The therapeutic relationship is, among other things, a social and interpersonal enterprise. There are certain givens in the nature of the relationship, but lots of room remains for individual differences. Some clients are suspicious of the therapist and some are trusting. Some are compliant, some are rebellious, and some are self-respecting and cooperative. As the therapist sees the client behave in certain ways in therapy, it becomes easier to picture the client relating to others outside therapy. The following example illustrates this last reason for exploring the client's feelings toward the therapist.

Robert told his therapist of being ill-treated by family and friends; he had no idea why this was occurring. One day, he mentioned that he had been to see another therapist "for a few visits." In the ensuing conversation, it developed that he had gone to the other therapist "to see if everyone would be as hard on me as you are," that the other therapist "saw things more clearly," and that he had not mentioned it before "because I knew how jealous and critical you would be."

The therapist was in fact angry and told Robert so, pointing out how he had been provocative. Fortunately, the therapist's anger was not so great as to interfere with her communicating clearly. She was able to maintain an objective stance focused on the client's provocative behavior. Robert saw what he had done to set himself up as the victim and eventually was able to look at that process nondefensively. For months after that, this example of Robert's provocative behavior served as a reference point that therapist and client had both experienced firsthand. Never again could the client recite, with injured innocence, his lifelong refrain: "I don't know why he got so angry at me." Whenever he would start, his therapist would raise her eyebrows questioningly and both would laugh.

This is just one of many examples in which behavior in the therapy session can be used to help understand behavior outside the session. The translation is not always one for one, of course. A very ingratiating client may be ingratiating with authority figures but bullying with subordinates. A quiet client may be talkative and noisy in more comfortable settings. Nevertheless, there is much that can be extrapolated to other situations from behavior in therapy. Similarly, clients can practice behavior with the therapist that they would like to make a part of their normal repertoire.

Another reason for carefully examining the client-therapist relationship during the middle phase is that the safety that makes much of this hard work possible can also lull the participants into bad habits. A certain tension between client and therapist needs to be maintained if the therapist is to exert a pull on the client to change. The client's resistance will create enticements for the neurotic needs of the therapist. The therapist must stand aloof from offers to get into comfortable but unproductive *folies à deux,* such as victim and rescuer, or casual conversational friends. Even constant conflict can be a comfortable neurotic niche. Client and therapist can fight endlessly without risk, thought, or resolution. This, too, represents a failure of the therapist to stand aloof from, but in tension with, the client's neurotic ways and thoughtfully to present a better alternative.

The irony in this is that the very safety that makes the middle phase so potentially productive can also make possible this comfortable collusion to escape the tension that creates change.

Early Memories and Intense Feelings

The middle phase of therapy typically is marked by extensive work on early memories and their accompanying intense feeling-expression. It is usually necessary for the therapist to push the client persistently to recall early memories.

Let us return to the example of Peter.

Peter's therapist had read his sensitivity regarding being controlled and knew she would need to postpone a major engagement of that issue until enough trust had developed to minimize the risk that Peter would flee therapy. By the tenth session, Peter had expressed a good deal of anger toward a number of people whom he felt had been controlling. These included his former wife and his mother. The issues with his mother involved contemporary interactions as well as memories of her during his adolescence. We regard such basic issues as having their roots in much earlier times. We use these later memories primarily as a safe forum for practicing feeling-expression and as a bridge to the earlier, more important memories.

Peter told a story in the tenth session of how, when he was in high school, his mother would listen in on his phone calls and would not let him use the car if he were dating a girl of whom she did not approve. He was angry and was expressing it well, yelling at her and smashing the mat. His therapist asked him if he remembered feeling similarly toward his mother when he was younger. He moved back in time by steps, recalling memories from age 12, then from age 7, and finally from age 4 or 5. This took some time because, at each step, his therapist encouraged him to feel his rage. As he got to the earlier memories, there was a subtle change. Instead of being angry about being controlled, he began to get angry about only getting love if he did what his mother or older sisters wanted him to do. It was not simply a matter of being controlled, as it so often felt to him in the present. He became more aware of wanting love as a young child, and his rage stemmed from not getting that love unless he allowed himself to be controlled.

Peter came to his next session eager to work. During the week, whenever he had felt angry about being controlled, he also had identified within himself the wish to be loved. He talked about this for a few minutes and then the therapist suggested that he work on the mat. She told him to lie down, close his eyes, and try to recall those memories he had discovered a week earlier. As he did this, he got angry with his mother and then sad that they had had so little time together that was simply loving. He felt keenly how good it had been when she had attended to him lovingly and how much it had hurt when she had turned away or bartered love for control. Peter cried hard some of the time and sobbed out his hurt. At other times, he screamed with pain. He was rageful only at the beginning. After that, he felt his pain and sadness.

These two sessions formed a particularly clear sequence in which the focus moved from rage to pain, from present to past, and from control to absence of love. There were many subsequent sessions in which these connections were developed further as the core issue was reworked in various ways. At times, for example, the initial focus was on Peter's feelings toward the therapist, rather than on feelings toward his mother or older sisters.

This type of intense feeling work usually occurs only in the middle phase of therapy, when there is enough time and safety to allow full exploration of whatever is uncovered. It is very important work. Expressing feelings only about events from late childhood on does not seem to lead to the same transformative change as does work from early childhood.

When clients cannot remember those early years, we often ask them to make up very detailed imaginary memories. As they do so, they usually recognize that many elements of the imaginary memories are in fact real. Even when that does not happen, the convention of agreeing that they are made up seems to free some clients from an excessive concern for historical precision and to give them permission to feel. If they make up a story that has emotional meaning for them, it makes little difference whether it was their mother or father who really hurt them or whether they were laughed at in the kitchen or the living room.

Behavior Change

For meaningful personality change to occur, understanding and the expression of feelings are not enough. In addition to these, specific attention must be paid to behavior. What does the client do that perpetuates isolation? How could she/he speak differently so people would respond more warmly? What cues does the client give that say to others "Stay away!" or "Let's fight!"

Neurotic behavior can be viewed as a way of coping that was originally adaptive but that has outlived its usefulness. Measures that were designed to avoid pain now cause more pain than they prevent. Working through the conflicts that resulted in the neurotic behavior does not automatically end the behavior. This is one reason why we need to attend specifically to behavior change. Another is that asking clients to behave differently can lead to useful feelings and understandings. An example of this behavior-to-feeling connection follows.

George's most obviously disturbed behavior was his struggling with people and his tendency to get angry and leave people and situations.

After this pattern became clear, his therapist urged George to refrain from struggling with and leaving people. They spoke concretely about what kinds of responses were proscribed and with whom George could safely practice these new ways of responding. He decided he felt safe enough with a woman he was dating and with a couple of friends to try new ways with them. He agreed that he would not struggle with these people under any circumstances. Whether it was a decision about what to do, a political argument, or even a statement by a friend that George struggled a lot, he was to agree and show no disagreement by grimace or tone. What's more, he was to be enthusiastic in his agreement.

Although he was faltering and hesitant at first, George experienced two sorts of successes. First, when he tried out these new ways of behaving, he found that his fears of totally losing his autonomy were unfounded. People did not seize on his agreement to make him more and more subservient to their will. Second, he uncovered feelings by overcoming his usual defense. He came to therapy angry and frightened after he had changed his usual response, and moved his therapy ahead by expressing those feelings and exploring their roots.

Ultimately, behavior is maintained by its consequences. In areas of conflict, however, people are rigid and do not see or dare to try all the possible responses available to them. Moreover, when they do try something new, the anxious chatter in their own minds often drowns out the real responses of other people and so they cannot accurately evaluate the payoff of their new behavior.

Another problem is that our language of behavior is often crude and imprecise. We frequently tell people to "reach out" to others. Yet there are many ways to reach out. Some attempts to do so convey so much fear, anger, or reluctance that they are not really reaching out at all. One of the advantages of groups and workshops is that the therapist gets to see the actual behavior rather than simply having the client's report of it.[1]

Despite these problems prescribing and proscribing behavior is a very useful tool. It is used most during the middle phase largely because there is a need for repeated sequences of prescription-trial-report, with each report shaping the subsequent prescription and with ample opportunity to express the feelings aroused by both the prescription and the trial.

Symptom Relief and Character Change

Early in the middle phase, a subtle transformation takes place. The

[1]See Chapter 7.

client realizes that many of the symptoms that first necessitated treatment have largely or wholly disappeared. Yet the character structure that is the basis of the trouble remains. The depression or anxiety is gone, but the client's long-standing ways of relating to others and of viewing the self have not yet changed. At this point, some people stop therapy, either because they got what they came for (relief of symptoms) or because they dread what lies ahead. Others feel like stopping but do not. Staying with therapy at this point requires courage on the client's part and a clear vision of the entire therapy process on the therapist's part.

The therapist must: (1) help the client to distinguish between symptom relief and personality change, (2) have some basis for optimism that personality change can in fact be achieved with this client, and (3) watch vigilantly for coded messages that the client is having trouble making the transition. The therapist's own feelings can make this task more difficult. When the client is resistant and wants to leave therapy, the therapist's own fear of being left can interfere with clear thinking. The therapist may block out clear messages of incipient flight which, were they dealt with, could result in renewed commitment to therapy. Or the therapist may respond defensively to such messages with anger or a cool, "who cares" attitude. Less dramatically, the therapist's hurt about being left can interfere with hearing the client completely and empathically and can muddy explanations of what remains to be done in therapy should the client choose to stay.

Negative Transference

In general, positive feelings predominate in the early stage of therapy while more negative, or at least mixed, feelings emerge in the middle phase. This change is another hurdle that some clients do not overcome. For therapy to progress, the client must risk sharing those angry feelings and the therapist must hear them and encourage their vigorous expression. Both must be willing to leave those sunny meadows of the early phase for the "savage, harsh and fearsome wilderness" of the negative transference that characterizes the middle phase. Making this transition is a challenge for both therapist and client. The client must share her/his anger or disappointment as clearly as possible, and the therapist must listen carefully for disguised and coded messages that tell what the client feels about the therapist beneath the level of conscious awareness (Langs, 1982).

Therapists have feelings, too, and they are often reluctant to search out and decode these angry messages. When therapists push past this natural reluctance and skillfully use what they hear, a number of benefits ensue. They may find ways in which they have not been dealing well with their clients. When this is uncovered and changed, the client feels better understood and more effective, and can re-experience childhood hurts with a more positive outcome.

Joining a Group

A final characteristic of the middle phase of feeling-expressive therapy is involvement in groups and peer-counseling. This is not simply a matter of joining a group or finding a peer-counselor. It is also a matter of attitude. When the middle phase is unfolding properly, clients develop a self-responsible attitude. They come to see that they, rather than their therapists, will benefit if the work goes well. Although that may seem self-evident, many clients' behavior reveals the opposite belief. Also, as the client works with other therapists and other clients, there is a tendency to attribute fewer magical powers to one's own therapist and to have more confidence in the process. Finally, there is a sense of common purpose with others and a willingness both to offer help to, and to seek help from, others. The client takes more charge of her/his own changing.

Let us now look at an individual client's middle phase of therapy and note the various hallmarks and tasks we have just discussed.

JOAN'S STORY

Introduction

Joan entered psychotherapy shortly before her fortieth birthday, saying that therapy was her birthday present to herself. She felt okay about her life, but wanted more—more feelings and especially more joy. Although her wish for growth was real, it soon became clear that Joan was also acutely troubled about her marriage.

Joan was working as a placement counselor in the personnel department of a large corporation. She had been married 16 years and had a son and daughter in their early teens.

In the first few sessions, Joan's sense of wanting more quickly focused on her husband. She said they had loved each other at first, but had not been very intimate since shortly after the children were born. They were involved in their careers and their children, but not with each other. She experienced her husband as distant, judgmental, and critical. When she told him of her dissatisfaction, he said that he, too, was unhappy. They began dissolving their relationship soon after that and six months after Joan started therapy, she had separated from her husband physically and legally, though not yet emotionally. The speed with which this was done suggested that a lot of the separating had occurred much earlier in unspoken form.

The months just before and after the separation were spent in working on feelings about her husband. Joan expressed her feelings of rage and hurt toward him, and she became aware that he reminded her of her parents and that his presentation of himself as righteous increased her sense of guilt. She felt her fears about separating and recognized that part of her grief was for her husband and part was for earlier losses. Joan worked hard, beginning sessions by describing some incident that had occurred with her husband and then following her feelings back to her mother and father.

After a year of therapy, Joan had come to grips with the end of her marriage. She had made important decisions, acted on them, and mourned her loss. In the process, she had also come to know herself much better. For example, she saw how her husband's self-righteous criticism hurt her more because of her mother's earlier criticism. She had also learned to track her current feelings to early figures and to use this insight to respond more flexibly in the present.

Now Joan was ready to turn her attention more fully to characterologic issues. These were primarily an exaggerated fear of losing control, a tendency to struggle with people, and anxiety that interfered with her enjoyment of life. She often felt rushed and pressured, hurrying to do one thing after another in the search for love and approval. Her mouth was sometimes dry from fear, and her conflict about being "good" and pleasing people often showed itself as somewhat unreal cuteness or as stubborn opposition to what others wanted. She struggled with herself about being perfect and with other people about whether to do what they wanted her to do. Her enjoyment of sex and of relationships with men were limited by both these conflicts. It was hard for her to relax with men, to let go and enjoy them rather than struggle with them. In her recent work with her therapist, Rachel, she had been focusing on these conflicts and specifically on her ability to initiate and enjoy a sexual relationship.

At the point we begin, Joan had been in individual therapy for nearly a year, had been in group therapy for three months, had attended a weekend workshop, had peer-counseled regularly, and knew how to express her feelings clearly. Consciously, the whole process made sense to her and she was committed to achieving her goals for personal change. Yet, part of her resisted change. Her conflicts regarding autonomy, struggle, and perfectionism continued both within and outside of therapy. The sessions described here dealt principally with this struggle, which sometimes took place between conflicting voices within Joan and other times seemed to be between Joan and her therapist, Rachel. However, the essentially intrapsychic quality of this struggle can be seen as Rachel expresses first one side and then the other of Joan's conflict. Whichever side she takes, Joan opposes her.

Session 43

Joan missed the session just prior to this one. She began by asking for a copy of her bill, which she had previously requested. Rachel said she had not had the bill made up and Joan said that was okay. The exchange was brief and matter-of-fact, yet it foreshadowed two important themes in Joan's therapy: her wish to control others and her wish to please others. Not surprisingly, these needs conflicted with each other!

Joan told Rachel of her impending vacation and mentioned having difficulty remembering her dreams. After a pause, she said:

Joan: I want to tell you that I . . . um . . . feel badly about missing my appointment with you last week. I felt really disappointed about it. . . . I felt really angry at myself.
Rachel: The "bad" about it. Is there something more to say about that? Were you angry at me?
Joan: I don't think so. I don't think I was angry at you or dreaded seeing you. I was thankful that I was going to have two sessions with you before I went away.

This focus on the therapeutic relationship, and especially on angry feelings toward the therapist, is characteristic of the middle phase.

Rachel: You feel OK about being charged for that?
Joan: Yeah. That's fair.
Rachel: Well, fair is one issue, but I'm talking more about. . . .
Joan: Anger with you for charging me?
Rachel: Yeah.
Joan: No. I feel OK about that.
Rachel: No anger at all, huh?
Joan: No.
Rachel: And about my not having the bill you asked for ready?
Joan: No, I just wanted it for the insurance company. No, I don't think I'm angry at you.
Rachel: Are you surprised at how badly you felt about missing the session? (Pause.)
Joan: No. I really looked forward to it. . . . Coming here is really important. Being with you here is really important. Working with you is important to me.

("Me thinks the lady doeth protest too much.")

Rachel: I'm sure that's true. I'm just curious about what old Sigmund Freud would say about it.

Joan: He'd say I didn't wanta come.

Rachel: Yeah. He would. An unconscious part of you didn't want to come. . . .

Joan: (Running over Rachel's last words.) And the only part that doesn't. . . .

Rachel: (Continuing to talk.) By the way, that's the same part that forgets your dreams.

Joan: I'm sure of that.

Rachel: Forgets—just blocks it out. Doesn't want you to know.

Joan (Speaking rapidly.) The one thing I think *does* have some bearing on that is that the appointment was on Thursday. It did not enter my mind after maybe Tuesday. It got transferred to Friday in my mind (Joan talks even faster and is sounding breathless). On Friday morning when I got up, still not realizing that I had missed the appointment the day before, I began to think about what I wanted to do with you in the session and I decided that I was really going to talk to you about terminating and coming back in September and October for four sessions. . . . When I realized later that I'd missed the session, I thought maybe I'd been afraid to talk to you about terminating.

The breathless speed of her talking, the run-on tone and the wish to flee therapy are all of a piece. This is the sound of a defense under stress. This child's sand castle is being hit with big waves. She is frantically patting new sand on the parts that washed out. It is a big job.

Rachel: Or maybe you want to talk about terminating for the same reason that you forgot the session—that there's some resistance to the piece of work we're doing. Which would certainly be my favorite hypothesis. (Slowly.) It's just hard. Your sex work is hard, scary. . . .

Joan: I'm feeling like I'm not getting anywhere. I'm bogged down.

At this point, only a few minutes into the session, the main themes had been established: (1) Joan's "forgetting" to come to the previous session and thinking about terminating because of feeling "bogged down"; and (2) Rachel's interpretation that resistance to working on sex was motivating Joan's missing the session, her wish to quit, her feeling of being bogged down, and her (not yet recognized) anger toward Rachel. Roughly speaking, these continued to be the battle lines for the balance of the session. As these themes developed, Joan's anger toward Rachel became anger toward her mother, and she worked on Oedipal issues of competitiveness, jealousy, and inclusion, with respect to both her parents and Rachel.

Rachel: I'd like to hear your anger toward me—the angry thoughts you've had.

Joan: All of 'em? Forever?

Rachel: The ones you've had since you've been into some resistance. (Pause.)

Joan: You're not helping me enough!

Joan went on to say that she was angry at Rachel for "not doing it right" and for letting her drift. She said she was worried about money; Rachel was not making the therapy go fast enough. Her voice was quiet and cute, not at all angry. Rachel pointed this out and then reminded Joan she was being charged for the session she had missed. Rachel went on to tell her how she planned to spend the money ("It'll help with our vacation") but Joan remained compliant. That is, she pretended to follow Rachel's suggestion, but actually undermined it by not letting herself really feel her anger. At this point, she was acting out her anger but not expressing it.

> *Rachel*: What's the dryness in your mouth?
>
> *Joan*: It usually means fear . . . but I'm certainly not afraid to get mad at you.
>
> *Rachel*: Get mad at me about something other than letting you down around your therapy. (Long pause.) That one! (Meaning Joan should share "that" thought—the one she just had.)
>
> *Joan*: OK. (She takes the plastic bat.) I get really pissed off (hits) at how warm you are with Matt (Rachel's co-therapist in Joan's group). You always agree with each other and have this big united front. Nobody gets between you! That really pisses me off!
>
> *Rachel*: Yes!
>
> *Joan*: It's just sickening sometimes—all that love and warmth! (Joan is hitting the bat hard, talking loudly, and sounding angry.) Ugh! I hate it! It's sickening! Like two little kids playing. (Hitting hard.) Ugh! I hate it!

Joan slowed down and sounded a little depressed, but Rachel encouraged her to go on. She soon resumed her angry tone and her hitting.

> *Joan*: I don't like it that you have a nice man to work with!
>
> *Rachel*: Know where I was just before I saw you?
>
> *Joan*: Probably hugging Matt and planning your joint strategy for how to handle the kids in group!
>
> *Rachel*: Mm-hmm.
>
> *Joan*: This goes back to that work on Tuesday night in group when Jeanette was working.

Joan recalled how Jeanette played out a scene wherein she competed with her mother for her father. Joan said that when she went off to peer-counsel with Jeanette afterwards, she found herself feeling competitive with Rachel—that is, she wanted to be more helpful to Jeanette than Rachel had been. She worked on this some, yelling at Rachel that she was stronger than her and would be a better therapist for Jeanette.

> *Joan*: I can do it better than you!
>
> *Rachel*: (Teasing.) I told her to work well with you. I said, "Be good to Joan."
>
> *Joan*: The hell you did! *I* was in control of that! Not *you*. (Pause.) And that's what all this is about, too. (Slower now.) It's control.
>
> *Rachel*: Uh-huh! . . . Uh-huh!
>
> *Joan*: And I'm telling you in one place to take over more control of my therapy

and I'm also telling you I'm in charge. . . . (Hitting again.) I'm going to decide that! Uhh! I'm better than you! (Pause.)

Rachel: Don't look for the right words to say. You're 4 or 6. . . .

Joan: (Hitting and yelling.) Leave it alone! I can do it better! You're doing it wrong! You're not doing it right! You're telling me wrong! Ahh! Ahh! (After a pause, Joan speaks in a quiet tone.) She (Joan's mother) would make me feel guilty and control me that way.

Rachel: I'm disappointed you're not going to the workshop. I thought sure you'd come.

Rachel then took up a real issue between them—Joan's decision not to attend a workshop—and role-played a disappointed, critical mother. This was an invitation to Joan to express her anger at whatever combination of Rachel and mother was most evocative. Throughout this section, Rachel's comments were delivered in a broad, slightly exaggerated manner, signalling to Joan that Rachel was indeed role-playing.

Joan: (Yelling and hitting again.) Uhh! I'm *not* coming. I'll decide what's right for me! Not you! You're not gonna lay what's good for me on me! Stop it! Uhh! I don't want to hear anymore of that! That's the same crap I' gonna get when I go visit her! Stop it! . . . Uhh!

Rachel: Everybody else is coming and you're not. Everybody else is optimistic, forward moving. . . .

Joan: Shut up! You don't know! Stop it!

Rachel: You've got a rebellious quality about you that we're gonna have to break.

Joan: Stop it! I'm in charge!

Rachel: (With an air of injured innocence.) I just assumed. . . .

Joan: Stop it! I don't care what you assumed! Ohh!!

Rachel: I said, "She'll get it together and make the right decision."

Joan: I hate you when you lay that stuff on me!

Rachel: I'm hurt. A little hurt.

Joan: Uhh! Don't tell me that!!

Rachel: Guess I expected too much. More than you could deliver.

Joan: That feels *awful*!! (Pause. Then, in a quieter tone.) That's it. By now, I should have myself together.

Rachel's tone suddenly changed from that of the disappointed, critical mother to one of a thoughtful colleague.

Rachel: Now that's quite similar to your mother saying, "Aren't you going to stay longer than three days?"

Joan: Right. "I should have done better."

Rachel: Is there a pained look on her face or pouting or what? Some with-holding of goodies?

Joan: It's like she's getting rejected 'cause I'm not giving her enough.

They talk about how Joan's mother's frequent disappointment with her was hard to fight—harder than outright condemnation. After a pause,

Rachel asked if Joan had more to say to her. They talked about Joan's competitive feelings and her concern about being a disappointment. When Joan discovered a particular way she had been seeking Rachel's approval, they both laughed at the twisted web in which Joan found herself with both Rachel and her mother. The more Joan sought their approval, the more angry she became and the more she needed their reassurance.

Rachel then returned to the jealousy that had been stimulated by Jeanette's work in the group.

> *Rachel*: So tell me what you saw when Jeanette was working. Describe it to me.
> *Joan*: I saw my mother getting in the way. . . .
> *Rachel*: (Joking.) Your mother came into that group? No, literally, tell me what you actually saw.
> *Joan*: Of course. She was right there. (They both laugh.) Interfering again!
> *Rachel*: OK. Don't go so quickly. Tell me what happened in group.
> *Joan*: You were selfish with Matt. You kept her (Jeanette) from getting close to him.
> *Rachel*: I was sort of laid back and subtle about that?
> *Joan*: No. You just put yourself between her and him.
> *Rachel*: What'd your mom do?
> *Joan*: I'd always slept with my dad when my mom went away and with my mom when my dad went away. And when I was about 11, she told me I couldn't sleep with him anymore.

Rachel then role-played mother saying that Joan could not sleep with her father. Joan raged, said it was insane, yelled, and hit. Rachel said she was protecting Joan from her father and her father from Joan.

> *Joan*: You control everyone, don't you!
> *Rachel*: So she really got to you, huh?
> *Joan*: No it was just . . . her control was so absolute, I was 18 before I began to get free of it.
> *Rachel*: But did you hear how you struggled with me about that? It was hard for you just to say, "Yeah, she really got to me." . . . She really did get to you.
> *Joan*: Yeah, that's right. She manipulated everybody around her. To this day, she still does. And there I was—this little dependent kid. A shit deal. I didn't get what I needed at all from her.

Joan began to cry about not getting the love she wanted from her mother and about having to accept being manipulated by her mother. She cried hard as she said, "I don't want to do it anymore."

After Joan stopped crying, she and Rachel talked about why Joan's mother had stood between Joan and her father. They agreed that, despite disclaimers to the contrary, her mother probably had done it for her own benefit rather than for Joan. As the session ended, Joan returned to the transference.

Joan: I was thinking about being better than you and stronger than you. And I was remembering when I was a little girl and the times I felt better and stronger than my mother—able to understand Dad better than she did—and the parallel there.

Rachel: It's wonderful, isn't it? (Pause.) It's our best tool. (Pause.) You're doing, by the way, very good therapy.

Joan: I'm ready to push the process and have it go where I want it to go.

The session ended on this enigmatic note. Had Rachel and Joan agreed that therapy was going well? Or had Rachel said, "You're not stuck in your therapy," only to have Joan reply, "It won't be okay till it's more under my control"? The answer emerged in the next session.

Session 44

This session occurred three weeks later, after Joan returned from New England with her children. She told Rachel that it had been a very satisfying vacation, that she had made contact with family members and old friends, and that she and her children had had a very good time together.

Joan then said that she had experienced some sexy feelings on vacation and that she was concerned about being behind on her bill. She told Rachel when she would be able to pay it and Rachel agreed to that arrangement. Then, going back, Rachel said:

Rachel: Tell me about the sexy feelings.

Joan: Well, you remember Clint? Actually he's my uncle, but he's not that much older than me. He's my father's brother. And . . . well . . . we just got very close. And we spent a lot of time together one night. We talked for a long time and I explored my sexy feelings with him.

Rachel: What do you mean, "explored"? You had sex with him?

Joan: Um . . . some petting with him and we talked about whether to make love.

In the next several minutes, the conversation went through several repeating loops. In various ways, Joan said, "This was a good experience, it was a start toward having sexy feelings toward other men and, if I had slept with him, it would have done no harm." Rachel said, in essence, "It's good you didn't sleep with him, it could have cost you a lot to do so, and such an experience would have been unlikely to lead to sexual relationships with other men."

Not getting the approval she sought, Joan confronted Rachel:

Joan: Um . . . you know, I'm feeling myself really defensive. I'm feeling like you're going to be really critical about me and tell me how I really shouldn't have shared these sexual feelings with him. I'm feeling a "but" before you even start talking.

Rachel: Well, I think I ought to share my "buts" with you so you don't have to read my mind and so we're really clear about what you imagine and what you're picking up from me. I have a sense that there's probably something you want from your uncle and it's not sex. . . .

Joan: Mm-hmm.

Rachel: And that it feels like sex . . . as there's stuff we want from our fathers when we're very little that feels like sex but is not sex.

Joan: Mm-hmm.

Rachel: And it would be costly to you to have it turn out being sex. And I would like you to get to what that is. Okay?

Joan: Mm-hmm.

Rachel: I don't think, like you do, that because you had sexy feelings about your uncle that you're now gonna go ahead and have sexy feelings toward other men.

Joan: Mm-hmm. See I see that as a bridge to places not quite as safe. . . .

Rachel: OK. Well let's look at that.

Joan: But I'm willing to go back and look and see what else is in there.

Rachel: Yeah . . . I'd be fearful that it would be the one thing that would get in your way—be a potential obstacle. I'm glad you felt sexy and I'm glad you told me. I'm also glad you didn't act on those feelings. So those are my thoughts—my most critical thoughts. How'd that feel to you—what I just said? . . . Who could I be, yelling at you that you shouldn't have done that?

Joan: Sounded like my mom. I clearly heard you when I was there with Clint. You were saying "Don't do it" just like my mom.

Rachel: That could make it more sexy.

Joan: Flirtation is dangerous. I was taking a risk with Clint.

Rachel: Yeah. More than most people!

Joan: What do you mean?

Rachel: There's a big difference between not doing anything with men and going to bed with your uncle. There's a big space there. I'd like to see you do something in between those two.

Joan: (Doubtfully.) Yeah.

Rachel: Some part of you wants to argue with me?

Joan: I want to be in charge of my own sex life. I've felt a lot of pressure the last couple of months about running out and finding somebody to go to bed with just to have it done.

Rachel: So you could say, "I found somebody to go to bed with! I found my uncle! . . . Look what I found! My uncle!"

Joan: (Laughs.) No, that's not what . . . I want to do this piece of work and I want to feel free to reach out to men . . . and to decide how and when to do that. And I believe that's gonna happen. But I don't want every week to feel like I've got to account—"I didn't find anybody this week and I didn't have sex yet."

Rachel: So your goal to work on sex feels like it's become my goal for you.

A case could easily be made here that Joan is right in defending her autonomy from a real, not imagined, threat to it from Rachael. Our view, however, is that Rachael is simply reminding Joan of a goal that she herself first espoused and of a strategy for achieving the goal that they agreed on together. In that context Joan's last statement is a resistance and Rachael's job is to confront it.

Joan was angry, perhaps partly because she felt Rachel was critical of her interaction with her uncle, but more because a defense had been blocked. The fear at the base of her symptom was experienced by her as anger at the person who made her confront her fear.

After Rachel's last comment about Joan's goal becoming Rachel's goal there was a pause. Then Joan responded:

Joan: What I want to do is work on my feelings about sex—where it's coming from and what's in there. I don't want to go out and screw somebody to get in touch with those. . . . And somehow I have felt that's been an expectation . . . that the only way I could get in touch with some of my feelings around sex was to go out and have it.

Rachel: I don't know about sex. Sex is the least of it. I don't know if it has that much to do with intercourse. It may, but I think it has much more to do with trusting and letting go and giving up control. . . . And . . . yeah, we can work on sex, but it's not going to be anywhere like the same work as if you do behavior change and then come in here and work on the feelings. I'd be happy to putz around (note Rachel's thoughtful choice of words) and talk about feelings and stuff, but it's just not the same kind of therapy. The best way to work on relationships is to go out there, find a relationship, come in here, shake, shiver, scream, and yell. Then go out there and do it again. Discharge by itself doesn't work that well. It needs to be combined with working on a relationship.

Joan: I think if you really believe that, that I might need to say, "Okay, I'm not ready to move into that behavior right now." I don't want to putz around for six months until I'm ready. What I might need to do is to come back later.

In the next few exchanges, Rachel said that that would be okay with her. Joan said she was afraid that if she left, she might not ever do the work. Rachel replied that if she really wanted to do it, she would, but that there was a large, very real part of her that wanted to avoid the work and she should be realistic about that. She also said that stopping therapy could make her feel lonelier and thereby provide the impetus she needed to work on getting closer to men. Rachel's tone was friendly and cooperative as they talked about the costs and benefits of leaving therapy. Then Rachel said:

Rachel: Let's have one more session after today no matter what. And spend some time now being mad at me. I think I hear some of that. Pushing you, bugging you about your uncle. . . . (Joan is silent.) And you may decide never to do that work. That would be okay, too.

Joan: Not with me.

Rachel: It *would* be okay with me. . . . You could decide not to do that and still have done a huge amount in your therapy.

After a pause, Rachel again invited Joan to express her anger. Joan did so, vigorously hitting the pillow and yelling. She did not yell about being controlled, however, but rather, about the other side of the struggle:

Joan: I don't like it when you just go along with me! Tell me you don't want me to stop! I don't like it when you go along with me. Don't let me go! Hang onto me!

She went on in this vein for awhile. Then Rachel asked:

Rachel: What does the little kid say?
Joan: (Crying.) The little kid's saying, "Don't leave me."
Rachel: Mm-hmm. "No matter what, don't leave me."

Joan held onto Rachel and cried hard for several minutes. As she stopped, she said it scared her to think of not coming to see Rachel anymore.

Rachel: It must feel like an unreasonable price to have to work on sex to get to see me.
Joan: Yeah. (Laughing.) That's right.
Rachel: It'd be nice if we could do some magic wand stuff so you could see how that's for *you*—how that would be good for *you*.
Joan: (Laughing.) I'm gonna do that—just not now.
Rachel: I've never heard it so clearly—"*Just not now.*" (Pause.) Is it too terrifying?

Joan gave a long explanation having to do with not yet being officially divorced, not wanting to embarrass her children, and so on, ending with:

Joan: When the children are gone, I'll have more privacy. It's just gonna be easier for me to have an active sex life.
Rachel: You don't have to have an active sex life to do this work. Reach out to a man, whether you have sex or not, once a week, and the feelings will come up. It's really funny how you. . . . (Now with a tone of surprise.) You see what just happened? I started pulling on you again to change. How did you get that to happen? You must feel very loved and wanted now!

They laughed, recognizing what had happened, and ended the session.

In this session, resistance was again the focal point, but it took a somewhat different form than it had in session 43, where Joan had sounded more concerned about being stuck in her therapy. Here she said little about being stuck, struggling instead about whether she would do the real-life reaching out to men that was her goal. Session 44 lacked even the apparent agreement present at the end of session 43. It was obvious that the struggle would go on in the next session.

This session shows particularly clearly the costs of an active, interventive therapy. Rachel engaged Joan about whether it would have been a mistake to sleep with her uncle and about the importance of seeking relationships with men as a part of her change process. In both cases, Joan resisted strenuously. Considerable time and energy were spent in this struggle. Less active therapists may view this session as a good illustration of the pitfalls of excessive intervention. We believe that while there are clear costs associated with this sort of intervention, the benefits usually outweigh them. Our view is that Joan's reaction to the above interventions reflected her fear of close engagement with men and that without such confrontations she would be less likely to change. The issues of sleeping with her uncle and her reluctance about seeking relationships with men represented two very real ways for her to avoid reaching her goal of being close with men. The first involved acting inappropriately—for example, choosing an unsuitable sexual partner—and then saying, "I knew it wouldn't work." The second involved avoiding any romantic/sexual contact in order to separate her real-life behavior from her in-session feeling-expression and insight, and perhaps even to use the latter as an excuse for putting off real contact.

We believe that a more passive approach eventually might have led Joan to see how she was resisting, but that could have taken a long time. Despite its disruptiveness, we think the type of active intervention that Rachel used usually saves time.

Session 45

In this session, the resistance continued, but two salutary events occurred. First, the heart of the conflict became clearer and, second, there was a resolution that permitted therapy to continue.

The first few minutes were taken up with Joan saying essentially, "I want more space and I want you to agree with me that it's OK to stop."Rachel's reply was basically, "Whether you stop is ultimately up to you, but I regard it as resistance and there is therapy work to be done whether or not you decide to do it." Joan sought reassurance that she could return and work with Rachel. Rachel gave her that reassurance, saying, "We want to be sure that if you decide to end today, we end in such a way that you can very easily decide to come back."

They talked for a few more minutes about what might happen if Joan stopped and what might happen if she did not. Joan was experiencing the choice as monumental. Rachel was saying that it was not monumental. Rachel said something about Joan's resistance being unconscious.

Joan: I need a way to break through that.
Rachel: It's awful for you not to be able to control your unconscious! (Joan laughs.)

This comment focusing on Joan's control struggles set the tone for the long middle part of this session. Rachel told Joan that she had worked well on the crisis issues that had brought her in, but that she now faced the prospect of basic personality change, which elicited much greater resistance. She said that part of facing this resistance was feeling stuck.

Joan's most characteristic adaptation was being "good," doing the "right" thing, and controlling herself and others. Rachel knew of Joan's unstated, unconscious belief that she was basically unworthy of being *given* love, which led her on a frantic search to earn it. She knew that in order for therapy to change this belief-behavior system, Joan had to experience its futility. Joan had tried to be a "good" client just as she had been a "good" wife, mother, and employee, working overtime and feeling tired and resentful. Rachel knew that Joan's experience of being stuck in her therapy stemmed from her repeated unsuccessful efforts to earn Rachel's love by being a "good" client. She therefore welcomed the stuck feeling as a good sign, while Joan felt frustrated and angry that what used to work did not seem to anymore.

Joan: I want you to tell me there's something I can do. And that if I really want to struggle with that, that there's something I can do different. . . .
Rachel: Struggling is the problem. Struggling is what gets in your way. *Being* is what you need to do. Chores, assignments, activities just aren't what you need, Joan. (Joan listens silently. Rachel speak slowly and quietly.) I can hear that's frantic for you—not to have something to do. But I wouldn't give you something to do anymore than if you were an alcoholic I'd give you a drink.
Joan: It feels like I can't do anything about it. . . .
Rachel: Right.
Joan: I can't do any more. I'm doing all I can do. (A concise statement of Joan's quandary.)
Rachel: I don't expect any more. . . . Actually, I might expect less. . . . Being better is not one of the things you need to be. And coming in with a plan is not one of the things you need to do.
Joan: (After a pause.) I don't want to stop before I'm ready to stop.

Joan said this last statement softly and with certainty. Although there were details to be worked out, this statement forms the basis for her decision to stay. We do not know why it came at this point instead of at some other, but Joan had listened very thoughtfully to Rachel as she spoke. She had slowed down enough, and perhaps felt safe and loved enough, to see clearly how she *usually* defended herself and, alternatively, how she *could* be.

They discussed how long they would work together and decided on six months. Then Joan said:
Joan: I trust you. . . . I like having you help me make the decision.
Rachel: We did a good job together.

Then Rachel reminded her that after the struggle they had had last time, it would not be surprising if Joan felt angry. Joan examined her feelings and slowly came to feel her anger about having Rachel tell her what to do. Joan was able to connect these feelings to experiences she had had with her parents, whom she had experienced as self-righteous and controlling. She seemed genuinely angry as she expressed these feelings.

Near the end of the session, they returned to their contract. They set a specific date to end and agreed that they would keep working on the intertwined issues of control, sex, and reaching out to men. They agreed that success in these areas involved Joan trusting herself enough to let go of her tendency to be overcontrolling.

Unlike the previous two sessions, this session ended with a sense of closure. Rachel and Joan decided to continue therapy, and Joan's resistant, anxious urge to flee therapy or to turn it into a battle was resolved. Moreover, insofar as the process of making the resolution required Joan to relinquish some control, it advanced the very goals being sought and provided Joan with an example of how she could give up control without losing her self, her dignity, or her ultimate control over her life.

If space permitted, it would be interesting to follow Joan's course in detail. We would hear her "forget" that she had made an agreement to work on sex only two weeks after session 45. We would also hear a fascinating string of reasons why now was not a good time to meet men, as well as a comical description of her disastrous first "date." These were only skirmishes, however. The war itself had a more favorable outcome.

Rachel discovered that all of Joan's close friends were women and, furthermore, that she only peer-counseled with women. She urged Joan to peer-counsel with men as well, and to make friends with men. Although predictably angry at being told to do something, Joan did begin peer-counseling with a man and that seemed to increase her sense of safety with men. She also began going to bars and talking with men. About two months after these sessions, she dated a man she had met at a bar and then others she met through friends. Her goal at this point was to get moderately close to a man.

Prior to meeting her husband, she had been deeply infatuated with one other man. Otherwise, she had had very little romantic or sexual contact with men. Her plan was to get close to men without immediately closing off her choices by falling in love and getting married. She and Rachel regarded this pattern of falling in love as a way of avoiding the give and take of two adults in intimate exchange.

Each time she dated, she shared her experience with Rachel, learned something about her way of behaving with these men, and became softer, more confident, and more trusting. Her progress was not smooth, in that she frequently raged at Rachel for "making" her do these things, even though the goal was her own. By the time she stopped individual meetings with Rachel (six months after the sessions reviewed here), she had begun a promising relationship with a man about her age who also had two children. Five months later, when she finished group therapy, the relationship was continuing and was quite rewarding for Joan.

Joan's struggles over control did not cease. They did, however, become less frequent and she was more often able to see what she was doing and stop herself. She was less hectic and anxious and less bent on pleasing people. In both her individual and group sessions, she was more open. When she was angry, she showed it, and she seldom "faked" how she felt.

SUMMARY

Joan's story illustrates several of our points about the middle phase of therapy. Most clearly, we saw resistance in various forms: repeatedly forgetting the contract, missing sessions, thinking of stopping therapy, and frequently struggling over control. Also, Joan's feelings toward her therapist were carefully examined and vigorously expressed. Resistance and transference are often prominent foci of the middle phase. Work on early childhood memories, another focal point of this phase, was present in smaller measure.

In the middle phase, issues get worked through in a spiral: the same issue is repeatedly reworked, each time somewhat differently, with a resultant increase in understanding and insight. In Joan's story, we saw issues of control and of closeness with men surface repeatedly, each time a little differently and with a clear movement toward resolution as time went on.

Exploring the therapeutic relationship was the major focus of the sessions we reviewed. Carefully examining this relationship tends to prevent premature termination, as it did with Joan, and teaches the client the very vital lesson that feeling and behavior can be separated. One can recognize a feeling and express it without acting on it. We also saw how the client's feelings toward the therapist can be used to help understand the client's relationships with parents and current life figures. We saw this in the way Joan experienced Rachel as righteously critical, like her father, and as selfish and controlling, like her mother.

One important characteristic of most clients' middle phase that was not especially prominent here is intense, focused work on early memories. Although these particular sessions did not happen to have much of this material, it formed an important part of the middle phase of Joan's therapy.

Finally, the issue of symptom relief versus character change was clearly demonstrated. Joan's course in therapy was much smoother, and her relationship with Rachel much more positive, earlier, when they were dealing primarily with depression and pain stemming from her separation and divorce. The focus on personality change is hard work and tends to produce more negative feelings.

Joan's story illustrated many characteristics of the middle phase: the repeated working through of conflicts and feelings, the focus on transference feelings, particularly negative ones, and the emphasis on behavior and character change as opposed to mere symptom relief. Group work and intense feeling-expression stemming from early memories were less evident in this example, but were a part of the middle phase for Joan as they are for most clients.

Langs, R. *Psychotherapy: A basic text.* New York: Jason Aronson, 1982.

6

The Termination
Phase—Suzanne's Story

> to make an end is to make a beginning.
> The end is where we start from . . .
> We shall not cease from exploration
> And the end of all our exploring
> Will be to arrive where we started
> And know the place for the first time
> Through the unknown remembered gate
> When the last of earth left to discover
> Is that which was the beginning;

> T. S. Eliot
> *Little Gidding*

The main task of therapy—letting go of parents—is recapitulated in termination as the client lets go of the therapist; a loved person who knew, who cared, and who set limits. Both relationships were safe and both were complementary, with the client/child in a dependent position. Both must end.

Throughout the therapy experience, the therapist has been a guide, and in a way a transitional object like a child's favorite blanket. While the client has been grieving the loss of parents and letting go of childish expectations, the therapist has been there as a mentor and caregiver. When therapy ends, that relationship, too, is lost. Much of the anger and pain experienced earlier regarding the loss of parents is now focused on the therapist. There is thus a chance for termination to be a "corrective emotional experience" (Alexander & French, 1946; Davanloo, 1980) in which feelings of love, loss, and rage can be expressed directly to the therapist in ways they could not have been expressed to parents.

Working these issues through completely is hard work and is seldom fully accomplished. The challenge is to create enough safety to allow the client to feel the loss while keeping the loss real enough so that it cannot be denied. If the loss is not felt, there is nothing to grieve, yet if the loss is too overwhelming, the client is likely to feel numb and deny the sig-

143

nificance of the loss. In either case, feelings are not fully expressed and the client misses a valuable therapy experience. Maintaining the right balance is a major challenge of the termination phase.

The therapist's feelings must also be considered. Someone the therapist cares about is leaving. The client may not be completely cured or may have outgrown the therapist. The therapist needs to listen and be thoughtful and kind with a client, who is apt to be volatile—angry one minute, greatly in love with and needful of the therapist the next, and then suddenly eager to leave. It can be a confusing and unsettling time for the therapist. Thoughtfulness and self-examination are especially important in this phase of treatment.

WAYS OF TERMINATING

All it takes to end therapy is for the client to stop coming. This occasionally happens without so much as a note or phone call. In such a case, therapy has ended, but none of the psychotherapeutic operations that we believe should occur in connection with terminating have taken place. There are many other ways for therapy to end which include some, but not all, of these operations. Finally, there is what we whimsically call the "full-term finale"—termination at the end of a productive course of treatment which includes all the essential operations. This is not an unattainable ideal, but an ending that should and often does occur. Perhaps 30% of our clients end in this way.

In the following sections, we will describe a variety of ways to end therapy, listed roughly in ascending order of desirability.

Not Connecting

Very early endings to therapy contacts can better be understood as failures to begin rather than terminations. Sometimes, at the end of the first session, a client will say she/he is not coming back because the therapist is too young, the fee is too high, the client wants to see someone of the opposite sex, or working on problems is too upsetting. Or, in the second or third session, a client will say that she/he came for advice (e.g., about a job) and does not want to sit around just talking about feelings. Even after the fifth or sixth session, either therapist or client may have a feeling that there is a failure to fit and that discontinuing therapy is indicated. The failure to fit may be personal, but is more likely to involve a major difference between client and therapist about how therapy should be conducted. For example, the therapist may say, "It sounds as though you mostly want your daughter to treat you better and are not interested in looking at what *you* can do to make it go better. If that's true, then I cannot help you." If the client says, "Well then, I guess I better look at my part," therapy can continue. If not, the client will probably decide to stop.

Most contacts terminated in less than five sessions represent a failure to connect. Obviously, there are other settings with different goals where this would not be true. For example, many crisis interventions have a beginning, middle, and end in less than five sessions. For a setting such as the Therapy Center, however, where long-term definitive therapy is the norm, such a brief series of contacts are more a failure to start than a true termination.

This sort of ending usually is quite rudimentary, with little said about the process of terminating. It is important, however, that the therapist do as much as possible to have the client leave feeling good about her/himself and about the process of seeking help. The client should not leave with a sense of diminished available resources. Whether or not the door is left ajar for the client to return to that therapist, the client should leave with a sense that help is available. If the client appears unable to accept something about the particular therapist, type of therapy, or conditions offered, referral is in order. If, on the other hand, the client either seems capable of resolving the presenting problems with no further professional help or appears to prefer suppressing these problems, referral is liable to be either unnecessary or rejected. It is important not to convey the idea that help is unavailable or that it is hopeless or stupid to look for help.

Flight

This type of ending occurs when a client stops therapy primarily because of resistance. What is actually happening in resistance is that the client is frightened and is making a very human and understandable response—leaving the fear-producing stimulus. In the last few million years, a lot of our ancestors have avoided being some animal's dinner by doing exactly that. Remaining in a situation that elicits fear is difficult and goes against much of our conditioning.

While it is difficult at times to know how much a client's decision stems from resistance and how much from more legitimate reasons, there are enough clear examples of resistance to allow us to see the process in relatively pure form. Defensive terminations are marked by suddenness, rigidity, and furtiveness. In the last chapter, for example, Joan's announcement that she wanted to stop had two hallmarks of flight: it was sudden and it was rigid. A third hallmark not present in Joan's case is furtiveness—for example, announcing the decision at the end of the session.

A client may say, "I feel pretty good, I'm sleeping better, and I think it's about time to stop. I know you're gonna think it's resistance, but I just feel good." If the therapist says, "Okay, let's take a few sessions and say goodbye," a resistant client is likely to get angry and/or refuse. If the therapist interferes in any way with the client's flight, anger is likely to be a first response; fear or even sadness may follow. We saw this clearly with Joan when Rachel stopped her from leaving.

A perceptive therapist often can identify the conflict precipitating the flight. The conflict may be obvious—for instance, a particularly intense session, the introduction of a threatening topic, or unusual anger between therapist and client. If such evident precipitants are not present, it is well to inquire about what could be causing the flight from therapy. Such resistances are unlikely to be fully conscious, so simply asking may not be enough. If the client can be cooperatively engaged, useful answers may come from questions such as: "Just suppose, for the sake of argument, that you are avoiding something. What would it be?"

Even if no specific resistance can be found, a strong case can be made that the hasty way the decision was made and presented suggests resistance, and that time should be taken to check out that possibility or to say goodbye if termination is ultimately decided upon. Some clients will still insist on leaving, but many will stay if gently but firmly confronted.

This sort of termination can cause problems for the therapist and eventually for the client. The sudden rejection can hurt the therapist, especially if the therapist is vulnerable at that point or does not clearly see the resistant process for what it is. Feeling hurt, the therapist may behave rigidly and respond aggressively. At a minimum, the therapist may not think clearly and flexibly at the very moment that such thinking is needed most. Ideally, we should have a broader repertoire of ways to reach a resistant client that would circumvent both the client's fear and the therapist's wounded pride. The therapist must be especially aware of the client's dynamics, firm and persuasive in countering the resistance, and careful not to let her/his feelings hurt the client.

If the client ultimately decides to leave, it is important for the therapist to do whatever termination work there is time for, and especially to make clear, as much as possible, the cause of the leaving and that it is okay to return.

A final note about flight: therapists often carelessly attribute many terminations to resistance. Any time clients end therapy, they probably harbor some feeling of "Whew! Now I won't have to deal with that stuff anymore." Yet to call all such decisions flight dilutes the meaning of the term, obscures the other reasons clients terminate, and keeps the therapist from looking at what she/he contributed to the therapy's untimely end.

Impasse

At times, therapy ends because it is stuck. Perhaps some blindness in the therapist prevents making the right intervention or series of interventions that would get the process moving again. Perhaps the client and therapist have come to a point where both agree what the next step must be, but the client cannot or will not make it.

Consider the case of Tony.

Example

Tony knew that his marriage would not improve as long as he kept seeing his girlfriend, yet he was afraid to leave his wife. Unhappy in each relationship and with his life in general, he knew that little would change until he left one or both of the women he felt caught between. His therapist tried various approaches, some focusing on his early history, some on what he got from each relationship, and some on the decision itself. Tony and his therapist worked on the fear Tony felt when he was by himself and the anger he felt when he was with either woman. They examined the triangle he was in and explored similar, earlier relationships. Although Tony was cooperative in most of these ventures, he would not make a commitment to either woman or leave either woman. He also was unable to leave the issue alone and make peace with his life as it was. Eventually, his therapy ended haphazardly. He interrupted the sessions to have an operation and never called back for an appointment. We can assume that he felt stuck, much as his therapist did, yet neither said to the other, "This is going nowhere. Let's stop." Perhaps each believed that change was just around the corner and that a little more work would finally bear fruit.

Saying it is time to stop when goals have not been reached creates a situation in which each of the participants may feel like a failure. It may be that such situations drag on as long as they do, so that neither therapist nor client needs to face that possibility. Tantalizing, too, are the cases where success is achieved after a period of seemingly hopeless impasse. Determining whether an impasse can be resolved is difficult; there are no clear guidelines.

As long as a client like Tony is in therapy, he is somewhat insulated from the full effects of his choices. He can say, "This is awful, but I'm working on it," and he can interpret some of his pain as the result of sickness rather than choices he is making. Of course, if he is stuck in therapy, he is unlikely to seek other, more useful help. These costs are not so great as to make it dangerous to work at length on resolving an impasse, but they are considerable enough to warrant occasionally raising the question of whether a client has already gotten whatever she/he is going to get out of therapy. One advantage of doing this is that it allows at least some of the tasks of termination to be performed (as they were not in Tony's case). Also, talking openly about the impasse and the possibility of ending therapy sometimes helps to resolve the impasse. At a minimum, such a discussion prevents or dispels any collusive denial of the impasse. If termination is decided upon, a clean break can make it easier for the client to return to this or another therapist with a better chance of making progress.

Intervening Life Events

Occasionally, therapy ends primarily because of intervening life events such as moving, career change, marriage, or divorce. At times, the pull of the external event seems genuine, as when a client moves out of town to take an attractive job. At other times, the realistic component is less significant than resistant processes or symbolic meanings associated with the external change. Clients, for example, sometimes stop therapy when they get married perhaps because they have a sense of starting a new life or a feeling that it would be insulting to their mates to imply they need another person. Other life changes may lead to termination, either for realistic reasons or because they offer substitute gratification that lessens the motivation for personality change.

These terminations can happen at any point in therapy. The degree of resistance involved varies widely, as the following examples illustrate.

Examples

At the nonresistant end was Jackie, who, near the end of her therapy, sought and got an excellent job out of town. It represented a big step up and was exactly what she wanted to do. She had been meeting every other week, but asked to meet weekly for the last six weeks before moving so she could complete her termination work.

Eddie was at the opposite extreme; his termination, though triggered by an external event, was largely due to resistance and unrecognized identifications. Eddie had started therapy at a point when he believed his marriage of 22 years was about to end. After two months, he left his wife, but a month later, he moved back in with her. When he returned home, he cancelled his appointment and said he would not be returning. Although his therapist had no particular sense that Eddie would be better off if he left his marriage than if he stayed in it, the therapist evidently had become identified in Eddie's mind with one side of his conflict—leaving his wife. When Eddie decided to return home, he felt he needed to dissociate himself from that symbol of separation and divorce.

Most terminations associated with changed life events fall somewhere in between these two extremes, i.e., they are less resistant than Eddie's, but more resistant than Jackie's.

When therapy is nearly finished, as in Jackie's case, we simply treat it as a full-term termination. But when clients clearly wish to continue therapy somewhere else or to use some less expensive form of therapy such as group work, we help them to make whatever arrangements their changed circumstances dictate and then work with them on termination issues as time permits and as their changing status requires. For clients who plan to leave without finishing their therapy, we talk more about which goals they have achieved, which remain, how they can decide whether they need more help, and how they can get it.

Symptom Relief

Another group of clients leave therapy after they have gotten help with symptoms, but before they begin serious character change. Anxiety and depression, sleep problems, sexual difficulties, psychosomatic conditions, and marital or family problems are prominent in this group. These and many other symptoms are often ameliorated in five to twenty-five sessions. Some clients want only these changes and when they achieve these limited goals, they leave therapy. Some may give lip service to the personality change that their therapist is purveying, but their basic focus is on symptom relief and they leave as soon as that has been achieved.

Many therapists would regard this group of clients as our most efficiently treated group: they get what they come for and they leave. We believe, however, that for most of our clients, this course represents a missed opportunity and contains the seeds of a later recurrence of difficulty. We would much prefer to go beyond sleep problems to the chronic worrisome sense of impending danger that lies behind them, or to the underlying fear that life can easily get out of control. An episode of depression can usually be resolved quite easily, but changing the underlying habits of how anger is channeled and how guilt and responsibility are dealt with is quite another and more arduous matter.

Clients who talk about leaving after they achieve symptom relief present a therapeutic challenge. The therapist feels that more work is needed and would like to make that point forcefully. Yet, since some clients ultimately opt for symptom relief only, the therapist does not want to make their lives more difficult by presenting that option as second-rate or dangerous. The therapist's task is to state persuasively the case for continuing on in therapy and seeking personality change without adding any additional burden of blame or failure to clients who decide to stop.

The issue is especially complicated for the therapist without a steady stream of referrals who may have an economic incentive to keep clients in therapy. There also may be a sense of failure on the therapist's part if clients do not remain in treatment. These conflicting professional and personal motivations make it especially important for the therapist to be disciplined and thoughtful in order to serve the client's best interests. If the therapist is aware of her/his feelings about these matters and finds appropriate people with whom to express them, there is a better chance that the therapist will be clear, a good leader, and affirming of the client regardless of which decision is made.

Clients in this category have connected with the therapist and the treatment modality. While they may be leaving partly because they see unpleasant issues looming ahead of them, they are not primarily fleeing from, or stuck in, therapy. Life events are not interrupting their therapy. In their eyes they are successes and in ours they are qualified successes. Nothing to be ashamed of, a perfectly respectable outcome.

We turn now to the last category—the "full-term finale"—those who have taken the whole trip. These clients have sought basic personality change and are leaving at the completion of their work.

Full-Term Finale

This is not an abstract ideal, but actually occurs with a certain percentage of our clients. These clients still hold back or feel bad about themselves sometimes and they are occasionally defensive. However, they have stayed with the process through symptom relief, through the storms of negative transference in the middle stage, and through the full termination stage. They have completed a profound course of self-exploration and change that usually has focused on one or two themes.

When we speak of a theme being "completed," we mean that many of the myriad connections have been felt, expressed, and re-examined. For Joan, completing therapy required expressing feelings of anger, sadness, and fear toward her therapist for judging her, controlling her, and leaving her. It also meant expressing similar feelings toward her mother, father, and husband. She examined her feelings and behavior toward people in her present life to see what was rational and appropriate, and what was based on early fears and hurts. Finally, she changed many of her irrational ways of being with people by trying out new behaviors and attitudes and adopting those that worked for her. The result of completing such a theme of self-exploration and change is substantial change in both the specific, targeted goals (e.g., having an intimate relationship with a man) and in a broader sense of well-being in relation to that area of life (e.g., trust versus fear of being controlled).

In the full-term finale, client and therapist share the understanding that saying goodbye is a therapeutic act. The very process of termination is itself curative. The relationship with the therapist is explicitly compared with the client's relationship with early caregivers. The emotional shading differs from client to client. The predominant feeling may be sadness that another nurturing and loving relationship is ending, or anger that once more one is being cast out. The client may try to disavow any feelings, saying that ending is no big deal anyway. If so, the therapist usually can show the client that that response is an echo of earlier coping mechanisms.

The therapist should expect an upsurge of irrationality from the client as therapy ends and not be surprised to be admired one day and hated the next. The child within us always feels abandoned regardless of who is actually doing the leaving.

In addition, termination offers clients an irresistible opportunity to trot out various issues that supposedly were laid to rest long ago. Questions of trust and confidentiality may arise. A client like Joan may find herself once again feeling controlled or a client like Michael may find himself getting depressed again. The return of symptoms at termination is a well-known phenomenon, but it usually is viewed as a way to prevent the termination. While this no doubt plays a part, we believe that separation is the number one, most painful human experience and that the simple impact of it tends to frighten people and send them back to old familiar defenses.

Another interesting aspect of termination is how the personality of the client shapes it, as the following examples show.

Examples

Jack was often conflicted about being included, whether in his family group or groups at the Center. His favorite defense was to distance himself. He worked well on this and made many changes in his way of being with people. Twice during his therapy he tried to flee, but both times he was confronted, saw what he was doing, and stayed in therapy. At the end, he worked well on terminating, yet he set his time to terminate a little earlier than many clients and gave himself less time to say goodbye than his therapist would have preferred. It was basically time for Jack to leave, so his therapist did not confront him. Still, he left in a characteristic and mildly defensive way.

Stephanie, on the other hand, struggled with dependency. While she, too, had made significant changes in therapy, she quite characteristically made her termination slower and more drawn-out than other clients.

In the full-term finale, a client who has completed a major theme of self-exploration and change makes a plan to leave and sets a termination date at least a month or two in advance. During this time, therapist and client work largely on the ending of their relationship. This work always includes reference to the loss of early caregivers and frequently provides a framework for some revisiting of conflicts and issues that have been largely resolved. Ideally, these terminations are definite enough for the client to feel the loss fully, yet sufficiently supportive for the client to express the feelings fully. This is a difficult balance to maintain and at any given point the client is apt to be closer to one pole than the other.

While the termination process rekindles old losses, it must also include an examination of the current therapeutic relationship. Asking the client how she/he is disappointed in the therapist is often fruitful, particularly if the question is "how" rather than "whether." Phrasing the question this way assumes disappointment and gives permission to admit and discuss it. There is always some disappointment and anger, as well as love, pleasure, and sadness. We help clients express all these feelings fully, and we work hardest on the ones they seem most reluctant to express.

The full-term finale occurs when clients have stayed in therapy long enough to have worked through basic character issues with some success. This type of termination allows time to express feelings about separation, achievements, and disappointments and to deal with any symptoms that return as part of the termination process.

GOALS OF TERMINATION

Termination is reminiscent of early separations from parents and is a foreshadowing of death; it is often intensely painful (Searles, 1973). Most therapists know that they should talk about termination near the end of therapy, but they do not know exactly how or why. Frequently, their own hurt about separation interferes with clear thinking about the goals and techniques of termination.

The most basic consideration in terminating is to do no harm—to make certain that gains from the earlier part of therapy are not erased and that the client does not leave with negative views of self or of the process of seeking help. A more ambitious goal is to make the termination process itself a positive therapeutic experience. There are subgoals under each of these larger goals. Let us look first at the most basic goal—to do no harm.

Do No Harm

Therapy can end psychonoxiously if the client's self-concept is damaged ("I'm not okay") or if the client's ability and willingness to seek appropriate help in the future is impaired ("There's nowhere I can turn").

Client's self-concept

If a client appears to be running away from therapy, the therapist should point out unmet goals that seem to call for continued therapy. At times, if the client is strongly resistant, the therapist must present these facts forcefully enough to be heard. Yet, such confrontations must never condemn, punish, or invalidate the client. The client has a right to hear a statement like this:

> You came here because you wanted to be closer to people. Now you tell me in a panicky way that you want to stop immediately. You haven't met the goal you stated about being able to live with someone. I think you're running and I want to urge you in the strongest terms to stay in therapy.

This sort of statement is firm, but not invalidating. The therapist is calling the client back in a way that counters the defense, but does not imply that the client is worthless. In contrast, the client has a right *not* to hear this sort of statement:

> Well, if you leave now you are saying goodbye to ever being close to people. You're just saying, "I'm the kind of person who can't love anybody." Is that what you want to say? If it is, then quit, 'cause you'll never make it. Maybe you're just too defensive to be in therapy.

While this may seem exaggerated, therapists sometimes do become defensive and say destructive things to clients. However understandable therapists' feelings of hurt or anger may be, they must not be acted on in a way that is harmful to the client. Therapists must be especially careful when they feel angry or personally involved in the outcome. At such times, it is better to miss a potentially useful confrontation than to risk hurting the client.

There are dangers either way, of course. In one case, the client's resistance is not sufficiently confronted. In the other, the client's self-esteem is damaged. What rule of thumb can we use? In general, if the therapist has a feeling of "needing to straighten out" the client, that is a danger sign and suggests caution. Also, in general, statements about what the client did or does are more useful and less apt to be harmful than statements about what or who the client is.

A client who decides to leave, even for neurotic reasons, needs as much support as possible. However tough or confrontive the therapy may be, there should be an underlying respect for the dignity of the client which should be made particularly clear at termination.

Client's view of help-seeking

The acts of seeking help, receiving help, and discontinuing a helping relationship are significant but poorly understood. When a client appears for an initial interview, it is usually fairly easy to find out why. It is much harder, however, to know why others who are equally unhappy do not seek help. There is clearly no one-to-one relationship between degree of distress and seeking help. We believe that most requests for therapeutic help are legitimate and that, although they may contain aspects of magical thinking and unrealistic hopes, they are basically adaptive efforts that should be encouraged.

Any therapeutic contact has the potential for benefit or harm with respect to both the treatment goals and the client's attitude about seeking help in the future. We believe the therapist has a responsibility not only to help the client meet her/his goals, but also to legitimize seeking help. The client should end therapy feeling that help is still available and can be sought without loss of self-esteem.

In talking about what the client has achieved in therapy, client and therapist may develop a before-and-after mentality that paints the client as formerly distressed, but currently trouble-free. Each participant may have something invested in emphasizing this distinction. The harmful result is that the part of the client that hurts or needs help may be made into the "not-me" part of the self-system (Sullivan, 1953). The client may believe that "I used to need help, but now I'm all better." While not encouraging dependency, the therapist wants the client to know that help is available should it be needed later and that the client is under no obligation to be perfect.

This is obviously a balancing act. The therapist is saying, "Welcome to the world we all live in where there is pain as well as joy. I'm confident you will continue to do well." There should also be another message between the lines that says, "If you do need more help at some point, that's okay, too."

Termination should be carried out in such a way that the client ends therapy feeling good about seeking help and about ending therapy. In addition, the client should leave knowing that further help can be sought from this or another therapist without the client labeling her/himself a failure.

Termination as a Positive Part of Therapy

There are three potentially therapeutic aspects of termination: (1) the client can re-examine what has happened in therapy; (2) the client can experience separation, loss, and individuation directly with the therapist; and (3) the client can assume a more peerlike relationship with the therapist.

The client can re-examine what has happened in therapy

Termination should include a review of changes the client has made, issues that have been addressed, and the vicissitudes of the relationship with the therapist (Langs, 1974). We supply some structure for this by going over goals and areas of satisfaction with clients as a routine part of termination. By going over these goals, client and therapist are able to see clearly how much change has occurred. Areas that have remained unchanged also become evident. Occasionally, after such a review, the client decides not to terminate, but to stay and work longer on certain goals.

Another part of the review process is sharing memories of high points and low points in therapy. Questions and directives such as, "What did you find particularly useful?" and "Tell me some of the ways I disappointed you," are likely to elicit interesting and often quite unpredictable responses. We are frequently surprised to hear that some casual comment uttered months earlier has been enormously supportive and affirming to a client. The client has carried it with her and nourished herself with it repeatedly since. Or some confrontation was felt as particularly apt and was remembered and used as a guide for evaluating and shaping behavior. Talking to clients about their disappointments yields a rich store of information, especially if the subject is broached in a matter-of-fact way that assumes they have disappointments. Some disappointments are banal and safe, such as, "I'm disappointed that you won't take care of me." Others are already well-known to the therapist and have been worked on extensively. Still others are fresh and surprising. They have been missed somehow, perhaps pushed aside by both therapist and client in the movement toward termination. Voicing these disappointments has a cleansing effect on the relationship and promotes openness and a sense of equality between client and therapist.

Perhaps most important in this review process, the client has a chance to step back and look at the therapy process, to see how the specific operations of therapy have contributed to the outcome. It is an opportunity to synthesize. David's comments illustrate this:

> All that hassling about getting here on time was me saying, "You gotta love me as I am." And when you let me have it that day and insisted that I shape up I realized that you did care about me. I was really mad at you that day, but that session made a big impression on me. I don't know how many times since then I've said to myself, "You're gonna make yourself late. What are you trying to do? Find out if Jane loves you?" I do that sort of stuff a lot less now. Sometimes I tell whoever it is that I'd like a little love or appreciation. Other times I tell myself I'm okay and that does it.

The most crucial task of this review process is for clients to see what changes they have made, understand roughly how they have come about, and feel confident that they can continue to make further progress and cope with new problems that arise.

The client can experience separation, loss, and individuation directly with the therapist

Regardless of the client's specific goals, therapy that goes beyond symptom relief necessarily deals with the loss of parents and the loss of one-way nurturance. As we grow up, we are each presented with "an offer we can't refuse." We exchange dependence for independence, and nurturance for freedom. The bad news is that if you do not work, you do not eat. The good news is that you get to decide your own bedtime. This is a choice that is forced on us and no matter how good or bad our parents were, the basic movement is the same. Some people grieve about the loss of what they had and some grieve about never having had it, but we believe that everyone has the potential to feel a great deal about being thrown into adulthood.

The therapeutic relationship mimics many of the qualities of the parent-child relationship. The client is cared for and attended to without reciprocating in kind. The client is encouraged to need and trust the therapist, and to view the therapist as a source of wisdom and strength. The power of this setting to mobilize childlike feelings toward the therapist is profound. When therapy ends, the client quite naturally is going to re-experience the loss of parents and early nurturance along with the loss of the therapist and the special relationship. Termination offers an opportunity to re-experience and master emotions that were largely suppressed during the original loss. When termination is used in this way, regret, loss, and resentment can be replaced by a mature acceptance and appreciation of independence, freedom, and responsibility.

Often when people leave us, we hold back our feelings and either express them later or not at all. In termination, however, as a real loss is experienced, the feelings about it are expressed at the same time and with the person toward whom they are directed. The therapist must be sensitive to the client's rapidly shifting feelings, which may change from love to fury and then to fear that the anger will drive the therapist away. It is most important for the therapist to let all of these feelings flow and not take them personally. Most of the feelings come from early experiences with caregivers. At times, that connection is evident to the client, but, at other times, the client may insist passionately that the feelings are really for the therapist and not the parents. In general, it is well for the therapist not to argue these points, but to keep in mind the powerful way the therapy situation imitates the early child-parent bond. If the therapist is consistently accepting of these feelings about the impending separation and can help the client to connect some fair percentage of the feelings to early parental memories and images, it is safe to assume that good work is being done.

Some clients totally disavow strong feelings about terminating. This, too, is usually analogous to how the client handled early separations, and the therapist should suggest that there may be stronger feelings hiding somewhere. Reworking the loss of parents through the loss of the therapist is a major source of gain in psychotherapy.

The client can assume a more peerlike relationship with the therapist

However democratic, fair-minded, and respectful a therapist is, there are inherent asymmetries and inequalities in the relationship. Therapy, by its very nature, encourages regression. As therapy comes to a close, however, client and therapist can begin to experience themselves as equals. Imagine two members of the cast of a play who are involved with each other through their roles as father and daughter. After the play, they take off their makeup and change out of their costumes. Perhaps they leave the theater together to get a snack. Particularly if they are heavily invested in the parts they played, they may make the transition gradually, slowly letting go of one identity and taking on another.

In a similar way, the client comes to the therapist as an equal adult who contracts to pay the therapist to perform a service. During therapy, they play their roles as therapist/parent and client/child. At the end of therapy, they each resume their roles as equals. This important transition is smoother when the therapist encourages it. It is important that this process of re-emergence as peers not be thwarted either by the therapist's insecurity or need for power, on the one hand, or by the client's insecurity, need for continued nurturance, or fear of the therapist, on the other.

One difficulty in fostering this process is that it tends to occur outside the main verbal dialogue. It is subtle and attitudinal and is expressed in such social conventions as asking the therapist a personal question, e.g., "How was your vacation?" or "Is that your car in the driveway?" During the middle phase, the therapist might or might not answer such questions, but surely would look hard at their transference meaning. As therapy ends, however, equality can be re-established if the therapist responds to more of these comments in purely social terms, as one person to another. The therapist may also choose to be increasingly self-disclosing toward the end of therapy, conveying more personal information and a sense of "we're both in this together." Obviously, an atmosphere of mutual respect should be present throughout therapy, but the shading varies and should shift toward greater equality as therapy ends.

THE THERAPIST'S ROLE IN TERMINATION

The therapist's role in termination is to direct the client's attention to the impending loss and to keep countertransference feelings from hindering the process. Unfortunately, separation can elicit strong feelings from the therapist as well as the client (Freud, 1912). The therapist, too, was once a little child, has lost caregivers over the years, and may not have mourned these losses thoroughly. Thus, the therapist is vulnerable to feeling hurt and to causing hurt as termination nears. The therapist needs to be especially vigilant at termination and should have a supportive relationship to work through feelings of hurt, anger, or deadness as they occur.

There are many ways that the therapist's countertransference feelings can interfere with the successful completion of therapy. First, the therapist's fear of being abandoned can result in various maneuvers that make it difficult for the client to leave when it is time. Alternately, a counterphobic defense against clinging to the client may keep the therapist from confronting a client who is fleeing therapy. Sometimes the therapist comes to have goals for the client that the client does not share or even know about. For instance, the therapist may develop a Pygmalion-like need to perfect the client and find it difficult when the client makes her/his own decision about how much improvement is enough.

Another way the therapist's unexamined needs can interfere with termination occurs when the therapist feels defeated by the client's pathology. In some cases where little or no progress has been made on major problems, the therapist must face termination knowing that the client's pathology has triumphed over her/his therapeutic potency. There is a temptation to blame the client, subtly or otherwise, for the lack of progress. Obviously, the client who terminates without achieving her/his goals has enough problems without serving as the therapist's scapegoat.

While there are many other ways that the therapist's unresolved hurt can hamper termination, one deserves special note. That is the annointing of certain clients as special. The conferring of this status is often subtle and is accompanied by positive feelings. It is limiting, however, in various ways throughout the therapy and especially at termination. While it is inevitable that some therapist-client pairs will be more compatible and warmer than others, it is a countertransference reaction when a client comes to have very personal meaning for a therapist based on the therapist's history. A client may represent a particular parent, sibling, or child to the therapist. An unconscious part of the therapist is trying to complete some unfinished business through loving, dominating, or curing the client. At times, such extraordinary energy is useful to the client. More often, however, the therapist's agenda interferes with giving the firm confrontation the client needs. At such times, being "special" can be a special burden on the client. It is the therapist's duty to rectify this situation.

The therapist has a great many specific duties in the termination process. If the therapist has taken care of personal needs and feelings well enough to think clearly about the client, the process will be greatly facilitated. The therapist must keep the client's attention on the impending termination. This may mean making plans for leaving, crying about the early loss of parents, or yelling at the therapist for being heartless. The focus will shift from moment to moment, but as long as the therapist is not deeply enmeshed in countertransference feelings and can keep the client's attention on termination, useful work will be done.

Let us now look at an individual client's termination process, which illustrates many of the issues we have just described.

SUZANNE'S STORY

Introduction

Suzanne, a 40-year-old mother of two and a middle-level executive at a bank, began therapy to seek help with alcohol and Valium abuse, a shaky marriage, poorly controlled rages, and stomach pain that her physician had told her was a preulcerative condition. At her first session, she was very tense, smiling nervously and talking rapidly as she spilled out her story. Though bright and attractive, she was clearly very pained and deeply tangled in the cross-currents of conflicting emotions.

Suzanne was torn between the demands of her job and those of her family. She deeply mistrusted her ambition and her wish for power and recognition. She feared she would lose love or her femininity if she worked too hard or became too successful. Her conflict over achievement was rooted in her experience of her parents. Her father was passive, accepting, and not very successful while her mother was bright, critical, and ambitious. Her mother was also resentful about not having a channel for her ambition while her husband did so little with his.

Suzanne got married at 23, had sons two and four years later, and resumed her career at 35, when her younger son was eight. The three years between Suzanne's resuming her career and beginning therapy were the most stressful of her life. Her new job was very demanding and she felt guilty about neglecting her children and her husband. She felt alternately like an irresponsible mother, a careless employee, and a lonely wife. She was depressed and discouraged by her failure to juggle the competing demands in her life more skillfully, and resented her children and husband for pulling on her. A child's inquiry ("Have my jeans been washed?") could sound like a condemnation of her as an uncaring mother. She felt caught between self and others, remorse and fury, apology and attack.

Suzanne decided to seek help after a particularly painful weekend. That Friday, her boss told her that the quality of her work was deteriorating. After work, she came home, got very drunk, threw things at her children, and provoked a fight with her husband that resulted in mutual threats of divorce. She spent Saturday and Sunday in thought, and in long conversations with her husband about what to do. She decided to get help and called the Center Monday morning. Two days later, she saw Mark for her first session.

She spoke first of her anger and guilt, and of her increasing dependence on alcohol and Valium. She said she drank most nights, got drunk about twice a week, and used 20–30 mgs. of Valium daily for sleep and to relax. She described her marriage as conflicted, empty, and with very little satisfying sex. She told of having persistent stomach pains over the past few months which, according to her internist, were due to stress and could result in an ulcer.

Her past history revealed a child and young woman with many strengths, but also some chronic difficulties. Her father had died when she was seven, and the resulting stress had caused her to do so poorly in school that she failed the second grade. After that, she did well scholastically and socially, although she became compulsive about doing schoolwork. She told of being so anxious about one paper in the sixth grade that she copied it over twelve times trying to get it perfect. Ultimately, she got a "D" because it was so late.

Suzanne worked hard for her mother's approval, yet regularly engaged in control struggles with her. She admired her mother's strength and self-assurance, yet feared her criticalness and vowed never to sound like that herself. When, as an adult, she heard herself using the same tone with her children, she hated herself for it.

She remembered her father as a big, quiet man who liked her, but who offered no effective counterweight to her mother. Suzanne saw her parents as mirror images of each other. Her father was warm, but weak, while her mother was strong but judgmental and critical.

After college, she married a man more ambitious than her father and less critical than her mother. Like Suzanne, Will was eager to have children and was quite fearful of intimacy. Thus, while they were very loving toward their children, they maintained a distant relationship with each other and often felt alone.

Suzanne's therapy began with three individual sessions with Mark, followed by six conjoint couple sessions with Will. The latter sessions were quite successful in improving the marriage by helping each partner to express anger and disappointment and then feel more loving. Suzanne and Will rediscovered the immense reservoir of love and respect they had for each other and, as they started to experience and show each other their warm, tender, and needy feelings, their sexual satisfaction improved. After the six couple sessions, Suzanne returned to weekly individual sessions and soon started weekly group therapy as well.

Suzanne spent a lot of time grieving her father and disentangling the anger, fear, and love she felt toward her mother. She attacked therapy the same way she attacked life—she worked hard, but often doubted whether she was doing well enough. She paid attention to her feelings, reported them in conscientious detail, and read relevant books about therapy. As time went on, she became more relaxed in her attitude toward therapy and, as she stopped working so frantically at it, she benefited more from it. This more relaxed attitude generalized to her work and family life, where she found herself becoming easier, more flexible, and more efficient. As she became less frantic about achievement, she stopped undermining herself and got a promotion. Within a year of beginning therapy, she stopped using Valium and used alcohol only moderately and socially.

In her second year of therapy, she mentioned terminating a couple of times. Each time, she talked about the progress she had made and the goals she still had to accomplish. Near the second anniversary of her beginning therapy, she said she soon would be starting a six-month training program at work. She thought that when she entered the program, it would be a good time to stop therapy. As she and Mark talked, it became clear that there was nothing frantic about her wish to stop, that most of her goals had been achieved, and that there would be realistic limits on her time once her training program had started.

The agreement to terminate occurred in Suzanne's 89th session. She and Mark decided to meet four more times to complete the termination process. Here is what happened in those four sessions.

Session 90

Mark: So here we are—the first of our last four sessions.

Suzanne: Yep! I had a number of thoughts about stopping. One of them was, "You agreed too soon! (Laughing.) You shouldn't have let me go like that!" Then I thought, "Oh boy, therapists can't win." If you'd said, "I think you're not finished," I'd have said, "He's just trying to hang onto me" or "He thinks I'm sick." This way, I said, "Gee, he really agreed to that fast. Must be he wants me to go." (Laughs again and stops talking.)

Mark: Say more.

Suzanne: That's about it. I had those thoughts pretty fast.

Mark: So you got what we might normally call perspective on it. But that might have taken you away from some feeling you had . . . being unloved? . . . kicked out?

Suzanne: No, I think what the thought was more (sounding sad and beginning to tear.) . . . oh, over the last two months, I've been really wanting to come for my sessions. Not like the early times when I didn't want to. I'll just miss you. I think it was a thought to keep me from being sad.

Mark: Uh-huh!

In her next remark, Suzanne returned, somewhat gingerly, to the idea that she was being evicted or was unloved. This was a very important part of Suzanne's response to termination and one we will hear more about later. Although this fear went underground for awhile, it was part of her first comment in the session—"he wants me to go." Also, as Suzanne prepared to leave, we could hear her collecting insights—like packing a lunch before starting on a hike.

Suzanne: I will miss you and it's been very helpful, the thought you mentioned last time, that if I think you don't like me, it's just my own anger. It's really basic. Something I can apply a lot of the time. . . . I like spending the whole hour with you.

Mark: Sounds perverse. Now that it's fun, it's time to stop.

Suzanne: Yeah. But that's not the way my life is. My life feels good. I've gotten a lot of what I came for. . . . I realized another thing this week. You know how we've worked a lot on being loved and being powerful and which do I want and which parent will I be like? Well, I can see that as I've really said goodbye to both of them and really got it in my head that they are not going to be around to take care of me, that that whole conflict has simmered down. They're not going to take care of me anyway, so it's no big deal whether I'm like one or the other.

Suzanne's insight had a liberating and energizing effect on her. People seldom keep such a clear perspective for very long, but the more they can grasp it, the better.

Suzanne: I've known that before, but I really felt it this week. I worked on it, too, with my peer counselor. I had a clear picture of my mother waving goodbye to me—goodbye forever. (Starts crying.) She's letting go of me. I'm letting go of her. (Cries quietly.) I talked to her the other night and she congratulated me on being accepted into the training program and then she told me that Mrs. Blotz had died. She was around a lot—sort of a family friend and babysitter. (Crying harder now.) And I was remembering that I think she was around a lot after my father died. I think she was one of the people who knew how much I was hurting. I remember her holding me close and rocking me when I was pretty big—eight or nine.

Suzanne began to cry hard. She and Mark sat on the mat and she held onto him and sobbed. For about 15 minutes, Suzanne talked about Mrs. Blotz, crying hard as she remembered the loving way she had cared for her—rocking her, baking pies with her, and even bringing Suzanne to the hospital one time in an emergency. She also talked about the last time she saw her a year or two earlier—old, sick, and unable to remember Suzanne clearly. Near the end of this segment, Suzanne pictured Mrs. Blotz and called "goodbye" to her.

As this section ended, Suzanne became less sad and more discursive. She described a recent confrontation with some friends and then spoke about some conflicts with her husband. She was pleased that she had been able to stand up for herself without losing her temper. She also mentioned lessons she had learned in therapy that had helped her. She was thinking about going out on her own and was assessing her resources.

Suzanne was talking quietly now, with long pauses between thoughts. She had been holding onto Mark since she started crying hard about Mrs. Blotz. She moved and sat facing him on the mat. After a pause, Mark said:

Mark: I was just thinking about our history together. It would be good to review it at some point. You feel like going over that now?
Suzanne: Sure. (Pause.) When I first came here, I was frantic and scared and wanting help. And I was so delighted to find you.
Mark: Why delighted?
Suzanne: You looked like someone I could talk to and when I told you the mess I was in, you looked as if you really cared. Then I said something about how hard I'd worked to have a career and a loving marriage and that maybe my mother was right and I couldn't have both. And it looked to me like you cried a little about that and I said, "Geez! A therapist with feelings! This is someone who can help me."
Mark: So we got off to a real good start together.
Suzanne: We sure did!

Mark: Then what?

Suzanne: Well, I remember early in our time together, when things were rough with Will, you helped me see how much I loved him. And that my mother's critical stance toward my father didn't need to be the way I treated Will. You also helped me see that her hopelessness about having a career and a family didn't need to keep me from having both.

They then talked about the couple sessions they had had and about how quickly her basically good relationship with Will had been re-established. Suzanne recalled starting group therapy soon after ending the couple sessions and resuming her individual sessions. She reminisced about a few other incidents from her therapy. Suzanne then talked about the possibility of returning at some point if she wanted more therapy.

Suzanne: My friend Sarah was saying the other day that I could think of it as something I could come back to periodically if I wanted to.

Mark: Like a 15,000-mile check-up.

Suzanne: Yeah. I'm not terminating with the thought that I'd never need to do it again.

Mark: Do you have any sense of disappointment with what you got from me?

Suzanne: I don't think so, Mark. I'm real pleased. You encouraged me to be angry with you. . . . You helped me feel good about myself. . . .

Mark heard Suzanne's statement about returning sometime as a statement of disappointment. When she said she was not disappointed, he filed the thought away to be considered later and went on to a second possibility.

Mark: Do you think you are stopping before you're ready?

Suzanne: (Pause.) Hm . . . um . . . the only thing I want different in my life is a greater sense of ease and finesse in balancing the parts of my life. I can do it, but it's hard. . . . But I don't see that I need more therapy for that. I'm getting better at it all the time. I think I just need practice. If I stopped improving, then I'd want more help. The thing I mentioned earlier about getting it into my head that my parents are gone—if I can keep hold of that, I'll be okay. That's the key. . . . I just realize how good you are as a therapist for me.

Mark: And you're going to be leaving me.

Suzanne: Yeah. I'm going to be leaving you. I had a thought this morning: "Oh God, I can't stop now!" But I knew that was just not wanting to say goodbye. . . . (Pause). I'll miss you a lot. You're not just smart. You're warm, too. (Crying softly.) And you help me see myself more clearly—you've taught me some good things. Like if I think you don't like me, it's probably *my* anger, not yours, that's bothering me, or how I'm partly this dynamite woman overcoming obstacles and partly a small-town girl who wants hearth and home. . . . I'll miss you.

Mark: I'll miss you, too.

Suzanne: That's nice. I believe you. That's what I wanted to be able to do.

Mark: Mm-hmm. (Pause.) It's surprising to me realizing that we've worked together just under two years. It seems longer. You've done a lot in that time. . . .

Well, same time next week?
　Suzanne: Yeah.
　Mark: That'll be session two out of four.

In this session, the main task of termination was attended to: Mark kept Suzanne aware that therapy was ending. For her part, Suzanne shared her initial fear that Mark wanted her to leave; expressed her sadness at earlier losses, particularly Mrs. Blotz; and saw clearly that her parents could no longer take care of her no matter whom she chose to be like. Mark inquired about whether Suzanne was disappointed or angry about what she got in therapy. Although she said no, we will hear more of this issue in later sessions. Throughout the session, there was also a *leitmotif* of collecting insights. Suzanne seemed to be making a point of remembering and treasuring thoughts and connections they had made earlier, as if to save them up for later use.

Session 91

This session had two themes. One was, "Am I leaving too soon?" The other was, "Have I changed enough?" Most of the session was spent working on these themes.

　Suzanne: Well, I've had a lot of thoughts this week about what you said last time . . . about how you were surprised to realize I had been in therapy less than two years. I thought a lot about whether I was leaving too soon. I saw myself still pretty compulsive about work and I realized that money was playing some role—not a big one, maybe, but some role—in my decision to stop. . . . I was talking to Jean at work about it—going back and forth, "What should I do?", etc. All of a sudden, I thought if I let you decide when I should stop instead of me deciding, that would just scare me to death! Whew! . . . That was Monday. Tuesday was the most compulsive day I've had in a long time. I got up at 5:30 to do work I brought home, I skipped lunch entirely, and just felt driven!
　Mark: What happened with your being driven? How did that turn out?
　Suzanne: Well, by Thursday, I was pretty well back to normal, although, as we've said before, normal for me is not where I'd like to be.
　Mark: Mm-hmm.
　Suzanne: The thoughts about letting you decide were that either you'd say, "Well, stop. There's no reason for you to do more therapy," or you'd say—you'd make me stay in therapy for years . . . but, that's just my not trusting you. . . . When I say, "Mark's a person I can trust to know what I need in my therapy," that's what scares me. (Pause.)
　Mark: So all these thoughts you've been having . . . symptoms returning . . . wonderings. Sounds like that would be enough to keep a person in therapy for awhile! (Both laugh.)

At this point, Mark was fairly certain that it was wise to continue toward termination and that Suzanne's reconsideration of ending stemmed from her fear of losing the closeness and support she had found in therapy. Such hesitancy is common during termination. Yet Mark did not want to dismiss Suzanne's concerns without investigating them further. He needed to assess: (1) how far short of her goals she was, (2) whether there were significant irrational elements in her decision two weeks earlier to stop therapy, and (3) whether she could contact feelings of loss and fear about stopping.

Mark spoke slowly, trying to establish a cooperative, investigative atmosphere.

Mark: Do you have a feeling that you have hurried the decision or pushed me into it or something like that?

Suzanne: Well . . . I've been going around and around about this. Is this a way to not stop? I don't know. One of my goals was to be less compulsive about work, and I am, but I'm still more compulsive than I'd like to be. (Long pause.) The thing that made the most sense to me is just to let you decide. That's noncompulsive, noncontrolling, and scares me. So either way you decide, my leaving it up to you would be good for me.

While appearing to cede control to Mark, Suzanne was, in fact, seeking to control him. "You decide" was an imperative. If this were the middle phase of therapy, Mark would explore this at length, but because they were terminating, he decided to step lightly around it. He did so by asking Suzanne to talk about her unmet goals. She said that her need to be perfect no longer pushed her to substance abuse or irrational attacks on others, but that she still sometimes worried needlessly about work, woke up early in the morning, and enjoyed herself less than she would like to. She talked about the training program she was being sent to by her employer. She was eager to get the most out of it and found herself wanting to start it "with a clean slate," having overcome her problems and having finished therapy. She laughed at herself when she recognized the compulsive categorizing and efforts at neatness that were present in that very wish. Yet she was easy about it, saying that she probably always would be a little compulsive. She said she was making progress currently, could feel herself becoming more relaxed, and wanted to keep changing. She wondered some if she could continue to change after she stopped therapy and gradually decided she probably could. At this point, Mark summed up what Suzanne had been saying and then said:

Mark: I understand that your leaving the decision with me represents some openness and trust in me and that's good. . . . But I think ultimately the decision needs to stay with you. If I thought stopping was a terrible idea or very resistant, I would have said so. I think it's just a judgment call. If you want to work more, try to reach more of your goals, that's fine. If you feel more like stopping now, that's okay, too. I would have told you if I thought it was a nutty idea.

Suzanne: OK . . . back to me, then. Well . . . (Sighs.) . . . I think I'll go ahead with my plan to stop. . . . It's good to know that you would have told me if you thought I was running. . . . It scares me. (Shivers.) Feels like I'm going out in the cold . . . on my own . . . far from home. I feel real sad. I can feel a lump in my throat. I'll miss you a lot.

Suzanne cried for a few minutes and then talked about leaving and how she was doing. The thoughts of leaving were accompanied sometimes by a mild fear and at other times by an eagerness to be totally on her own. The thoughts about how she was doing were largely positive. A third point she touched on occasionally was her trusting Mark to make a good decision for her and her pleasure that he trusted her to make a good decision for herself.

Mark's response to Suzanne's request deserves some comment. If he had made the decision for her, he could have been seen as infantilizing her, being manipulated by her, or both. Yet, categorically refusing to comment on whether she should leave would have opened up many issues of dependence and control—a good strategy in the middle phase, but not at termination. Since Mark believed that ending was appropriate, he did not want to engage Suzanne in a lengthy examination of why she had asked him to decide for her. What he did was put the decision back with her, but simultaneously give her reassurance that he would have told her if he had thought she was fleeing treatment. In a sense, he did make, or help her make, her decision, but he avoided the two worst obstacles—deciding for her or engaging her in a lengthy exploration of why she wanted him to decide for her.

Near the end of the session, Suzanne discussed her insight that when she felt critical of people, it was usually because she was frightened. It was a sign of how far she had progressed that she recently had stopped herself from being critical by remembering the connection to being scared. She seemed to be preparing for ending by reviewing the insights she had achieved. Then at the end of the session she returned to the ending of therapy.

Suzanne: I'm glad I did this therapy. I'm real glad I did it. (Mark and Suzanne hug.) You've been real good for me. . . . If I needed to come back sometime, I could.

Mark: Absolutely. . . . You know, just the way you are right now. . . I don't see any of that driven, compulsive stuff. You seem totally easy and at peace with yourself.

Suzanne: That's right.

Mark: It may be that when you get near work, you may get speedy and tense again, but it must be nice to know that you can be totally relaxed . . . and not at all driven.

Suzanne: That's right.

Mark: Ready to stop?

Suzanne: Yeah.

Mark: Next time will be next to last.
Suzanne: Okay. See you then.
Mark: Bye.

A major plus in this session was that Suzanne kept the focus on termination. Clients sometimes want to work on "just one more" issue as a way of avoiding the reality of termination. In this session, we sensed Suzanne getting ready for her first parachute jump. As she got ready to jump, she turned to her instructor and said, "You sure this thing will open when it's supposed to?" She had made a good decision earlier, but as the reality of termination approached, she got scared. Mark said essentially, "It's up to you whether you jump, but I would let you know if I thought it was a really bad idea." A case could be made for Mark leaving it even more up to her. In any case Suzanne decides to stop and the Termination Express keeps rolling.

Session 92

The next-to-last session is usually the time we go over the client's goals and the Personal Satisfaction Form. Mark and Suzanne spent about half the session reviewing Suzanne's goals and half dealing with her feelings about termination. At the start of the session, Suzanne returned to one of the main themes from the previous session, i.e., whether she should be stopping now.

Suzanne: I really think I'm scared to stop. I was scared this morning thinking about it being my second to last time.
Mark: You'll be on your own.
Suzanne: I know. It feels like it doesn't fit with what I know rationally, but the feeling is, "I'll be on my own. Oh, my God! I hope I can make it." (Pause.)
Mark: Well, let's see what you'll have to cope with. (Mark picks up the card with Suzanne's goals on it.)
Suzanne: Okay.

Here Mark chose to focus on the task at hand, although he recognized that Suzanne would rather talk about her feelings. He read Suzanne's goals out loud and asked her how she was doing with them.

1. "Stop abusing alcohol and Valium." Suzanne said she now used no Valium and only drank socially. She seldom had a drink after work. She said most of her wish to escape was gone, although she sometimes read in a way that felt escapist.

2. "Save my marriage." Suzanne was very pleased with her marriage, enjoyed her husband, and saw him as a help to her career rather than hindrance.

3. "Get my stomach relaxed." Her stomach was much better, although it occasionally still felt tight. The frequency of this symptom had dropped from three times per week to twice a month.

4. "Be less driven about my work and stop trying to be perfect." This was clearly the goal on which Suzanne had made the least progress. She was often able to keep work in perspective, but when she was under stress, she regressed in this area. At such times, she worked hard, although not very efficiently, and was hard on herself as well.

5. "Be less critical. Stop sounding like my mother." Suzanne did well with this goal and had a clear understanding of what circumstances tended to make her critical.

Mark then reminded Suzanne that she had been feeling scared. She thought for awhile and then said that she appreciated Mark keeping the decision about whether to stop with her. She said she felt respected and could feel Mark's interest in what was good for her.

Mark: So you're feeling pleased about me right now.

Suzanne: Mm-hmm. I also thought about how last time I said something about your not trying to get rid of me and I thought how sad it was that I'd have a thought like that—that people would be trying to get rid of me. (Cries softly.) And I was trying to think of where that would come from. You know, I must have been really young.

Mark: Mm-hmm.

Suzanne: Probably my parents were like other parents. Sometimes they wanted to get rid of me. Sometimes my father was real glad he had a little girl and sometimes he was just—I was in the way. It was probably pretty regular.

Mark: But it hurts.

Suzanne: Yeah . . . but I think I can feel the hurt and know it's just regular . . . it's not me. It's not that there's something wrong with me. (Still crying as she talks slowly.) It's like every parent feels that way and every kid feels that way. It wasn't that I was bad.

Mark: Mm-hmm. . . . It also could be that some children will get more rejection than others without being bad. Their parents were just more hurting or distracted or whatever.

Suzanne: Right.

Mark: The important thing is for you to know you were okay.

Suzanne: Right.

Mark: There wasn't anything about *you* that made people want to push you away.

Suzanne: (Pause.) You don't want to get rid of me.

Mark: No, I don't. Not at all.

Suzanne: I believe that. I don't have to be perfect to have people want me around.

Suzanne then talked for awhile about the progress she had made recently in regard to feeling driven. She had been feeling "more okay" about not being perfect. She then branched off and began to talk about her job and the training program she was about to start. Mark entered into this conversation like a peer, asking her questions about her work and her training program and telling her about a recent article he had read about banking that he thought she might be interested in. He did this more than he would during the middle phase as a way of moving their relationship from a superior-subordinate one to a peerlike one.

After a while, Suzanne stopped talking about these issues and said:

Suzanne: I'm gonna be on my own, Mark.
Mark: Looks like you are. How will that be for you?
Suzanne: (Pause.) I'm gonna do well.
Mark: You have some disappointed thoughts about me or our work together?
Suzanne: (Pause.) I can't think of anything. (Pause.) I really wanted to stop being compulsive when I was here. I wish that had happened. (Pause.) I don't know. I got a lot of what I came for.
Mark: Yet something important to you, you didn't get.
Suzanne: That's right.
Mark: So it's disappointing to you. In some ways, you must feel like if I'd done a better job, you would have gotten all you wanted.
Suzanne: I guess so. . . . I don't know. . . . Rationally, it doesn't make much sense. I got a lot from you, but . . . yeah, I guess I could. (Beginning to sound angry.) When Lorraine left group the other night, I thought she'd died and gone to heaven. Everybody said *how much* she'd changed! (Sarcastic. Quite angry now.) How great she looked! (Louder.) How much softer she was! I said to myself, boy, I sure as hell haven't changed that much! And she's your client, too. Did you work better with her? Or do you like her more, or what?
Mark: So I gave her more than you?
Suzanne: You must have. Even if some of that was for show, she really has changed a lot. Sometimes I wonder if you really worked as hard with me as you could have . . . or as you did with her.
Mark: Grab the bat and hit as you talk to me.
Suzanne: (Hitting the pillow.) You piss me off! I didn't get all I wanted! I didn't. How could you let me go without finishing? (Still hitting.) I'm angry at you! Uh! Uh! Uh! Uh! (Hitting the pillow hard.) Uh! Uh! I wanted more! Goddamn it! I've gotta go out of here and still be compulsive. Uh! Uh! Uh! (Suzanne is slowly running down.) Uh! Uh! (Long pause.)
Mark: I'm glad you could let yourself feel that.
Suzanne: Me, too. . . . I do wish I'd gotten more. . . . I'm also appreciative of what I did get, which is a lot.

Near the end of the session, Suzanne again talked about her upcoming training program and her professional goals. She then mentioned that she would like to learn to fly a plane. After a pause, she looked at the clock and said, "It's time to stop." She had seldom, if ever, been the timekeeper before. It seemed propitious that as she prepared to leave therapy, she took charge of ending the session and told Mark that she was "going to fly." Someone once said that parents can only give their children two things: roots and wings. Suzanne was feeling her wings and, as we will see in the next session, she was appreciative of her roots as well.

Session 93

The last session is often difficult because the loss is so real that clients do not have enough safety to let themselves experience their feelings fully. This was not the case with Suzanne, who contacted her feelings strongly, made feelingful connections with early loss experiences, and demystified her therapist. In addition, she had a confident vision of herself and her future. In short, she had a very productive last session.

Suzanne: (Slowly.) I don't know what to do in the last session except say goodbye. (Pause.) and Say, "Thank you."
Mark: You're very welcome.
Suzanne: I'm real scared, Mark. I'm scared of being on my own . . . planning my career long term. Last night, the car broke and I had to get it fixed myself. I said, "Shit! I have to take care of everything."

Suzanne then talked about responsibilities connected with work and her training program. Mark soon brought her back.

Mark: So you're leaving therapy . . . and starting a new chapter of your life.
Suzanne: I'm excited and real scared. (Pause.) I'm different from my mother.
Mark: How so?
Suzanne: She went off to school one summer to try to get a career going, but she never went further with it. She just let it go. I'm going after what I need. . . . I'm going to get it, too. Instead of being resentful and blaming, I'm going to be pleased and have what I want. (Long pause.) I liked the last session—the fact that you pushed me to say what I was disappointed in. That was true. I was disappointed.
Mark: Uh-huh. (Pause.) You sad now?
Suzanne: (Crying.) Uh, it's complicated. It feels like a loss of innocence more than a loss of you. It's like there are no magic people and I've known that . . . that's sad. (Crying harder.) It's sad that you aren't magic like you were when I first came. You were real magic then . . . and somehow it's just sad giving up magic. (Sobbing hard now.) It's giving up being a little girl. I have to take care of myself everywhere. (Sniffling.) It scares me.
Mark: You used to think, "If things get tough, I'll go to Mark. He'll know what to do."
Suzanne: That's right. I could hardly wait for my appointment 'cause I'd think you'd fix it.
Mark: Mm-hmm. I'd know just what to do to make you feel better.

These words of comfort and assurance evoked enough of the "good daddy" Suzanne had been remembering to let her sob hard. She held onto Mark and experienced the comfort and the loss. She talked a little, but mostly cried. As she finished crying, she got the insight, perspective, and humor that often follow heavy discharge.

Suzanne: I know the magic is in me, but it scares me. It's hard to really believe it. (Pause.) That's a funny kind of paradox: I'm willing to believe someone else can make it happen and they can't. I'm the one that can make it happen and I won't believe it!

Suzanne then talked about how she was similar to and different from her mother. She finished with:

Suzanne: I don't *need* her. I've got my life going fine. It just gets lonely sometimes. (Pause.)
Mark: A little reluctant right now to say "goodbye."
Suzanne: "A little reluctant." That's right. . . . Goodbye, Mark.
Mark: Goodbye, Suzanne.

Suzanne cried softly at first and then hard. As she stopped, she said:

Suzanne: I've been coming here every Tuesday for almost two years and next Tuesday I won't be here. It's over. (Cries hard.) I'll miss having you think with me. You care about me, how I'm doing. . . . (Cries.) And an hour of prime time . . . (Pause) I'll miss that. An hour just for me.

Suzanne then talked about her job and training program, again feeling both frightened and excited. She sounded optimistic as she remembered another time she had met a new challenge successfully. After a pause, Mark suggested that Suzanne try being alone. She agreed and he went to the other side of the room.

Suzanne: (Beginning to cry.) I just got a real warm picture of my family (of origin) being behind me, just . . . oh . . . supporting me with warmth. It didn't feel at all burdensome. Like sometimes I've had thoughts I had to do it for them, you know?
Mark: (Mm-hmm.)
Suzanne: I had to go out and be who they . . . didn't know how to be . . . but, ah . . . it seemed easier for me to be warm if I had warmth behind me. (Crying softly.) So, I'm on my own . . . and I come from . . . good roots . . . and I've had good help here . . . from you. (Long pause.)
Mark: I've heard you say something about help—getting help—and I want to be sure you don't sell yourself short on how much you can do for yourself.
Suzanne: Yeah. What I was saying was that I don't have to have a chin-out attitude like, "I don't need anything from you." I've done that kind of attitude sometimes. Maybe I need to emphasize that I have what it takes myself.
Mark: Yup. You have everything . . . already there. You've got a knapsack on your back and everything you need for the trip.
Suzanne: Actually, I have a terrific new briefcase.
Mark: Do you? Everything you need is right in it. You have a sandwich . . . knowledge, confidence . . . power. . . .
Suzanne: Intelligence. I have everything I need. I have the magic . . . I'm pretty enough.
Mark: Plenty pretty! Warm. You've got it all.
Suzanne: (Crying.) I do have it all. . . . I'm ready to graduate. . . . I'm going to fly to Chicago to start my training . . . confidently.

Mark: There's nothing that can hold you back.

Suzanne: That's right. Nothing. I'm gonna keep flying.

Mark: Mm-hmm. So as you fly there, imagine yourself calling back, "Goodbye, Mark."

Suzanne: Goodbye, Mark. . . . Goodbye, Mark.

Mark: Louder.

Suzanne: Goodbye, Mark! Goodbye, Mark! My voice cracked.

Mark: That's right. Say it some more.

Suzanne: (Suzanne starts sobbing loudly.) Goodbye, Mark! Goodbye, Mark! (Sobs.) Goodbye, Mark!

Mark: Real loud!

Suzanne: GOODBYE! GOODBYE! (Sobs heavily now. The only sounds are of her crying.) GOODBYE! (Sobs more.) GOODBYE!!! . . . Oh boy.

Mark: That's good. Holler out, "I love you."

Suzanne: I LOVE YOU!! (Very loud, punctured with sobs.) GOODBYE!! I LOVE YOU!! GOODBYE!! I LOVE YOU!! Whew! (Quietly now.) I'm saying that to a lot of people.

Mark: Who?

Suzanne: My children in some ways—they're growing up—my parents, Mrs. Blotz, the little girl in me who used to have magic helpers, you. . . . Goodbye, Mark.

Mark: Goodbye, Suzanne. I'll miss you.

They stood up, hugged, and said goodbye.

Suzanne was able to let herself feel strongly even in the last session. As she said goodbye to Mark, she had a sense of being on her own and of saying goodbye to various caregivers in her life. She also said goodbye to being a child. In this way, she made the most of termination by continuing to work on basic issues literally up to the last minute of therapy.

SUMMARY

The issues involved in termination—letting go of a helper and taking full responsibility for one's own life—are the core issues of therapy. Termination is therefore both a great opportunity to deal with these issues and a minefield of dangers. Perhaps it is best thought of as a difficult opportunity. In this chapter, we described the various ways termination can occur:

1. *Not starting*—when the therapist and client never really engage and therapy ends after a few sessions.

2. *Flight*—when the client decides to leave suddenly and primarily for avoidant reasons.

3. *Impasse*—when therapy stops, by plan or otherwise, because the parties are stuck.

4. *Intervening life events*—when termination is caused by events such as moving out of town, marriage, or childbirth. These terminations may or may not be motivated by resistance.

5. *Symptom relief*—when clients get help with the specific difficulties for which they sought help and choose not to go on for longer-term character change.

6. *Full-term finale*—when termination occurs at the completion of a major focus on self-exploration. This termination process includes examination of feelings about the ending of the relationship and about any symptoms that may re-emerge.

We outlined two broad goals of termination: (1) the termination must not harm the client either by lowering self-esteem or by interfering with the client's willingness or ability to seek help in the future; and (2) the termination should function as a positive part of therapy by helping the client to review what has happened in therapy, by giving the client a chance to experience separation from the therapist, and by shifting the relationship with the therapist to a more peerlike level.

Finally, we emphasized the importance of keeping the client's attention on the termination process. We pointed out some ways the therapist's own hurt could sidetrack the process and discussed how the therapist could prevent this.

In the last half of the chapter, we got to know Suzanne and followed her progress as she ended her therapy. Although she took the initiative to stop therapy, she was afraid to leave, feared she was not wanted, and thought about changing her mind. As she worked through these feelings, she grieved the loss of her therapist, her parents, and another early caregiver. She expressed some anger toward her therapist for not helping her more and shared her warm feelings for what he had given her. She talked enthusiastically about plans for her future and stored up pearls of insight for the times when she would not have her therapist's help. She grieved the loss of her childhood, her innocence, and her magic belief that parents or therapist could take care of her. She let go of parents and parent surrogates and took hold of her own life. Her termination ratified, strengthened and extended the work she had done during her therapy. And that is what termination is supposed to do.

REFERENCES

Alexander, F. The principle of corrective emotional experience. In F. Alexander and T. M. French (Eds.) *Psychoanalytic Therapy*. New York: Ronald Press, 1946.

Davanloo, H. *Short-term dynamic psychotherapy*. New York: Jason Aronson, 1980.

Freud, S. (1912). *The dynamics of transference*. Standard edition, 12. New York: Hogarth Press, 1955.

Langs, R. *The technique of psychoanalytic psychotherapy*, Vol. III. New York: Jason Aronson, 1974.

Searles, H. F. Concerning therapeutic symbiosis. *Annal of Psychoanalysis*, 1973, *1*, 247-262.

Sullivan, H. S. *The interpersonal theory of psychiatry*. New York: Norton, 1953.

7

How Clients Help Each Other: Group Therapy, Peer-Counseling, and Workshops

> No man is an island
> Entire of itself
> Every man is a piece of the continent
> A part of the main.
>
> John Donne
> *No Man is an Island*

Any therapy that focuses on private experience and on uncovering and expressing feelings runs the risk of becoming self-absorbed. The same separation from everyday reality that allows full emotional self-exploration can become destructive if that separation leads to divorce. While feeling-expressive therapy does concentrate on individual experience and catharsis, it also uses a variety of interpersonal methods that foster an awareness of others and a sense of community.

In group therapy, peer-counseling, and workshops, clients interact with other people whose needs and pain they must somehow recognize and respond to. This interaction not only counteracts the tendency toward self-absorption but also teaches clients about themselves and how to give as well as receive help. In order to see how we combine these group methods with individual treatment to form a total therapeutic regime, we will describe schematically an individual client's use of these treatment modalities during his therapy.

Warren began individual therapy, he was depressed over his lonely isolated way of life. At 27, he had a good job and lots of casual friends.

177

He had no close friends, however, and never had formed a close relationship with a woman that lasted more than a few months.

Warren met weekly with his therapist starting in October and attended his first workshop in February. At moments during that weekend workshop, the wall between himself and others seemed to have a door in it and he felt close to others. The door opened briefly and he felt a connection between himself and his pain, and other people and theirs. This was a remarkable experience for Warren, and the memory of how things could be provided a fulcrum for his subsequent work.

He found the workshop so helpful that he decided to join a group in March. By this time, his depression had lifted and he was working full-time on getting closer to people—trusting them and opening himself up to them. He used both forms of therapy well, getting the safety he needed from individual sessions, and getting the opportunity to be close to others from group sessions.

In August, Warren attended a four-day workshop in which he frequently experienced the openness with others that he had felt first in the February workshop. Now more able to integrate such experiences into his everyday life, he began dating a woman with whom he was alternately quite close, and then fearful and rejecting. At the workshop, he connected his current fear of closeness with childhood experiences of being abandoned. He had discovered this earlier in individual and group therapy, but his feeling experience of the connection was much stronger at this workshop. He began peer-counseling at the workshop and continued it on a regular basis afterwards.

Warren continued in individual and group therapy until February, at which time he cut down to one individual session every other week. In April, he stopped individual therapy altogether. He attended a weekend workshop in May and continued in group till the following October—two years after he had begun. During his second year, he consolidated his gains. He continued to work mostly on issues related to being close to people and trusting them. There was a crisis in his relationship with the woman he was seeing when she considered leaving town, and then another crisis regarding their decision to live together. Both were resolved positively and, in the process, Warren had a chance to work through the fears that had kept him distant from people for so long. Even after Warren ended his therapy, he continued to peer-counsel on a weekly basis.

Writers often comment on the cost of group therapy as one of its advantages vis à vis individual therapy. This was clearly illustrated in Warren's case. Of his total hours in treatment, he spent 80% in group modalities—workshops, groups, and peer-counseling—yet only 35% of the money he spent for therapy went to pay for these services. Without questioning the value of individual therapy, we can appreciate the importance of group methods, which frequently are ignored or viewed merely as minor aids to individual treatment.

Although Warren's involvement in several treatment modalities is typical of clients who come to the Center, there are some who do not become involved in any group approach. Some of these seek only symptom relief and remain in contact with us too short a time to join a group or attend a workshop. Others are not able to listen to other people without becoming distracted. A minimal level of empathy for others is necessary for clients to participate in group therapy. A few of the clients who do not have attention for others are psychotic or borderline, but others are simply too anxious, depressed, or self-absorbed to listen well to other people.

GROUP PSYCHOTHERAPY

Feeling-expressive therapy groups meet for two hours in the evening. There are two leaders and twelve group members, all of whom are or have been in individual therapy at the Center. Groups meet in a special group room quite bare of decoration but well-supplied with mats and pillows.

Standard-Format Groups

Most standard-format groups begin with a "go-around" in which clients talk about what they plan to work on. This tends to focus the group, to stimulate group members to think about the feelings and issues they want to work on, and to give the therapists a chance to make a brief assessment of each client. After the go-around, we typically give each member 5 or 10 minutes to work in the group. Other group members listen carefully, occasionally responding or making suggestions. Mostly, however, they just listen intently. This concentrated attention impacts so strongly on the person working that feelings are often felt and expressed more quickly than in one-to-one work. When each client's turn is finished, she/he chooses another group member and they go off to another room to peer-counsel. The member who has been working continues to work. The helper typically does not work at that time, but rather, after her/his turn in the group. The peer-counseling pair returns to the group after 15 to 20 minutes. People also occasionally leave the group to peer-counsel before they work in the group or when feelings come up while someone else is working.

This format means that there is a constant circulation of people in and out of the group. A group of twelve will often have six or eight members present in the group room with two or three pairs of peer-counselors scattered around the building. There are obvious costs in this procedure. Each client misses some of the other clients' therapy. In addition, a client could spend a considerable amount of time away from the group on a given evening, missing a sense of community. The benefits are that the client has a chance to work each week in group for a longer time than would otherwise be possible. Going off to peer-counsel can easily double or triple the total amount of time a client has available to focus directly on her/his feelings. Moreover, the additional peer-counseling augments the client's initiative and responsibility.

An occasional feature of our group format is the opportunity for a client to spend almost the entire group meeting in therapeutic work. The client who chooses to do this takes her/his turn first after asking four or five group members to serve as peer-counselors. After the client works, she/he goes to one of the other rooms in the Center and those who have agreed to be peer-counselors take turns sitting with the client during the rest of the group meeting. This enables a client to have occasional opportunities to work uninterruptedly on a single theme or set of related feelings.

Primal-Format Groups

Another group format we use from time to time is the primal one—a method derived from Janov's work, but differing somewhat from his original form. It works as follows.

First, each client is asked to talk about what she/he has been feeling and would like to focus on. Then clients find places in the room and lie down on their backs, making sure there are mats or pillows nearby to hit. The room is darkened and clients are asked to close their eyes, to imagine their parents or other early significant figures, and to see what feelings emerge. They are encouraged to talk to those imaginary figures and to express the feelings necessary to finish their business with them. Gradually, there is a buildup of sound as clients express their feelings more and more vigorously. Although clients are dealing with figures in their own histories rather than each other, there is a contagion of catharsis that creates an evocative climate for the expression of feelings. Some clients who get stage fright when expressing feelings in front of other group members find the semidarkness and relative isolation of the primal format congenial to full feeling-expression. After about an hour, the loud sounds gradually subside and clients enter a quieter, more reflective phase. The leaders slowly turn the lights up and invite people to sit up and reconvene as a group. Generally, group members feel peaceful and quiet. They hold each other closely and talk about what they have experienced.

One very striking aspect of the primal format is its power. Clients both fear it and benefit from it. Before the primal, group members joke about it and are often quite frightened. Afterwards, however, most have a strong sense of peace, well-being, and accomplishment. Occasionally, people leave the primal because they experience their feelings as too strong and upsetting. At such times, the leaders talk with them and make a clinical judgment about whether to urge them to return or to invite them to relax and talk separately with a therapist. Since a small percentage of clients do not do well with primals, and others strongly resist them, we have developed a method whereby clients can choose between a primal-format group and a standard-format group on a given evening.

Process Groups

A third format we occasionally use is much more like traditional group psychotherapy. Members are encouraged to address each other about any anger, concern or hurt they feel in their relationships with each other. Unlike our standard format groups, in this sort of group, interaction, response and confrontation are encouraged. Leaders and other group members comment on these interactions sometimes viewing the group as a family-like system and sometimes in terms of the individual feelings and defenses of the participants. While this sort of group is lively and useful in its own right, we use it primarily to clear up issues between group members that could cause them to feel unsafe and hence unable to work well in their other group meetings.

Guidelines for Group Interaction

Standard format

What a client actually does in group varies, but fits within certain guidelines. In the standard format, clients sit on a mat, face the group, and talk. Talking usually leads fairly quickly to expressing feelings. They may cry or rage, scream or shake. They may hit the mat, lie down and kick as if having a tantrum, or hold on to other people. In general, the goal is feeling-expression, but occasionally clients spend their time looking at their behavior and planning strategies for changing or interrupting it. The latter type of session is less intense, more thoughtful, and more likely to include discussion between group members. If a client were planning

to spend a holiday with parents, for example, there might be some prep-
aratory sessions focused on feelings and other sessions focused on how
to behave so as not to fall into childish or neurotic old habits.

A third way to work is to focus on the present situation within the
group. There are times when a client's feelings involve other group members. For example, if a client does not look at other members, addresses
only the leaders, or proclaims a wish to be close to people while acting
coolly toward members of the group, then the therapeutic intervention
must focus on the present situation in the group. That often involves
having the client behave in a manner opposite to the present, comfortable
but neurotic, way. It may also involve exaggerating the defense or simply
being aware of the conflict and letting the feelings come. In this process,
the therapists vary from being quite active and directive to fairly passive.

The group provides a laboratory for both diagnosing and changing a
client's unsuccessful ways of being with others (Lieberman, 1970). At
times, a client pushes everyone away or is "nice" to everyone in an unreal
way. At other times, particular group members emerge as the "good guys"
or "bad guys" in a client's drama. Most of our work with these feelings
is intrapsychic rather than interpersonal. We ask the client who is working
to look at what characteristics make Jack seem mean or Jill seem kind.
The person who is the object of these reactions may express how it feels
to be seen that way or may wonder why she/he is so often seen that way.
Thus, each person in such an interaction has an opportunity for useful
learning.

Primal format

The primal-format group by contrast, involves a very different way
of working. Therapists are very inactive and clients work on their own,
seeking to remember and encounter their parents or other significant
people from their childhood. In a sense, they are encouraged to leave the
present setting and focus on the people who shaped their earliest years.
The presence of other clients near them crying and screaming exerts a
powerful influence on them to do likewise. The ease with which this
regression occurs and the power of it suggest that the social influence is
more in the nature of an invitation than a demand. Other than this general
invitation to express feelings fully, clients are on their own to talk with
imaged parents or to grieve lost ones, to condemn or to reach out with
love. They are seldom given directions during the primal.

Therapists set the stage and may suggest an exercise prior to the session
to help clients attend to and remember their early family experiences.
During the sessions, we sometimes used to go around the darkened room
making suggestions to clients or touching them in an effort to aid their
work. More recently, however, we have not done this. Instead, we wait
in the next room for the occasional client who feels so stuck or frightened

as to want help. Our rationale for this is that the basic thrust of the primal is to say goodbye to parents and to come to terms with the aloneness and freedom of adulthood. To "help" people with this can create a confusing message in which process and content contradict each other. In addition, some clients become distracted by the therapists' presence and worry about "doing well," giving or withholding the good work they think the therapists want. While these performance concerns may be worth addressing, they also create a diversion from more important foci.

Although primals classically involve clients working alone, we have experimented recently with formats in which clients hold or help each other. These and other innovations are ways to vary the degree of isolation clients experience in an effort to find the most useful combination of an awareness of pain and a sense of safety.

Once the actual session ends, the therapists again become more active. They bring the group members together and initiate a sharing of what the members felt and what their experience meant to them. Therapists and clients discuss what the primal experiences imply for changing behavior and attitudes.

Example: Standard-Format Group

In the next few pages, we will describe a standard-format group meeting. Although groups usually have twelve members, this description includes only eight members for simplicity and brevity. Also, we do not detail all the specific movement in and out of the group as pairs of clients leave to peer-counsel and return. Finally, each client is presented as fairly well-focused in her/his therapeutic work. In actuality, on any given evening, perhaps two or three group members are somewhat groping or stuck. Otherwise, the description of the group is intended to be accurate and representative of a real group session.

It is 8:25 Monday night in the waiting room at the Center. A few people from the early group are meeting and chatting with members of the late group who are just arriving. There is more nervous joking among arriving members of the second group than among members of the first group, who seem more relaxed and peaceful. Gradually, members of the early group drift out and second-group people move into the group meeting room and arrange themselves in a circle. The therapists Lee and Gary join them and, after a couple of minutes of conversation, Lee suggests they get started.

In the go-around, members state briefly what issues they expect to work on. Marty says he is now more hurt than angry about his wife leaving him and would like to continue to work on that. Ellie says she wants to pursue some feelings of love toward her mother that she uncovered in the last primal. Each group member makes a statement. Then Gary says, "Okay, we've got about eight minutes apiece. Any pairs want to peer-counsel first?" George and Jill leave the group to peer-counsel and Art decides to take his turn first. He sits in the center on a mat, with another mat behind him on the wall. He leans back against the wall. The group is gathered close to him in a semicircle. He begins:

> I've been thinking about my father a lot this week. It seemed like he was never there. He would travel and come home on weekends and then leave again. And while he was around, it was hard to know what he was thinking. He was always working on the house or taking naps.
> I gotta do some archaeology on him—find out what was going on between us. (Pause.)
> Gary, would you sit over there in the chair near the corner and be a sort of absent father? I want to talk about him, or to him, or whatever.

Gary does so, facing away from Art and not moving. Art tells the group some biographical details about his father and then talks about what it felt like on weekends when his father came home. He tells how his father made him stay around in case he needed him to get something, but would not talk with him or help him feel included. Then Art begins talking to his father:

> "Why wouldn't you talk to me? Why wouldn't you touch me? I wanted you to touch me! That scares me. . . . Please touch me, please touch me, Dad!"

Art stays with that thought, repeating it and shaking and crying as he says it. He reaches out to his "father," asking to be touched. When his time is up, he talks for a minute or two about how scared it makes him to ask his father for love. Lee asks Art with whom he wants to peer-counsel. Art indicates David and, as they leave, Gary says, "There are lots of tears there, but don't hurry yourself. Stay with the fear as long as you want to."

Next, Sharon moves to the center and says she is ready. She talks about the recent ending of a relationship with a man she cared about. While describing her hurt and sadness, she cries a little, but gradually her feelings turn to anger, first toward the man who left her and then toward the therapists. She smashes a pillow and says:

> I did all the things I was supposed to do! I reached out! I let him know I cared! (Louder and louder.) I came to all my sessions! I came to the group! I expressed my anger!! And what goddamn good did it do me? I'm alone just like I was before! Goddamnit! I'm pissed at you! (Looking at Lee and Gary.) I'm pissed at both of you!

Sharon continues hitting and shouting in an uncharacteristically powerful way. In the past, when she got angry, she frequently also got frightened and her anger had a tight, squeeky sound. She could not express her anger fully because her fear blocked it. Tonight, she has left her fear behind and is clearly intensely furious. When her turn is over, she talks a little about her work and then goes off to peer-counsel.

George comes forward next and begins to talk about his mother, who died a few months ago. He says that he has been reading her diaries recently and remembers some phrases she used to describe him when he was little. The group members sit close to him, holding his hands and touching him warmly. He sobs hard for most of his time, remembering phrases she used to describe him. Over and over, he says, "It was a whole world—my mother, my father, and brothers—that house. It's all gone . . . a whole world." As George gradually ceases crying he holds onto the people near him. While he does members of the group talk about the death of a parent during the course of therapy. Gail says she thinks it tends to focus a person on the loss of parents, which we all experience growing up, but which can often be denied while parents are alive. George says he now can distinguish more clearly between the mother who brought him up (toward whom he still has angry feelings) and the old woman who recently died, who had become his friend in many ways.

Marty, who was crying during George's turn, says he wants to be next. He says, "While George was talking about his mother, I got really sad . . . really sad. (Starting to cry.) That sense of being wanted. . . ." Marty holds on to the people on each side of him and begins to cry hard. Through his sobs, he tells how his wife wanted and loved him early in his marriage and how sad it is to have lost that love.

> I'd put my head on her lap and she'd stroke my hair. . . . (Marty's voice breaks and he sobs harder.) There was a way she looked at me—so loving. . . . (Laughing and crying.) She called me her cupcake! (He laughs very hard for a minute without talking and then sobs some more.) She was my friend, too! We told each other things we'd never told anyone else. We had so many plans! (Marty sobs hard.) We even imagined what it would be like when we were old together. (Crying hard.) That's not going to happen. We're not going to be old together!
>
> (Marty gradually stops crying and says slowly.) I guess a lot of that loss must go back to my mother. Denise (his wife) really mothered me in those early days. That sense of connection—of a real close, tight connection—must be what I felt with my mother when I was little. I've felt that a few times about my mother during primals, but it's a lot more available right now towards Denise.

Lee says, "It may take awhile to get to the early connections. You're feeling a lot about Denise right now. Don't push yourself to work it back further right now. It'll come."

Marty goes off to peer-counsel while some of the others return.

Jill speaks next, picking up on a theme she has stayed with consistently for a few weeks. The theme is her tendency to be critical and rejecting when she is afraid of being rejected and abandoned by others. The self-fulfilling quality of this "You can't fire me—I quit" strategy is clear to her, but changing her long-standing response style is not easy. She says:

> In my individual session this week, I decided that I needed to just open myself up to people. And I have and everybody's loving me. Bill's been very tender and caring. And we've been very sexy together—unusually sexy. It scares me! We've been so close! And my son came up to me when I was lying on the couch and sat down on the floor and put his head on my shoulder like he used to when he was little. I stroked his hair and he just stayed there for a long time. I don't know how he knew that I was so open but he must have seen it somehow. It felt really good, but it made me shiver after. We were so close.

As Jill says these things, she shakes some and cries a little. Then she falls silent. After a minute, she looks up and says, "I was afraid to come to this group tonight. I almost cancelled twice." (Jill is normally in the early group, but came to the late group because of scheduling conflicts.)

Gary says, "When I came in and first saw you, you looked terrified. I wondered what was up."

"Yeah. I just was really afraid to come here. I thought I might feel like an intruder."

"You're really welcome here," Art says, and Jill starts to cry hard. It is just the reassurance she needs to let her feel and fully express her fear of rejection. When Art holds his arms out to Jill in a welcoming gesture, she goes over to him and he holds her as she sobs. She cries hard without stopping for several minutes. Whenever her crying begins to subside, Art says, "You're very welcome here" or "I'm glad you came to this group," and she cries hard again. Paradoxically, she can feel her pain about past rejections most keenly when she feels sufficiently safe and welcome in the present. Jill is still crying when her time is up, so she asks Art to peer-counsel with her.

After a pause in which no one comes forward, Gail says timidly that she is ready. She looks at Gary and says, "I've been thinking about what you said to me a couple of weeks ago." (He told her that he found her warm but very cautious in her dealings with him. He urged her to take more risks in her comments to him.)

> *Gail*: I think I made some modest progress.
> *Gary*: Well it wasn't quite the off-the-wall stuff I was hoping for.
> *Gail*: I know. (Gail blows out through her mouth—a half-scared, half-frus-trated gesture.) I know it wasn't off the wall. I had a joke I wanted to tell you, but I forgot it. Let me see if I can remember it.

Gail looks at Gary and blushes, "unable" to remember the joke. After a minute or two, Gary says, "Just look at me and say, 'I won't give to you'." Gail does so a few times and then Marty suggests, "Try saying, 'I won't give you me'." Gail does so repeatedly, getting more and more in touch with her stubborn anger and wish to withhold. As she says the phrase louder, her usual, compliant, passive holding-back stance is transformed into a hard, flinty "No! I *won't* give you me! No! I *won't*! I *won't*! You can't make me do it! *No!* You *can't have me!*" Gail says these words loudly, directly to Gary, and with facial expressions that are mostly congruent with her words. There are some transient smiles and grimaces that say, "I don't mean it," but mostly her face and body convey the same angry refusal as her words.

As she finishes, there is some group discussion that reflects a consensus that this is a useful direction for Gail and that as she feels safer to say "No" openly, she will have less need to act it out sneakily. Gail asks George to peer-counsel with her and, as she leaves, David goes to the mat.

> I'm the youngest in my family. That meant that I was cute . . . and got people to laugh . . . and was a nuisance sometimes. But I wasn't taken seriously by them and sometimes now I'm cute for people instead of insisting that they take me seriously and treat me respectfully. So I want to work on that.

Group members nod and listen, waiting for him to go on.

> *David*: Oh . . . let's see . . . I'm not sure how to work that. . . . (He lets out a playful mock scream for help.) Anybody have any suggestions?
> *Lee*: Just like a youngest child. "Tell me what to do."
> *David*: Shit! . . . Oh shit!

David recognizes the truth of what Lee has said, but he remains stuck. His speech becomes increasingly "cute."

> *David*: I don't know! I don't know what I'm supposed to do! I never was an older brother. How'm I supposed to know how to do that? . . . Jeepers!"
> *Gary*: (Turning to Lee.) Isn't he a cute little fella? Couldn't you just put him in your pocket and take him home?
> *David*: Stop it! (Grinning, laughing, and getting angry all at once.) Okay! Goddamnit! Just give me a minute.
> *Marty*: (With mock concern.) Give the little guy a minute. His legs are short and he can't keep up.
> *David*: (Visibly angry.) Goddamnit, shut up! . . . Stop it! I know what to do and I don't need your shit! Take your condescending tone and shove it!

David is yelling now, no longer laughing or pausing. He continues for a minute or two, smashing the mat with a plastic bat and with his fists. As his anger subsides, there is a pause. Then Gary speaks to him.

Gary: Okay. So contacting your anger and feeling powerful is one way to step out of your little-kid role.

David: Right. . . . It feels good . . . and you're saying, How else can I do that?"

Gary: Yeah.

David: Well I can do it by being certain and not hesitant in introducing Jane (a woman friend) to my family like I did this weekend.

Gary: Good.

David: And I can do it by saying what I know. At lunch yesterday, I was with a bunch of people and they were talking about woodworking and I knew more about it than any of them, but I was afraid to say anything. I just sat there. So the next time, I'm going to talk. I'm going to let them know what I know.

Gary: Good. Who would you like to peer-counsel with?

David: Art, will you work with me?

Art agrees and they leave together.

Ellie says she wants to work more on her divorce. The decision to get a divorce was her former husband's and she has been struggling with feelings of being abandoned and worthless. In addition, her children, who are nearly grown, are gradually moving away from home and leaving Ellie to confront herself, her loneliness, and questions of who she will be and what her life will mean. Often, she has responded to her loss by being bitter and critical. Recently, she has tried to move beyond this to positive feelings.

Ellie: Since the primal last week, I've thought a lot about the phrase that came to me then: "I love my mother." I do love my mother and there's a lot about me that's like my mother. So I better love her or I'm in trouble with myself.

Gary: What do you love particularly about your mother?

Ellie: Oh, you want me to get specific, huh? Next thing I know, you'll want to hear what I love about myself. (With mock horror.) Where will it end?

Ellie thinks for a minute, looks at the ceiling, and says:

Once when I was, oh, maybe six, I was sick and my mother had earaches so she couldn't hear well. My room was next to hers but she was afraid she couldn't hear me, so she tied a string to her ankle and to my bed, so if I wanted her I could pull the string. . . . I like it that she was thinking about me and about what I needed. . . . That seemed very loving. . . ."

Ellie's eyes get moist. She doesn't really cry, but she clearly is loving her mother.

She would sometimes take me out of school for the day and we would go on the subway all the way out to the end of the line—just the two of us. Then we'd walk some more and end up in the country. And she'd have brought a picnic lunch and we'd sit there and eat and talk. Once she fell asleep and I sat and looked at her face for a long time. I remember thinking how beautiful she looked.

Ellie goes on in this loving tone for the rest of her time. What is remarkable about it is her staying with the theme of loving her mother. Previously, she tended to become anxious when she was so open and loving, and would revert defensively to a critical, complaining mode. Tonight, she reaches and sustains a new level of vulnerability and lovingness.

The group is nearly over. People look around and nod at each other, holding hands and sitting close together. There is a peacefulness and a feeling of completion. Lee reminds the group of the sign-up sheet for the coming workshop. Sharon asks a question about when the Center is open for peer-counseling. Then the group ends with members hugging and saying goodbye to each other. Ten minutes later, the last people leave.

The Group Leader's Role

The leader's role in a feeling-expressive therapy group has several quite distinct features. First, as with any group, the leaders bear certain responsibilities for group maintenance. They decide who is invited to the group, who is encouraged to terminate, and who is challenged when she/he wants to leave prematurely. They are largely responsible for deciding the time and place of meetings and for providing needed supplies. They also must ensure that the group room is isolated or soundproof enough so that there is no threat of interruption from people outside who might be upset by the sounds emanating from the group. Although these group maintenance functions are largely taken for granted, if they are not carefully attended to, the group suffers.

Another obvious task is to facilitate feeling-expression using the various techniques of individual therapy,[1] as well as other techniques that are particularly suitable for groups. For example, feelings of embarrassment are easily elicited in groups. Embarrassment involves being looked at and a group can look at a client with so many eyes! Often embarrassment attaches to loving or sexual feelings people are ashamed of and wish to hide. When a client lets the group see these warm feelings and feels the embarrassment, she/he can end up feeling good rather than shameful about them. There is also a tendency to "catch" feelings from other group members in the group's permissive atmosphere. Knowledgeable therapists can use these and other qualities of groups to promote feeling-expression.

Partly because of the power of groups to move in a feeling way it is also important for group therapists to teach clear thinking (Lieberman, Yalom and Miles, 1973). At times, one or more clients go off on nonproductive pathways and must be confronted. Since group members are

[1]See Chapter 3.

also peer-counselors, they must be taught to think critically about what is being said. For example, clients often work well and productively on the idea of taking care of themselves. Most of what results is good for themselves and those with whom they live. Occasionally, however, self-indulgence masquerades as self-responsibility. One evening, for example, a group member was saying that his 12-year-old son, for whom he alone was responsible, was staying out nights and that he did not know where he was. He said further that that was something he was not going to worry about—that he was going to take care of himself. The leaders interrupted this client's work, saying that a 12-year-old needed more structure and support than that, and helped him to form a plan for dealing more responsibly with his child.

There are value judgments in such interventions. We believe, however, that such judgments of value are made whether or not one intervenes and that such decisions simply go with the job. We also believe that certain choices, such as letting a 12-year-old roam unattended overnight, fall outside a standard to which most reasonable people could agree. At other times, the stakes are not so high, yet we feel that thinking clearly with clients and teaching them to do so with each other can move therapy ahead dramatically. Often, it takes nothing more than the courage to say that the emperor has no clothes.

Another part of the group therapist's role is to encourage new behavior and new attitudes. Groups are an excellent place to test out new ways of being. Assertiveness or openness that might be too frightening to try in the outside world can be tried out in the group. Since behavior is largely determined by inertia and habit, frequently it is necessary for therapists and other group members to push clients to try out new behavior even within the relative safety of the group.

Finally, if clients are to work well with each other, the group leaders must teach them theory and show them techniques. Frequently, after someone works, we talk for a minute or two about the work—what helped them cry, how behavior change might move their work along, and so on. Group members, group therapists, and the client who just worked all take part in these discussions.

Let us look now at a second way clients help each other.

PEER-COUNSELING

Peer-counseling is a process of exchanging therapeutic help in which two people take turns as each other's counselor/therapist. Clients peer-counsel as part of their group and workshop experiences and independently, often on a weekly basis, at the Center or in their homes (Caplan, 1964). Typically, a peer-counselor works for 30–45 minutes each as client and as counselor, but the work period can vary.

Although we see ourselves as doing *therapy*, we use the term "peer-counseling" to convey a sense that the helper is somewhat more passive and less confrontive than we are while doing therapy. We place more emphasis on listening and facilitating than on confrontation and active intervention.

Purpose

Peer-counseling emphasizes the adult, coping, responsible aspects of clients. It supplements and extends the therapy process in many ways. It gives clients additional time to examine their thoughts, express their feelings, and try out new behavior in a safe atmosphere. It is also a reminder to clients of their ability, competence, and capacity to give to others. Finally, it is a demystifying experience that shows clients that the process is useful rather than that the therapist is magical.

There is a great benefit to be derived from telling someone one's thoughts and feelings and having them listen without argument or addition. At the most elementary level, people feel good about themselves when what they say is warmly and sympathetically received. It is so much easier to think creatively about oneself when one feels safe and accepted. Generally, however, peer-counseling goes beyond liking and support to expression of feelings. When therapy is going well, there are more feelings stirred up than can be expressed in 50 minutes per week. For example, in the group session we described, Marty was trying to heal himself after his divorce. This takes many hours of expressing feelings of love, anger, and perhaps fear towards his ex-wife. It is primarily a matter of going over his mental photograph album and letting go of each picture, discharging the feelings associated with those memories and following the feelings that connected his ex-wife with early caregivers. Such work can be accomplished in peer-counseling as well as in therapy sessions. In fact, almost any sort of grieving lends itself very well to peer-counseling. Plenty of time is needed to feel the loss, and peer-counseling can help with this task, freeing therapy for other work, such as examining transference feelings or making tough confrontations.

In grieving, there is work for both the therapist and the peer-counselor. People who have lost someone they love have a strong tendency to be angry, often quite indiscriminately so, at anyone who happens to be available. Helping the mourner to channel this anger so that it is fully expressed but does not alienate members of her/his support system is a complicated task that often is better left to the therapist than to the peer-counselor. The peer-counselor, however, can encourage the client to express sadness, fear, and anger over the person being grieved.

Another area in which tasks can be efficiently divided between peer-counseling and therapy is in helping the client to decide how to approach a particular issue. Let us take Jill's situation as an example. Jill came into her individual therapy session full of complaints about the people in her life. There were many ways her therapist could have responded to her. The most obvious responses would have remained at the level of Jill's complaints: "Who are you the most angry at?"; "What do you need to say to your son?"; "What does it remind you of?" Such responses are often useful. When instead, her therapist responded with, "What would you feel if you didn't feel annoyed?", she shifted to a different perspective in which Jill's anger was seen as potentially defensive. The question then was what more basic feeling was being blocked by the anger. This is not the sort of operation most peer-counselors are able to perform skillfully. It stemmed from numerous contextual and historical cues filtered through the therapist's experience. It was not a hard sentence to say, but it was hard to say it at exactly the right moment.

Peer-counselors helped Jill to carry out the work that sprung from this intervention. Jill's answer to the therapist's question turned out to be, "I would feel love and closeness and that would scare me." Jill felt safer being annoyed than being scared. In this session, she resolved to be close to her husband, children, and friends—to open herself to them. She agreed to appreciate them and reach out to them. Her peer-counselors could and did hold her to this resolve, reminding her of it on numerous occasions when she protested that this time, her family "really" was being bad to her and "What else could I do?"

Peer-counselors are also helpful at checking on progress with behavioral goals. For instance, a client may decide to be more outspoken at work or to maintain an exercise regime. Peer-counselors can ask about progress in these areas and help the client to work on feelings or attitudes that are blocking progress.

A unique advantage of peer-counselors is their occasional presence as "real-life" participants in each other's worlds. More than therapists, they are likely to see other clients at work or social gatherings. Thus, they are in a unique position to support and encourage other clients to try new ways of being. They may also function as observers who can say, "You're right, your uncle treated you very badly" or "Well, he wasn't that great, but I think you overreacted." This sort of information can be very useful and is often in short supply. Such feedback usually comes from other participants with their own interests and axes to grind. Of course, that may be the case with peer-counselors as well, but it is less likely to be so.

A special case of peer-counselors playing a role in each other's lives is couples who peer-counsel. Obviously, being husband and wife sometimes conflicts with being peer-counselors—for example, when the spouses are angry at each other. No one likes to hear anger, especially from someone close whom one depends on for love and support. There are other aspects of couple peer-counseling, however, which are very rewarding. It is often easier for a person to credit statements of love and support when they come from someone who has actually chosen to live with her/him. In addition, the possibilities for teamwork on major psychic or behavioral restructuring projects are much greater than among ordinary peer-counselors or therapists and clients. In a couple, the other person is there most of the time to reassure the partner, to plan, or to remind the mate of a direction that has been forgotten. Achieving this level of cooperation in a mine field of potential zero-sum games is not easy, but it is very rewarding.

Limitations

Having described some of the uses and benefits of peer-counseling, we must also look at some of the limitations and potential problems. Peer-counselors seldom seem to confront each other as strongly, firmly, and lovingly as good therapists confront their clients. The peer relationship seems to lend itself less to such confrontation than does the client-therapist relationship, with its more clearly demarcated roles. Another limiting feature is that, although transference does develop in peer-counseling relationships, it flowers less and is examined less than in therapy. This may result in part because the object of these transference feelings so regularly and visibly becomes a hurting child in the next half hour.

The relative lack of confrontation in peer-counseling means that one can go on longer working an unproductive vein or mistaking a defense for genuine feeling-expression. These factors limit the usefulness of peer-counseling, but do not seem to pose much possibility of outright harm.

There is an aspect of peer-counseling, however, which does have the potential for harm. That is the acting out of unexamined transference feelings. These can be divided roughly into anger, dependency, and sexual feelings. The peer-counseling relationship, like the psychotherapeutic relationship, requires safety if the client is to be vulnerable and open. The mixture of sexual and dependent feelings that such a relationship allows can only be fully felt and openly examined in an environment separated from action. A person cannot openly express and safely wonder about anger if a physical fight may result. Nor can needy and sexual feelings be freely expressed and examined without confidence that the peer-counselor will not act on them.

Our advice to clients about this issue is aimed more toward avoiding harm than toward using transference therapeutically. We think it is a rare peer-counselor who has the vision and restraint to elicit transference feelings and work them back and forth between childhood and current experiences as we would in therapy. Therefore, we suggest that transference feelings be focused primarily on the relevant parent from the client's childhood, rather than on the peer-counselor. Similarly, we make a clear statement that people are not to have sexual relationships with others at the Center, including with their peer-counselors. It is easy and natural to develop strong, warm feelings toward one's peer-counselor: "This person listens and holds me and is on my side. She/he is the perfectly loving person I've always looked for, but never found." Whether or not all the subtleties of this attachment are explored in the peer-counseling session, the harmful acting out of these feelings must be prevented. If the feelings are acted on, it usually means the end of both the peer-counseling relationship and the process of expressing these feelings in a self-examining way. When this happens, or when anger or disappointment ends a peer-counseling relationship, an effort to step back and look at an interpersonal process has become simply one more cyclic repetition of that process.

Despite these limitations, we find peer-counseling to be a very valuable adjunct to therapy; it is used by well over half our clients during their time at the Center. For some, peer-counseling is a major part of their therapy experience and an important source of gain.

Recommendations

Our ideal, widely observed by therapists at the Center, is for peer-counseling to become a regular, ongoing routine like exercising or brushing teeth. We see peer-counseling as a permanent part of our way of living. Of course, the frequency of the sessions may vary over time. A few clients who share our viewpoint have continued to peer-counsel years after terminating formal therapy. Our impression, however, is that such a consistent use of peer-counseling occurs in a relatively small minority of clients. For a large number, peer-counseling continues on an occasional, as-needed basis (e.g. to help in dealing with crises).

WORKSHOPS

Our workshops range from one to four days and use various constantly evolving formats. At the time of this writing, a typical workshop might begin on Friday evening and end on Sunday afternoon, with most participants staying overnight at the Center. There are usually thirty clients and three therapists. After an introductory meeting, small 3-hour groups meet Friday night and again Saturday morning. These meetings are like weekly group meetings in that they involve feeling-expression, insight, and attention to behavior change. They tend to be more emotionally charged than weekly groups, however, because of the intensity generated by the workshop setting. Saturday afternoon we have a primal and, after a short break, small group meetings until dinner. After dinner, there is another 3-hour group, and another on Sunday morning. Sunday afternoon we have groups focusing on behavior change and re-entry. In that group, clients make plans to implement changes they have decided on during the weekend.

The tone of the workshop is generally informal and friendly. There are shared assumptions that we have all been hurt and that we are all working on our feelings and behavior to make our lives better. During breaks, clients talk, laugh, hold each other, snack, or quietly rest and think. Many find themselves trying out new ways of being with other people and feeling closer than usual to other people.

Like individual therapy, group therapy, and peer-counseling, workshops provide an opportunity to look at oneself, to express feelings, and to plan personal change. Workshops also have the following unique qualities:

1. The extensive and intensive character of workshops helps to break down defenses against feeling and allows thematic work.
2. Workshops are interpersonal laboratories permitting the diagnosis of, and prescription for, interpersonal difficulties.
3. Workshops build a sense of community and provide a good starting place for peer-counseling and group participation.

We will discuss these points in order.

Workshops Break Down Defenses Against Feeling and Allow Thematic Work

By extending over a much longer time than a single therapy session, and by eliminating distracting and competing cues and frames of reference, a workshop comes to have some of the powerful characteristics of a total institution described by Goffman (1961) and Le Vine (1966). While isolation from competing frames of reference can be used for repressive purposes, it can also be used to help people. Thus, a rigidly obsessive client who has great trouble contacting feelings may be able to cry in a workshop where other people are crying. The cautious, critical parent who usually perches on this client's shoulder, saying, "Be sure you don't look foolish," can be ignored more easily in the presence of such powerful group support. This effect is by no means limited to a few clients with tight defenses. Nearly everyone becomes more feelingful in a workshop atmosphere that supports feeling-expression. The following example illustrates this point.

Ben had been in therapy for about two months when he came to his first workshop. He had cried a little in his first session when he had talked about how unhappy he was with his life. Since then, he had not cried, but instead had presented himself as too worldly and sophisticated to feel hurt. As he sat in a group at the workshop, he listened to another client cry about a sister with whom she had been very close when they were children. She talked about what good friends they were to each other and how sad she was that they had grown so far apart.

Listening to this, Ben was reminded of a parallel experience with a childhood friend. Along with several other members of the group, he began to cry. By the time the other client had finished talking, tears were streaming down Ben's face. He moved to the center of the group, looked at the soft, teary faces of those around him, and kept crying as he told his story about a friend who had loved him and was gone.

Workshops also offer the possibility of doing thematic work because, even in a short workshop, clients have multiple opportunities to explore their experiences. There is a greater chance of discovering thematic relationships when they occur closely together than when they are spread out in weekly individual therapy sessions. This thematic consistency may have to do with a feeling (e.g., all work is focused on anger), a significant person (e.g., all work is focused on mother), or a way of being (e.g., all work is focused on reaching out to others). It may also tell a kind of story. For example, a client relates a symptom (e.g., indecisiveness) to a feeling (e.g., fear) in the first session. In the second session, the fear is experienced in relation to someone in the present. In the next session, the client traces that sense of fear back to a critical father. Finally, she finds that her fear stems from anger toward that critical father, and the expression of that anger helps to resolve the indecisiveness with which the chain of related sessions began.

The following is an example of thematic work that occurred at a workshop.

Early in the workshop, Elise worked on how conflicted she was about feeling sexy and, even more, about letting other people see her as sexual. She worked on this issue for the rest of the workshop, frequently starting her turn with a statement such as, "I'm a sexy woman." She sometimes stayed with that sentence or related ones, shivering and shaking as she let go of her nonsexual "I'm just a mother" facade. At other times, she told the group about her sexual experiences, thoughts, or wishes, thus presenting herself to others as sexual. In other sessions, she recalled experiences with her mother in which she was told in various ways to deny and hide her sexuality. Sometimes she yelled at her mother and sometimes she cried as she said goodbye to the mother who both had taken care of her and had told her not to own and enjoy part of her self. Each session was related quite directly to the theme Elise had enunciated at the start of her work.

Workshops Are Interpersonal Laboratories Permitting the Diagnosis of, and Prescription for, Interpersonal Difficulties

By interpersonal difficulties, we mean both outright symptoms (such as debilitating anxiety in social interactions) and more insidious difficulties in relating to people which keep relationships from being fulfilling. For example, some people who feel very lonely will not reach out to others. Others who are bored with their lives rigidly control people's access to them, thus cutting off sources of stimulation. Some people who yearn to be close to others persistently see others as wanting to use them or do them in.

Difficulties such as these often can be seen more clearly in clients' behavior at workshops than in other formats. The social interaction that is a natural part of living with others allows these warps to show clearly. The one-to-one therapy session is ideal for eliciting problems the client has in relating to authority figures. Often, however, it does not reveal much about difficulty with peers. Since we spend much more of our time relating to friends, lovers, and colleagues than to bosses and policemen it is important that this aspcet of a client's functioning be available for evaluation. The following case examples illustrate how to make behavioral prescriptions suited to each client's personal style.

Michelle worked in individual therapy for about six months before she attended a workshop. Her relationship with her therapist was basically cooperative. Near the start, she was somewhat cautious and fearful in committing herself to therapy. She was also a little more dependent than some clients, asking frequent questions and seeking reassurance. This was all subtle, though, and not particularly remarkable. At her first workshop, however, Michelle's shyness became much more noticeable. She seldom looked at people when she spoke and she sat by herself most of the time. When she worked in group, she looked down or at her therapist, but seldom at her peers. Even when a group member spoke to her, she would turn to her therapist as she made her reply. The annoying, self-defeating quality of her behavior was pointed out to her and she was encouraged to express the fear she had felt as a child whenever she had left her parents to make her way among playmates. For her next group session, she wisely chose to work in a group that her therapist was not in so that she would be less tempted to hide from her peers.

Janet, who was uncomfortable with men, was paired with Harry, a shy man, in an interpersonal workshop experiment. The therapist suggested, and they agreed, to the following: During the workshop, whenever Janet wanted to use the bathroom, she had to get written permission from Harry. Whenever he wanted to eat, he had to get Janet to write him a note agreeing to it. Both the cooperative and the whimsical aspects of the contract were helpful as they created frequent opportunities for a light interchange. As the embarrassed laughter gradually dissolved some of their fear and shyness these clients became closer and warmer with each other.

Ted, whose anxiety led to a characteristic tense, fast-paced, somewhat frenetic interpersonal style, was asked to stop making jokes and to talk exaggeratedly slowly throughout the workshop. Ted conscientiously behaved as prescribed during the workshop. Two interesting results occurred. One was that he became much more aware of his fear; so much so, that he shook during most of his sessions. Deprived of the way he normally acted out his fear, he felt his fear *as fear* more keenly. Second, he saw other people react differently to him. They looked at him with more respect. His frenetic style conveyed a "please like me" message, but his anxiety to be liked ironically kept him from having real attention for other people and, hence, from being liked. When he was quieter, there was a sense of someone being there—someone self-confident and not so needy as to provoke suspicion ("What does this guy want from me?").

Once one sees how ubiquitous personal style is, the stage is set for behavioral prescriptions. Mothers who are resentful about doing housework and not being appreciated somehow find themselves setting up the food at workshops. If they are told to stop and to go tell someone an entertaining story that does not deal with their children, they are being encouraged to try a new way of behaving. Similarly, people who are working on feeling comfortable with being alone may need prompting to spend some time alone at the workshop, rather than chatting compulsively.

An advantage of the workshop format is the opportunity for sequences of behavioral prescription, observation, and refinement. Sometimes when clients are told to be more assertive, they become hostile instead. They confuse appropriate self-assertion with abusive treatment of others. Seeing this happen allows for quick clarification of how the new behavior needs to be modified to make it truly nondefensive, as well as personally effective.

Workshops Build a Sense of Community and Provide a Good Starting Place for Peer-Counseling and Group Participation

In the 10 or 15 minutes before each hour, the waiting room at the Center is usually active and friendly, with people talking, hugging, or laughing. Sometimes it has a quieter, more thoughtful tone and occasionally it is like a more typical waiting room where strangers sit uncomfortably, avoiding any eye contact. The latter occurs when the people in the office do not know each other; one of the main ways they get to know each other is through workshops. Clients who have been through a workshop together frequently go on to peer-counsel, meet socially, and join a group. For many clients, the workshop is an entry point to the whole community aspect of therapy at the Center. It is a powerful experience that makes clients aware of their shared humanity.

Most workshop participants feel a powerful bond and sense of kinship with one another. They watch and listen carefully while others work. They feel good when they realize that appearances and circumstances differ far more than human character. When they connect with each other on that basis, the defensive postures of "smarter than," "sicker than," or "deeper than" fade away. The intensity of prolonged, intimate interactions also strips away the defensive postures, leaving participants more open and alive. Discovering the kinship of common emotional experiences develops a spirit of community.

Of course, a few people attend workshops without feeling much sense of community, and a larger number somehow manage to avoid attending workshops at all. Some of the latter participate in other aspects of the community such as peer-counseling, but most simply miss out on an important part of what feeling-expressive therapy offers.

Another aspect of community is the community of therapists. Workshops are usually run by three or four therapists, so clients have a chance to get to know therapists other than their own. This tends to correct magical beliefs about one's own therapist and makes it easier to see one's therapist as a person. It becomes clear that there are various effective therapy styles, and one of the other therapists may see something, or find some new and productive way to work with a client, that the client's individual therapist had missed.

Special Therapeutic Tasks of Workshops

In addition to the therapeutic skills needed for individual and group therapy, workshops require two other specific therapeutic operations: (1) relating each client's work to her/his behavior and (2) monitoring the life of the group.   Since workshops provide much more opportunity to observe clients' behavior than do other forms of therapy, it is useful for therapists to notice how clients deal with such mundane issues as rules, meals, and sharing with others. Who shares in the clean-up chores and who does not? Who socializes only with peers or only with leaders? Only with men or only with women? All these "real-life" behaviors are before the therapist as in no other outpatient setting. The therapist needs to see them and to relate them skillfully and usefully to the client's therapeutic issues. It is by no means a matter of simply stating to the client everything one observes. Rather, the feedback should allow the client to see how her/his behavior in the social setting of the workshop undermines or supports the client's therapeutic goals.   The main obstacle to doing this is the therapist's own involvement in the social setting, with its rules about what can and cannot be commented on tactfully. Although the therapist takes part in that setting, she/he must reserve the right, and summon the courage, to point out how the client's behavior is related to the client's therapy. It is particularly hard to comment on "gifts." At one workshop, a client wanted to show the leaders some movies he had made. This was presented as a "gift" for the leaders and one leader, "under the influence" of social rules, agreed. Later, after some consultation, the offer was rejected and an interpretation was made to the client relating this offer to his wish to be the center of attention. The therapist is probably best able to make these interpretations about workshop behavior when she/he is comfortable with the idea of making the entire workshop a therapeutic experience.

The second task that emerges in running workshops is monitoring the life of the group. Group maintenance is even more critical in workshops than in weekly groups. The therapist must be aware of cliques developing, of anyone becoming isolated, of any scapegoating, and of the general mood of the group. Leaders must evaluate trends and decide whether or not to intervene. When a therapist makes an intervention, she/he should know whether its intent is primarily to stop something harmful or, rather, to engage clients in exploring their history and feelings in relation to a particular phenomenon. At times, the most important thing is to stop some angry or harmful behavior. If clients are becoming sexually involved, for instance, we first make a clear statement that that should stop. The expression of the clients' resulting angry, guilty, or fearful feelings may be therapeutic, but that is secondary. Our main goal at that point is to stop behavior we see as harmful and disruptive. At other times, however, we may ask a client about certain behavior ("Why do you eat alone?") primarily to explore that behavior rather than simply to stop it. Since workshops involve more people meeting for a longer time than is the case in weekly therapy groups, the need for constant monitoring of the group's mood and pulse is considerably greater than in weekly groups. The same power that workshops generate for feeling-expression and support can be used destructively to force conformity or feed neurotic needs.

The idea of community, sharing, and mutual aid may discomfit some readers who fear that individual initiative and responsibility will be diminished by a cultish focus on "The Group." Clearly, there *are* groups today, many under a religious aegis, which exert such a corrupting and infantilizing influence on their members. Their promise is, "Give all of yourself to the group and the group will take care of all your needs." Unfortunately, these groups flourish more than their members. Our groups do not function this way. Clients in our groups continue to live their lives independently, coming together briefly once or twice each week to help each other reach their own highly diverse goals. Further, no one comes to our groups forever. Most people stay a year or two, few more than three.

Imagine a continuum from isolation, to reasonable contact with others, to loss of individuality in some larger group. Most of our clients begin relatively isolated and in need of more awareness of and involvement with other people. We feel that the group and community aspects of our practice aid the growth of these important human qualities without interfering with individuality or personal responsibility.

SUMMARY

In this chapter, we discussed three ways that clients help each other: (1) group therapy, (2) peer-counseling, and (3) workshops. All are part of the community aspect of our therapy, which we believe encompasses two related but distinct processes. One is the actual help clients give each other. Clients gain from both aspects of the peer-counseling relationship. They not only have more time to work on their feelings, but also have a chance to be helpful to another person. This gives the helper a feeling of usefulness and value and a sense of responsibility for others that are often lacking in clients who have long been preoccupied with their own troubles. This kind of mutual support is good practice for successful living in an interdependent human ecosystem.

A second therapeutic benefit of community is the *sense* of community. It is good for people to realize that, as Sullivan (1953) wisely said, "everyone is much more simply human than otherwise." (p. 32). Seeing others' pain and connecting with it emotionally make it harder to treat people contemptuously or unkindly. The sense of being part of a caring, sharing community can blunt the worst of our selfishness both by making us less afraid and by making us more aware of other people and their feelings. Some otherwise useful therapeutic and self-help movements of the last few years have lost some of their value by focusing on individual concerns to the exclusion of social ones. Cooperation and sharing are as important as individual needs and rights. Both are good, but it is hard to balance them without a sense of community to keep individualism from deteriorating into selfishness.

REFERENCES

Caplan, G. *Principles of preventive psychiatry*. New York: Basic Books, 1964.

Goffman, E. *Asylums*. Chicago: Aldine Publishing Company, 1961.

LeVine, R. A. American college experience as a socialization process. In T. M. Newcomb and E. K. Wilson (Eds.) *College peer groups*. Chicago: Aldine Publishing Company, 1966.

Lieberman, M. A., Yalom, I. D., and Miles, M. B. *Encounter Groups: First facts*. New York: Basic Books, 1973.

Sullivan, H. S. *The interpersonal theory of psychiatry*. New York: Norton, 1953.

Yalom, I. D. *The theory and practice of group psychotherapy*. New York: Basic Books, 1970.

8

Couples: Strengthening the Emotional Bond

> Through the long years
> I sought peace.
> I found ecstasy, I found anguish,
> I found madness,
> I found loneliness.
> I found the solitary pain
> that gnaws the heart,
> But peace I did not find.
>
> Now, old and near my end,
> I have known you,
> And, knowing you,
> I have found both ecstasy and peace.
> I know rest,
> After so many lonely years.
> I know what life and love may be.
> Now if I sleep,
> I shall sleep fulfilled.
>
> Bertrand Russell
> *To Edith*

In order to feel better, it is first necessary to feel more. Unfortunately, most people do just the opposite: in order to feel better—that is, to suffer less pain—they try to feel less. In couples, this means avoiding chronic, unresolved problems. When they come for treatment, most couples have a long history of avoiding their unhappy feelings, if they acknowledge them at all. To bring them closer together—and, ultimately, to help them to feel better—we help them to feel more, beginning with their angry feelings and progressing toward their loving feelings.

Much of what we do in couple therapy is similar to what many other therapists do. We work to improve communication, reduce blaming, and help the pair meet each other's legitimate needs. We view the couple as a system and find how each member is behaving to keep the negative features of the system operating. We deal with sexual dysfunction using the behavioral approach developed by Masters and Johnson (1970), Kaplan (1974), and others. Perhaps roughly half of what we do is common to many other therapies. The rationale for these goals and methods has been discussed repeatedly elsewhere (Ables and Brandsma, 1977; Lederer and Jackson, 1968) and need not concern us here. This chapter focuses on the other half of what we do—the part that deals with feeling-expression.

RATIONALE

The purpose of arousing strong emotions in couple and individual therapy is somewhat similar. In individual therapy, strong feeling-expression is used to help people become more open to parts of themselves they have denied so they can enjoy themselves and others more. In an analogous way in couple treatment, strong feeling expression is used to break up a couple's rigid patterns of relating. In addition, however, in couple therapy one sees one's mate[1] crying and being vulnerable and this has a powerful warming and softening effect. Finally, the strong expression of angry feelings paves the way for loving feelings.

Let us look first at how feelings can break up rigid ways of relating. There are couples who are so devitalized by their problems that they have no emotional energy available to solve them. If a therapist can tickle the playful child inside these morbidly serious adults and get even one of them to laugh about their predicament, it will be hard for the other to resist laughing, too. Even an angry response is more alive and involving than the ponderous seriousness that prevailed before. Other examples of unfreezing responses are when the submissive spouse becomes defiantly angry and rebels, when the "good," long-suffering member of the couple lets the other one have it without being "understanding" or apologetic, and when the "naughty" spouse shouts indignantly at the "good" spouse, who is then suddenly transformed into the "naughty" one. Although these transformations tend to be transitory and often are followed by a return to comfortable old ways, they do show the couple how relative, changeable, and arbitrary their roles are, and they tend to expand the couple's behavioral and attitudinal repertoire.

A second benefit of feeling-expression in couple therapy stems from the powerful effects of seeing one's mate expressing pain, sadness, and grief. While couples tend to drive each other away with their anger, they draw each other closer with their pain and sadness. Often these vulnerable feelings go underground when a relationship stops feeling safe. Afraid to show their hurt, the spouses act angrily, which only drives the other one

---

[1]In this chapter, we will use the terms "spouse," "mate," "partner," and "husband/wife" as free variants of each other. No distinction is intended among these terms; nor is marriage necessarily implied.

further away. Couples who used to get close to each other through sharing hurt and comforting each other may now be afraid to show each other these feelings. In couple therapy, the support of the therapists often makes it possible for one or both members of the couple to cry. Unless crying has been used manipulatively, this is likely to have a melting and warming effect on the partner. Seeing the hurt child in any other person, particularly in one's mate, dissolves the barriers erected to defend against assault. Sharing the thoughts that provoked the crying further enhances this warming effect. A husband may have been remembering the way his wife was with him when they first met, or how supportive and loving she was when his father died. Or they may cry together about the death of a child. Whatever the particular thoughts, this sort of sharing often has a greater impact than words because tears are clearly genuine and not simply a wooden effort to say the right thing.

Wolves cease fighting when one lies down with its head back and offers its neck to the other. This gesture of vulnerability ends the fight. Similarly, the spouse who shares deep and painful feelings is showing a vulnerable part of the self and the mate seldom continues to fight. The only time we have seen a spouse turn away coldly from a genuine expression of sadness and pain is when she/he feared being manipulated. This occurs seldom, however, and is more the exception than the rule.

The third reason for urging clients to express unhappy feelings is that they open the way for positive, loving feelings. Warm, open, sexy, safe feelings tend to become unavailable when anger is blocked. We frequently hear clients say when they start couple therapy that they feel deadened—blunted and without much feeling of any sort. They may notice, vaguely, the absence of positive feelings in their relationship and then add, "But we get along very well. We don't fight and we agree about how to raise the children and about politics." These people would like to put aside their anger and resentment without giving up their longing. Unfortunately, they cannot do it! Our unconscious minds can do a lot, but they cannot bury just one feeling and let the rest go free.

METHODS

Anger

In our work with couples over the last decade, we have learned some ways to harness anger, and some untoward effects to avoid. One lesson is that the anger needs to be expressed angrily, not "considerately." It should be clear to both partners that they are not negotiating an agreement or conducting a feedback session about how each perceives the other. It needs to be clear that this is a time for feelings only. At such a time, it is not useful for a mate to say: "Well, I know you try hard, but sometimes . . . well, I don't know . . . The kids have mentioned it, too . . . You're weak and wishy-washy and a little bit annoying sometimes." It would be better to yell: "You weak, spineless jellyfish!! I hate you! You never say what you want! You make me sick!" Ironically, the first statement is harder to hear than the second. The first pretends to be caring, but is not. The second is a frontal attack that makes no pretense. The listener can brace for the worst and have no hesitation or guilt about making an angry reply. Also, the very childishness and overstated quality of the second convey the metacommunication that the speaker is mostly expressing feelings and is not asking to be taken too seriously as a thoughtful critic. On the other hand, the apparent balance in the first statement conveys the opposite metacommunication: "Take me seriously. This is thoughtful stuff."

The first rule, then, is that if the couple is working on anger, they should be encouraged to express it vigorously and to differentiate it clearly from other sorts of communication, such as negotiations.

A second rule is that the spouses should not threaten to leave each other. Since most people have been hurt deeply by being left, they are unable to hear such a threat without becoming extremely anxious and defensive. Although expressions of anger and threats of leaving frequently occur together, it is useful to separate them.

Some couples do separate and they need to communicate with each other about that, but those discussions should not be confused with therapeutic expressions of anger. As long as couples are working actively on their relationship, discussions of the possibility of dissolving the relationship are counterproductive. Most couples in therapy have thought of leaving each other, but while they are in therapy trying to heal their relationship, they should put those thoughts aside. We find that helping couples to break the associative link between feelings of anger and threats of abandonment helps them to fight better because they are doing so within an overall context of safety in which the relationship itself is not questioned.

A third rule is that there should not be too many rules. Some therapists urge fighting clients to make statements only about themselves or to attack what their mates do, but not who they are. We seldom impose such limits because those clients we teach to fight are usually inhibited about expressing their anger and too many rules can make their task more difficult. To ask that they let go, yet keep within the Marquis of Queensberry rules, is a tough assignment. We do what we can to make their task easier by not imposing too many rules. Our only prohibitions are against physical attack and threats of leaving. In addition, at times we have asked spouses not to use words with sexist connotations (e.g., bitch) and we may ask clients with particular vulnerabilities about sex to avoid that area in their fighting. With the exception of these rules, we invite clients to be angry in whatever way feels best. Even so, clients need continued reminders to talk loudly, to look at the other, and to avoid dropping back into a critical conversational tone.

An understanding that has emerged recently is that much of this expression of anger need not take place in the presence of the spouse. There is clearly some cost for the mates as they listen to each other's anger. Even if they remember that it is just a fight, it is often hard not to hear some of what the other person is saying and let it in where it can hurt.

To avoid that, we have begun experimenting with ways to get the greatest benefit from the expression of anger while doing the least harm to each spouse's self-esteem. We have asked members of the couple to express their anger in group, to peer-counselors, and even when riding alone in their cars. This has helped considerably. Although some ventilation of anger to a third person may be a useful beginning, it still seems to be true, that some toe-to-toe fighting between spouses is necessary for the anger expression to yield its dividend of love. Without it the anger has a gossipy hidden quality which limits its usefulness. Also, direct angry confrontation especially at the start of therapy when the rage has not been acknowledged, makes an unmistakable statement which neither can ignore: "We are important enough to each other to be very mad at each other and to risk expressing it." This statement can form a foundation for further work on the relationship.

Love

The obvious counterpoint to working with anger is working with affection and appreciation. At times, when anger is not blocking clients, or when they are scared of losing each other, they can be moved directly into their feelings of love and longing. We may ask them to say what they would miss most about the other if they were separated. Or we might ask them to tell the story of how they first met or what attracted them to each other at the beginning. Sharing this kind of material with each other is a step toward re-establishing the exchange of love they once enjoyed. Occasionally, we see couples who never were in love. These people are hard to work with in general and are not at all likely to respond well to this remember-the-good-times technique. Fortunately, such couples are rare.

Humor

Humor can be used to facilitate the expression of either angry or loving feelings. We once asked a woman to compose a letter of recommendation to her husband's next wife. Earlier in the session, each member of the pair had stoutly insisted that the relationship was finished and that they could each find a better mate than the present one. We had heard this before and knew that they were very much involved with each other and that their talk about leaving was defensive.

Male therapist: Well, Jane, why don't you tell us what you'd say if Harry came to you in a year or so and said his new bride-to-be wanted a letter of recommendation. What would you write?

Jane: (Laughing some.) I'd tell her she wouldn't have to worry about excessive sexual demands. (Pause, then laughing more.) And I'd tell her that he's good about putting away his socks—especially if she's careful not to tell him to.

Harry: (Laughing.) What about me? Do I get to write a letter for her?

Female therapist: Sure you do. What would you say?

Harry: I'd tell him that if he marries her, his worries will be over. He'll never again have to think. (General laughter.) She'll tell him everything—when to get up, what to do, what not to do, and when to go to sleep. No more beating his brains out deciding for himself. (Seriously now, and with a warmer tone.) I'd also tell him that she's very smart and pretty and he'd better treat her well. (Harry starts to cry, genuinely appreciating Jane. She responds warmly, taking his hand, crying, and smiling.)

Jane: I don't want him. I'd rather stay and fight with you.

An opening was made into the warm feelings Jane and Harry had for each other. It occurred because the therapist invited them to look humorously at what they had both regarded seriously. This shift disrupted the rigid defense enough to let them feel their caring for each other.

Prescriptions

These techniques can be understood as "pump-priming." The therapists say, in effect, "Since you two are so caught up in your pain and your defenses, we will prescribe what is needed. We will get you to *act* flexibly and lovingly and thereby start a positive, self-sustaining process." As long as each member of the pair behaves angrily, is rejecting, and shows no love, each one's negative beliefs about the other will be confirmed. "Why should I be nice to her (him)," the refrain goes, "when she (he) is treating me so terribly."

We may have the mates tell each other things they appreciate about the other or things that make them angry. Or we may coach the more dependent member of the pair on how to act more independent and less needy.

We can assume that any couple who seeks help has already tried most of the home remedies. Each has already tried being loving and has found the mate unresponsive. Usually these trials are too short to break the cycle of anger and recrimination. Such failures only confirm each mate's belief about the other's recalcitrance. Therefore, the therapists need to do more than say, "Be good to each other." They need to use the power of their office to give permission for the expression of anger and forcefully to prescribe the sharing of warm memories or the exchange of appreciative statements. They also need craft and cunning to prod the clients into unwittingly showing their caring and love. Because the therapists prescribe the first few steps, the clients do not have to take responsibility for what is being said. "Take your wife's hand, look into her eyes and say how lucky you are that you found her." The clients need not risk as much and be as vulnerable as if they were taking full responsibility for what they said. This makes it easier for the clients to speak. Each one hears what the other says and knows that at least part of the message is sincere. This is what makes the process self-sustaining. The therapists allow themselves to be used by the clients to get a positive cycle started and then the clients maintain it.

This same principle works with physical closeness, holding, and touch. Therapists can suggest that the pair hold hands, hug, or touch in a particular way. The therapists take responsibility for initiating the closeness: the couple need not risk that much yet. When the mates touch, they may come to feel closer and want to keep touching. They may let themselves feel some positive feelings or they may reject them entirely. This is basically an experiment. It is often hard to tell ahead of time how a couple will react to touch.

Couple versus Therapists

One useful response that occurs occasionally is when the partners join together in getting angry at the therapists. One may say, "I don't like them looking at us. Holding you is okay, but I don't want an audience." The other replies, "Yeah! Me, too." The couple changes from me-against-you, to us-against-them. This is not ideal because it bypasses real intimacy within the couple, but it is usually better than the previous impasse. It also invites interesting questions such as, "Do you have to hate someone to love someone else?" and "What would happen if you were pleased with everyone in the room at the same time?"

Negation

Negation is a method in which the presence of "no" or "not" in a sentence has an almost magical effect of freeing some clients of their otherwise rigid inhibitions.

Example

One couple, Phyllis and Bill, had trouble learning to fight because Bill had a great reluctance to show anger toward Phyllis. He did various passive-aggressive things such as forgetting to meet her on time or waking her by playing music loudly. He would even admit that he was angry at her and that his grin and refusal to fight were angry gestures. Yet he seemed too afraid of his anger to shout at her or call her names. One day, he was reassuring the therapists that he did not feel angry at her and "wouldn't hurt her." One of the therapists took advantage of this opening.

Therapist: What would you want to be sure not to do to her?
Bill: What do you mean?
Therapist: You said you don't want to hurt her. What hurtful things do you want to be sure not to do to her?
Bill: Well, I certainly wouldn't want to chop her in the neck! (Bill holds up his hands "karate-like" and laughs hard.)
Therapist: Where do you want to be sure not to hit her? Show me.
Bill: (Laughing hard.) Well, I wouldn't want to come across like this (he moves the edge of his hand slowly toward her neck) and hit her right here. (All four are laughing now. Bill goes on.) I also wouldn't want to stick my fingers in her eyes! (He makes a "V" with his index and middle fingers and points them at Phyllis's eyes. As the laughter subsides, one of the therapists asks how he would feel about throwing her down the stairs.)
Bill: Oh! I certainly wouldn't want to throw her down the stairs! (More laughter.) Or run over her with the car.

Bill went on in this way for some time, needing only slight encouragement to continue. He was discharging through laughter the tension that had built up because of his tight control over his anger. This experience also made Bill's anger more real for each participant and, by detoxifying it somewhat for Bill, served to facilitate more direct expressions of anger in the future.

Role-Reversal

Role-reversal is another method in which humor is used to break up stereotypic ways of relating. If one partner typically wants closeness while the other wants distance, we may suggest that they change roles. This gives each a chance to experience the other's perspective. We believe that many of these opposing roles represent divergent wishes that each partner has and that, as long as someone plays each role, it is not important who plays which. By opposing roles, we mean such old standards as controlling parent versus rebellious child; feeler versus thinker; spender versus saver; warm, close person versus distant, cold person; and disciplinarian versus friend-of-the-children. Exchanging roles lets clients feel the essential interchangeability of the parts they play so that they can view them with greater humor and detachment. Let us look at an example.

Example

In one couple, the wife, Linda, often felt out of control and weaker than her husband Herb. Linda's fear of being taken advantage of, hurt, or used made it hard for her to let go in many areas of her life, particularly sexually. One day, she mentioned that her gynecologist had just given her a pelvic exam. She looked at Herb and said teasingly, "I wish you had to have one of those things. I'd really like to know how you'd like it!" The therapists saw an opportunity to let Linda work through some of her fear and to let each experience the other's usual role. They suggested that Linda give Herb a pelvic exam. Herb remained dressed but, with coaching from Linda, assumed the position of a woman having a pelvic exam.

Linda was tentative at first, but soon warmed to her new role and profession. "Scoot down a little more please," she sang out happily, "this will only feel cold for a minute." Herb was a good sport about his unexpected visit to the doctor, but became uncomfortable as he actually began to experience the passive, fearful role in which he was so unaccustomed. Both laughed hard as power and sex roles were reversed and they each experienced "how the other half lived."

Exaggeration

Occasionally, we try to elicit humor and break up old ways of doing things by role exaggeration and "prescribing the symptom" (Ericson, 1967; Erickson and Rossi, 1979; Haley, 1963). In this technique, we ask both members of the couple to exaggerate their usual patterned role. For example, let us say that the husband acts like a little boy and the wife like a stern mother. He wants her to love and notice him, has a hard time taking care of her, and often worries that she will be angry at him. She is critical, denigrates what he does, and tends to push him away, saying that he is too dependent. We might ask this couple to spend some time in the session or at home exaggerating these roles. The husband would magnify his childlike dependency and the wife would become even more critical and rejecting. Like role-reversal, this exaggeration helps the couple to loosen their attachment to stuck and unsatisfying roles.

Contracts

We also work with contracts in a way that promotes feeling-expression and the loosening of defensive role-taking, as well as behavior change. Most couples who seek treatment are stuck in how they behave with each other. Each wants the other to change first; and as long as they both wait, the result is a stalemate. At times, therapists suggest contracts and trades that would give each person more of what she/he wants from the spouse. However, such contracts are seldom carried out fully. When they are, the spouses have found a new way to please each other without great apparent cost. When they are attempted but not carried out, that is useful, too. Therapists can work with the couple's feelings about what it was like to try to perform the contract. There is no benefit from the contract only if it was not serious attempted.

Often, when clients agree to act in a way contrary to their usual behavior, important feelings emerge. If a husband who never cooks agrees to do half of the cooking, or if a wife with frequent evening commitments agrees to spend a certain number of evenings per week at home with her husband, emotional tensions are likely to arise. It may be anger at "having" to do something or fear of being out of control of one's life. Feelings that emerge following the agreement to a contract are likely (1) to be at least partially based on early experiences, and (2) to play a role in keeping the couple stuck. Their expression and resolution enables members of the couple to behave more flexibly with each other and find more pleasure in their time together.

The Two-Therapist Team

We use two therapists, one female and one male, for several reasons. First, we think this makes it more likely that each client will feel understood. It is easier for a therapist to become involved as an advocate or vigorous confronter of one client if another therapist is there to lend support to whichever client may feel attacked or betrayed. Also, there are issues and feelings that are gender-linked and it is very helpful to have a therapist who can instinctively understand these feelings. When women clients are afraid of being used sexually, for example, it is helpful to have a woman therapist who can understand that fear. If she decides that the fear is irrational and defensive, she can confront the wife with much more confidence than a male therapist could. Similarly, a husband who is being pressed to share household tasks may be less defensive with a male therapist than with his wife or a female therapist.

Other benefits also accrue with the use of conjoint therapist teams. Many couples share a set of irrational assumptions, approaching at times, a folie à deux. Often, couples who fight over many trivial items come together as allies when these assumptions are questioned. A pair of therapists can support each other in challenging these irrational assumptions, as the following case example illustrates.

Example

Laurie and Eli were in their late twenties. They lived together and had no children. They had come to therapy to decide whether to stay together or go their separate ways. Politics was Laurie's job and hobby. Eli's major interest was people, feelings, and relationships. They enjoyed each other in many ways, but in some important ways, they did not fit together well. He was resentful that she spent so much of her energy on political concerns and she was much less interested than he in talking about their relationship. She felt hounded by his wish to examine feelings and their relationship so relentlessly and, ultimately, she became resentful as well. What made this such a sticking point was that their interests were more than just careers or hobbies. They were life styles.

One day, Eli and Laurie came for therapy bent on confronting each other about these issues. Within five minutes, each had laid out what she/he wanted while the other said she/he was not interested in changing. The shared irrationality was that they were both oblivious to the implications of their exchange. The obvious alternatives were: (1) to end the relationship, (2) to work to accept each other, as she/he is, or (3) to continue to struggle. When the therapists pointed out these options, Eli and Laurie alternately argued with the therapists, yelled, and cried. Because there were two therapists, the confrontation could be carried out actively and nondefensively. The therapists' shared view of reality was in marked contrast to that of the clients and they could pursue it forcefully because of their shared perceptions and mutual support. The result was that Eli and Laurie were eventually brought to recognize the importance of their impasse and the real options available to them. The clarity with which the therapists heard each client say, "I'm not changing," was conveyed to Laurie and Eli. This was possible only because there were two therapists vigorously confronting the clients' system. Both Eli and Laurie were afraid of being alone, yet neither was ready to make the basic behavior changes necessary for their relationship. It was easier to believe that, with enough insistence, the other would change.

Spacing of Sessions

Frequency of sessions and total length of treatment are other methods that spring directly from our use of two therapists. Although we charge couples somewhat less per hour than the combined fees of each therapist, the cost is still substantial. That makes weekly sessions difficult for many couples to afford. Partly for that reason, and partly because of the subtle ways in which couple therapy differs from individual therapy, we often meet with couples every other week. This means that our model of change emphasizes the couple's interactions outside of therapy. We see ourselves as providing the couple with experiences during the hour which are likely to provoke new behavior, new perceptions, and experimentation between sessions. In individual therapy, where the therapist has only one client's defense to overcome and there is more time, it is often feasible for power and determination to carry the day. In couple therapy, however, fortresses must be taken with trumpets, wooden horses, and other means employing stealth and cunning.

A further constraint is the usually much briefer duration of treatment. While some couples work steadily for a year, ten to fifteen sessions are far more common. Couple therapy often involves a degree of self-exposure not present in individual therapy because at any moment a client may "tell on" his/her mate and present the mate in a very unfavorable light. It also may be that individual therapy is more gratifying than couple therapy. There is so much nurturance and support, with the therapist so clearly on the client's side, that even fairly confrontive individual therapy is probably more immediately rewarding than couple therapy. Couple therapy offers considerably less dependent nurturance while demanding a self-examination as painful as that of individual therapy. Furthermore, since each partner is less in control of what happens in the session or of how the therapist will view her/him, the threat of exposure is greater in couple therapy.

Couples tend to stay in therapy for a much shorter time than do individuals. These two parameters of our work with couples—meetings less than once per week, and a relatively short total course of treatment—put limits on what can be done. So does the setting itself. With four people in a room, we are unlikely to stay very long with one client's intrapsychic issues. We may, however, look at those issues briefly, suggest they be worked on in another context, and note how they affect the workings of the couple.

Homework

One way to expand the effect of couple sessions is to use the time between meetings for therapy. One way to do this is through the use of suggested homework. At times, therapists offer explicit suggestions to be tried out before the next meeting. At other times, they are presented more casually as something that might be worth trying. Here are some suggestions we have made:

1. Spend ten minutes each day saying nice things about each other.
2. Don't initiate sex with her this week. Make sure the first move comes from her. You can say "yes" or "no," but do not be too eager.
3. Sit down and fight with each other three times before we meet again. Yell, call each other names, anything, but don't talk about leaving each other.
4. Anytime she says anything this week about leaving you, smile and say that you are too wonderful for her to leave you.
5. Go to bed as usual, but don't bring any reading material. You don't have to talk to each other or make love; just don't turn off the light for 15 minutes and don't read.
6. Wrestle gently with each other. Get a feeling of pushing against each other. He must keep one or both hands in his pockets to make the fight fair. Do not hurt each other. Just push.
7. You are the worrier and she/he is the happy-go-lucky one. Switch roles for a week. You take everything easy and let your spouse worry about what could go wrong.

Most of our suggestions are designed for one of two purposes: to encourage the expression of feelings, or to break up rigid perceptions and habits. By using homework this way, cooperative couples can move along much faster than they would otherwise, and resistant couples can easily be spotted and confronted.

PROBLEMS AND OPPORTUNITIES

The balance of this chapter deals with special problems that arise in couple therapy. These include: integrating couple therapy with individual therapy (i.e., bringing in the spouse of a client already in treatment), choosing goals, responding to sexist attitudes, helping couples to peer-counsel, and helping couples to express feelings without necessarily acting on them.

Integrating Couple Therapy with Individual Therapy

Frequently, we see a couple because one member of the pair has been in therapy at the Center, decides there are relationship issues to be dealt with, and invites the spouse to come in for a couple session. The first and most obvious problem with this arrangement is the potential for the newly arriving spouse to feel alienated and excluded. This spouse often begins treatment assuming, often quite correctly, that the mate has already said angry and unflattering things about her/him to the therapist. There is a sense of coming into the enemy camp which can produce outright defensiveness or resentful pseudocompliance.

The therapists must deal quickly and effectively with this if there is to be a successful outcome. One method is to suggest that the spouse who has not had contact at the Center have a session or two with the therapist who is not treating the other member of the pair. Thus, couple therapy starts with each member of the couple having at least some sense of safety with one of the therapists. However, by doing this, and by showing understanding and friendliness to the newly arriving member of the couple, the therapists may frighten and anger the spouse who originally issued the invitation. No arrangements will entirely satisfy both partners or obviate their fear and anxiety. It requires continuous effort to demonstrate understanding and acceptance of each client's feelings on the part of the therapeutic team. The spouse who is already in therapy does not want to lose a safe place where her/his feelings are accepted, and the newly arriving spouse will have a hard time trusting and being open without establishing a sense of connection with the therapists. In principle, of course, there is no reason why both cannot have what they need. Each has a perspective that is understandable given her/his history and each has a right to feel connected to a therapist. Yet, jealousy and rivalrous feelings often intrude, making it hard for each spouse to feel safe and understood.

Some of the difficulty stems from the shifting alliance and guilty loves and hates that occur within the client-spouse-therapist triangle. The client not only tells the therapist of anger toward the spouse, but may feel at times that the therapist is more supportive and understanding than the spouse. This is probably why the arrival of the client's mate for couple therapy is often as tense a time for the client as for the mate, and why it sometimes results in flight from therapy. When clients invite their mates for couple therapy, they run some risk of losing their individual therapeutic contact without establishing a connection as a couple. Perhaps as many as 20% of these individual-to-couple attempts end in early withdrawal from therapy.

Our awareness of this problem has made us careful to apprise the client of these risks when couple therapy is being considered. We also tell the couple of these difficulties at the beginning of therapy and ask them to let us know if either feels shut out. Finally, and perhaps most importantly, we look for evidence that individual clients are using the therapist as part of a "good guy/bad guy" triangle. Such triangles impede individual therapeutic progress and virtually insure that there will be little intimacy within the couple.

Choosing Goals

We find that in couple as well as individual therapy, it is important to have clear goals. Goals keep the work focused and can be used to remind couples who become resistant that it is they who want to change, not the therapists who want to change them. Clients come in with a wide range of goals, a sampling of which follows:

1. We want to get closer to each other.
2. He had an affair last year and I can't seem to trust him or really forgive him.
3. We want to communicate better.
4. She wants to leave and I don't want her to.
5. We want to be able to fight better.
6. I don't have enough freedom. He won't let me do what I need to do.
7. Our relationship feels dead. It's no fun any more.
8. We want sex to be better.
9. We want to have our relationship get good or end it.
10. He said if I didn't come for therapy, he'd leave me.

This is a representative, but by no means exhaustive, list of goals that bring couples to therapy. All goals need to be discussed and operationalized. The most critical part of the process is being certain that each member of the pair has a personal goal for the therapy. If one is there only to "help out" or has a hidden agenda to get the other into individual treatment, the treatment will not go well. At times, couples come for treatment because one member has decided to separate and wants to have someone around to support the spouse. These motives must be discovered and discussed in early sessions. Treatment can continue only when each client can find a nonmanipulative internal goal that he or she personally wants to pursue. For instance, wanting a more satisfying sex life makes sense as a goal, while finding someone to comfort an about-to-be-rejected spouse does not. The following example illustrates this process.

Example

Martha and Eric were in their fifties. They had been married nearly 30 years and had one grown child. He was a lawyer; she was a social worker. She had ended her individual therapy pleased with herself, but wanting more from her marriage. Less than a year after terminating, she had called the Center to ask for an appointment for herself and her husband.

When they came in for their first session, Martha said she wanted him to be warmer with her, share more, and give more to her. Eric's reply was that he was accepting of her, had no wish for her to be different, and was there simply to help her get what she wanted. Although apparently caring, this response was in fact self-protective and not very giving. There was nothing personal in Eric's response other than his fear. Clearly, he was dissatisfied with aspects of their relationship, but was too afraid of losing Martha to risk sharing his dissatisfaction with her. The therapists kidded Eric about having a perfect wife—a wife he in no way wanted to change. They told Martha how fortunate she was to have such a totally accepting husband. Eric laughed at this, but still could not say how he wanted Martha to be different. The session had a cautious, careful tone to it that Eric exemplified, but the therapists knew that Martha was as much a part of the system as Eric; if she were as daring and reckless as she claimed, she would have left him decades ago. They knew that therapy would only be useful to Eric and Martha if Eric set a goal for himself and Martha recognized her fearfulness and caution.

At the start of the next session, Martha and Eric took their accustomed roles—she as the one who wanted lots of interaction, no matter how angry, wild, or sexy it might be, and he as the good, kind, helpful mate who somehow was not able to understand or grant his mate's fervent requests. The therapists began to ask Eric about his apparent fear of Martha's disapproval. At first, he vigorously denied it, but finally he admitted that he would go out more often looking for fossils if he were not afraid of incurring her disapproval. Even though he then tried to cover his tracks by saying that he really enjoyed staying home with her, Martha got angry anyway. One of the therapists pointed out to Martha how her nagging contributed to keeping them stuck and asked if she would be willing to exchange a "free pass" to Eric to go fossil hunting for more love from Eric. She said she would be happy to do so. Then the therapist asked Eric if he would like the same deal. He agreed and seemed genuinely warmed by the idea and by their interaction. He said that his goal in therapy was to be able to tell Martha what he wanted without letting his fear of her hold him back. This modest goal represented an important move for a man quite frightened about being left, and in a couple strongly committed to the status quo. While it may be more satisfying for therapists to work on fundamental changes, couples deserve help with little changes as well as large ones.

Responding to Sexist Attitudes

In the last ten to fifteen years, people have become increasingly aware of the political dimension of how men and women deal with each other. Gender-based expectations of oneself and others are being examined and revised (e.g., Laws, 1975). This is true with respect to career, housework, childcare, and various social interactions between the sexes. Therapists working with couples necessarily make choices, consciously or otherwise, about whether to address these issues. Our stance used to be that the degree to which a couple adhered to traditional versus nontraditional sex roles was their business and that our business was helping them to make the relationship work. More recently, however, we have come to believe that this attitude is only appropriate within certain limits. We have identified some attitudes and behaviors that are so oppressive of one's full humanity that we believe they need to be interrupted in order for therapy to be continued. If we fail to do so, we become technical advisors and cosponsors of the oppression.

Example

Dan and Elizabeth had been married for a long time and sought help because of a sense of deadness and disengagement in their marriage. Both were loving people. Dan was a thoughtful, caring person who was involved in humanitarian causes—not the stereotypic oppressor. Elizabeth was an active, feisty woman—not a victim in the usual sense. Yet, they divided household tasks based on traditional sex-role assignments even though both now had full-time jobs outside the home. Elizabeth cooked, washed the dishes, and cleaned the house. Their children were mostly grown but, even here, Elizabeth was more involved with them than Dan and served as a conduit between the children and Dan. Elizabeth had been working full-time for about a year before they sought help.

The session described here was the sixth in a series of twice-monthly meetings. It was the first session in which issues of sex-roles came up. Elizabeth said she was sick of doing all the cooking and wanted Dan to help. She was tentative in what she said and he was joking in his response: "Geez, I don't know how to cook! You wouldn't want to eat anything I cooked!" Elizabeth remained tentative, saying at one moment that she just wanted Dan to talk with her while she cooked, and at other moments that maybe they should share the cooking equally.

The therapists faced a choice at this point. They could encourage the pair to express their feelings fully without regard to the specific issues that were arousing the feelings. Dan might get angry or frightened about being pushed and controlled, and Elizabeth might feel angry or hurt about being ignored and not supported. These are, in fact, battle lines along which Elizabeth and Dan fight. Another possibility, and the one the therapists chose, was to attend to the specifics of this argument and to state their own value position. They said that all of us carry a child within us who would like to be cared for without reciprocation. It was understandable that Dan would rather have his meals cooked for him than cook some of them himself. However, the life of an adult who has said goodbye to the dependent, cared-for child must be balanced between giving and receiving. Therefore, it made sense for each spouse to contribute equally.

The therapists also said that, other things being equal, it often was better to share jobs in ways that set both partners free of their sex-role prescriptions. It would be good for Dan to share the cooking, rather than to do all the yard work and fix the car while Elizabeth cooked. Otherwise, even if the workloads were equal, the partners would miss a chance to try new ways of being.

This value statement was presented as such, and both Dan and Elizabeth thought it made sense. Dan said again that he did not know how to cook and the male therapist said that he had had similar fears, but he guessed that if Dan could design high-pressure gauges, he probably could handle a recipe. The tension that had built up was discharged through laughter as clients and therapists made humorous remarks about the coming regimen in which Dan would do half the cooking. Dan and Elizabeth negotiated which nights each would cook and, after some discussion, they agreed that it would be best for Elizabeth to be out of the kitchen, but available for consultation, when Dan cooked.

In subsequent sessions, they reported that sharing the cooking had gone very well. They had had a couple of fights over it, but had worked them out satisfactorily. This intervention was different from most. While various value assumptions are implicit in much of what we do, they are seldom as overt as they are here and in other cases they are probably more universally held.

There are a few other issues we usually address because of their sexist implications. We often ask people how they share the care of their children and whether one spouse believes she/he can "make it" in life without a husband/wife. We find that there are both men and women who assume that, without a mate, they are no good and their lives can have no real meaning. Buried beneath the dependency and low self-esteem in this view are sexist assumptions that interfere with true intimacy. The mate is seen as the "good mommy" who cooks and cares, or the "good daddy" who brings the money home. We challenge such attitudes because they interfere with seeing and appreciating the actual mate and, hence, with making the loving connection needed for real intimacy.

While we have addressed ourselves primarily to sexism directed against women, it can be directed against men as well. For example, child custody cases that unthinkingly presume that women are better caregivers devalue men as nurturers. There are many other examples. Whenever people are dealt with categorically, they are not being seen accurately, and the potential for real intimacy is diminished.

The other main way we address sexism is by attending to language. Terms like "bitch," "dumb broad," "cunt," etc., carry so much anger and repressive history with them that we are very cautious about their use. Since we are not aware of similarly harsh sexist words for men, we view the use of these terms as inherently unfair. We always interrupt women who apply these terms to themselves and, when couples fight, we usually steer them away from these words, depending to some extent on how accessible their anger is. Once a couple has some facility to express anger, we suggest using other terms.

We find that sexist attitudes are so ingrained and harmful that at times we must address them directly and make our own position clear if we are to change them. In such cases, we see these attitudes as a fundamental part of what needs to change if a couple is to change. Ignoring these attitudes in the name of value-free neutrality allows a major part of the couple's pathology to remain unchallenged.

Peer-Counseling Between Couples

This final section deals with the opportunity in couple work to help two people build a subculture of shared beliefs, attitudes, and behaviors. A couple can learn how expressing their feelings softens them and makes them more loving and can choose to do that any time they wish. They learn the skill of separating feelings from action and can choose when to just feel and when to let their feelings lead them to some behavior.

A couple can be taught to think in these ways and to peer-counsel together, a difficult but rewarding task.[2] It is rewarding because each spouse always has someone nearby with whom to peer-counsel. It is difficult because it hurts to hear the anger or disappointment of one's mate without being able to yell back or explain oneself.

Therapists can help by communicating attitudes and beliefs about feeling-expression; for example, that expressing emotion fully fosters loving feelings, and that it is important to be aware of, attentive to, and interested in one's mate and to let this interest be clearly visible. Obvious though these attitudes may be, they are frequently ignored. Focusing on

[2]See Chapter 7 for a detailed discussion of peer-counseling.

them creates a strong, good feeling within the couple and helps them to develop a sense of being a minicommunity. The therapists must also convey some ground rules about how strong emotion should be expressed and what should be avoided. With this sense of community, the couple can leave therapy and carry with them powerful tools for tending the garden of their love.

SUMMARY

We believe full feeling expression strengthens the emotional bond between mates. When therapists create the conditions for members of a couple to risk expressing their feelings to each other in a fresh way, rigid patterns of relating are broken up. This allows the members of the couple to learn new, more satisfying ways of behaving.

This chapter describes various methods that help clients mobilize and express feelings they have held back and it suggests other ways of moving clients out of unproductive habits of relating.

REFERENCES

Ables, Billie S. and Brandsma, J. M. *Therapy for Couples.* San Francisco: Jossey Bass, 1977.

Erickson, M. H. *Advanced Techniques of Hypnosis and Therapy: Selected Papers of Milton H. Erickson.* Ed. Jay Haley. New York: Grune and Stratton, 1967.

Erickson, M. H. and Rossi, E. L. *Hypnotherapy: An Exploratory Casebook.* New York: Wiley, 1979.

Haley, J. S. *Strategies of Psychotherapy.* New York: Grune and Stratton, 1963.

Kaplan, Helen S. *The New Sex Therapy.* New York: Brunner/Mazel, 1974.

Laws, Judith Long. *A Feminist View of Marital Adjustment In Couples in Conflict.* Gurman, A. S. and Rice, D. G. New York: Jason Aronson, 1974.

Lederer, W. J. and Jackson, D. D. *The Mirages of Marriage.* New York: Norton, 1968.

Masters, W. H. and Johnson, Virginia E. *Human Sexual Inadequacy.* Boston: Little Brown, 1970.

O'Connell, D.S. Symptom prescription in Psychotherapy. *Psyotherapy: Theory, Research and Practice,* 1983, 20, 12-20.

[1]In this chapter, we will use the terms "spouse," "mate," "partner," and "husband/wife" as free variants of each other. No distinction is intended among these terms; nor is marriage necessarily implied.

PART III
SPECIAL ISSUES

9

Training Therapists to Work More Effectively with Feelings

> "There is this place the tears have unlocked that is endlessly rich, a spring."
>
> John Updike
> *Rabbit is Rich*

This chapter is intended as a practical guide for therapists who want to work more skillfully and comfortably with feelings. It contains suggestions for becoming more aware of feelings, more fluent at expressing them, and more adept at helping clients to integrate feeling-expression with other therapy tasks.

These skills usually are acquired in an apprenticeship where a learning therapist works closely with a teaching therapist and has frequent opportunities for observation, modeling, and dialogue. In this chapter, we suggest some things therapists can do, largely on their own, to expand their abilities to deal with feeling-expression. This is no substitute for the hands-on experience described above, but it is a place to start.

There are a number of ways that therapists can become more comfortable with feeling-expression. They range from brief, casual exercises to long-term psychotherapy. Many require the involvement of other people, although some can be done alone. Our intention is to present a wide enough range of possibilities so that each reader will find some compatible ways to become more adept at eliciting feeling-expression.

BECOMING MORE AWARE OF FEELINGS

There are a series of exercises that can increase one's awareness of feelings. Many involve noticing more clearly the quickly changing inner landscapes of feelings and moods that we move through constantly. Unfortunately, as children, most of us were trained not to notice these feelings. The exercises that follow provide ways to reverse that training and become subtler, more accurate observers of our own inner processes.

The No-Radio Trip to Work

Many people have more privacy in their cars than anywhere else. It can be pleasant to spend that time listening to music or to the news. Turning the radio off, however, makes available another opportunity—a chance to talk to ourselves about whatever we are feeling. Try it next time you drive by yourself. Have a conversation with yourself. Make yourself talk out loud about feelings and be sure to say whatever comes to mind without censoring or avoiding. As the feeling builds, go with it. It could begin like this:

> Let's see, what do I feel today? Geez, this sounds funny. I wonder if people in the other cars can see me talking. If somebody I knew saw me, I'd feel like a jerk. . . . Shit, I don't feel like going to work today. I gotta tell Gill the bad news and he's gonna be mad.

In addition to talking and becoming aware of feelings, it is also important to exaggerate feelings. Most of us tend to play down our emotions and show less feeling than we really have. This exercise is more useful when people push themselves to make their feelings dramatic—even stronger than they feel. If you feel a little frightened, say that you are terrified. If you are only annoyed, say that you are furious. If you feel blah, find it hard to talk, and feel a little depressed, then look for something you are angry at even if you do not feel it. Push yourself and let the feeling build. The freedom to shout is one of the facilitating aspects of working in a car and has led one client to suggest that the term "expressway" derives from this source. Next time you drive, try some feeling-expressway therapy!

Art as a Teacher

Artists, in whatever medium, often transform their personal experience—their feelings and pain—into a form that is available to others. As you watch TV, read books, and see movies you have feelings about the people and events being depicted. Music and paintings can have the same effect. For some people, these are the only stimuli that allow them to cry. They are defended against their feelings in a way that makes them unable to cry about the hurts in their own lives that would otherwise elicit sad feelings. For these people, more distant dramatic presentations are especially helpful as a doorway to their feelings. But all of us can benefit from our responses to these stimuli.

Remember what makes you cry in such stories or songs and see what common threads are present. There may be a phrase that repeatedly triggers a feeling. Or you may think of something you would like to say to comfort or confront one of the characters. As you remember and write down these feeling episodes, you will get a clearer and clearer picture of exactly what elements are needed to elicit the feeling. You may find, for example, that kindness elicits sadness only when exhibited by a strong person toward a weak one, or by a mother to a son. The more you observe these connections, the more you can pinpoint what lets you feel sadness, joy, anger, and fear. These gradually forming, increasingly detailed connections form the raw material for the next exercise.

A Trip Down Memory Lane

Having established the existence of these very specific connections between interpersonal stimuli and emotional responses, you can now try to figure out why one song makes you cry and another makes your husband cry. We all have different histories and different current life circumstances. Both contribute to our varying individual responses. Someone going through a divorce or custody fight is likely to respond more to "Kramer versus Kramer" than someone who is not. The impact of these current life circumstances, however, is usually quite evident and does not require much digging to uncover. Less apparent is the contribution made by early history. Often, even when a specific emotional response to a certain theme is very clear, the early memory or conflict remains obscure. At such times, we can increase our self-awareness by a trip down memory lane.

One way to do this is by the free-associative recital of childhood memories related to the theme or feeling being examined. This can be done alone or with a friend, but it should be vocalized even if no one else is there to hear. As much as possible, memories should be brought forth as they come to mind without being screened out by filters such as, ' Are you sure that really happened?" or "Don't complain so much!" It is even useful to make up memories about what might have happened. This can lead to real memories and can clarify wishes and fears.

Another way to explore these connections is by talking with parents, older siblings, or others who were around when you were young. Ask them questions about what your childhood was like. What you hear may not necessarily be factually accurate, but it is the viewpoint of one participant. Even the distortions are interesting and meaningful.

The point of all this exploring and remembering is to come to a better understanding of your unique makeup—how and why you respond as you do, and why you cry when they play *September Song* and someone else does not.

LEARNING TO PEER-COUNSEL

One of the best ways to become more feelingful is to peer-counsel. It provides a forum to explore and express feelings and gives a facsimile of the experience of being a client for those who have not been in therapy. Although peer-counseling is more easily learned from another person than from a book, we can help you get started.

First, arrange things so that you feel safe with your peer-counselor. Find someone you like and respect, and meet in a private place where you can comfortably make noise. Agree to maintain strict confidentiality so that each of you can say what is on your mind without having to worry about whether your secrets are safe.

The counselor's job is mostly to listen. Simply having another person listen attentively without interrupting is a rare and enlivening experience for most people. Feelings tend to follow naturally. At times, the counselor may inquire what something felt like, may reflect the client's feelings, or may ask what would frighten, please, or anger the client. Mostly, however, the counselor's job is to listen.

The client's job is to talk about what comes to mind, especially feelings, and to push gently toward fuller-than-usual feeling-expression. Like any skill, feeling-expression is learned largely through practice. To feel more, one has to express more. At times, the client's efforts may seem wooden or may embarrass the client. That is to be expected. The client must not let self-consciousness become a stumbling block.

Another potential difficulty concerns feelings between peer-counselors. Whether affectionate, angry, or fearful, it is usually best for the client to state and explore her/his feelings toward the counselor. The counselor should encourage feeling-expression within the limits she/he can tolerate and should not try to be a hero, listening to more of the client's feelings than is comfortable. The purpose of this discussion depends on the skill and maturity of the peer-counselors. Those who are not experienced generally should aim toward simple emotional ventilation; they should recognize that much of the feeling does not really spring from the current relationship but from early ones that are recalled by this relationship. More experienced pairs can go further, examining the feelings toward both counselor and parents in a thorough, intense, detailed way, as would be done in therapy.[1]

PERSONAL THERAPY

We believe that anyone who works as a therapist should also experience therapy as a client. There are several sources of gain. One, of course, is the chance to overcome neurotic or characterologic problems. In addition, being a client deepens a therapist's understanding of what clients experience during treatment. The sense of dependency, the attribution of magical powers to the therapist, the radical shifts in perception of the therapist (e.g., from good to bad, from strong to weak)—all these are part of a client's experience. A therapist who has not experienced them is less able to empathize with clients. Finally, almost any therapy provides an opportunity to explore feelings. While many therapists do not encourage high levels of catharsis, most encourage at least a conversational level of feeling exploration. Thus, personal therapy is a useful way to get to know yourself better.

The next question concerns where to get therapy. We believe that, other things being equal, therapists who work actively with feeling-expression will increase your comfort and fluency with feelings more than will traditional therapists. Other things are not always equal, however. Also important is your perception of the therapist's power, competence, and credibility. It is crucial to work with a therapist you trust and respect personally and professionally, regardless of therapeutic orientation. Such a therapist can provide the safety necessary for deep personal exploration and therapeutic regression. It is also important to choose a therapist distant enough from your own circle of friends and associates that you can feel free to confide even your most private thoughts. Be sure to work with a therapist who can give you as much distance as you need between your therapy and your everyday life.

Finally, plow into your therapy aggressively! Commit yourself to it! Don't worry about how you appear to your therapist. Say what is on your mind even if it embarrasses you.

---

[1] See Chapter 7.

WORKSHOPS

As mentioned earlier, workshops can create a community that very powerfully supports feeling-expression.[2] At the right workshop, participants can learn a great deal about intense levels of feeling in a very short time. Unfortunately, the intensity generated in a workshop is sometimes used by leaders to proselytize their particular point of view rather than to liberate and teach the participants about themselves. Choosing good workshops is therefore an area where *caveat emptor* is especially apt. Many brochures, even those promoting worthwhile workshops, are written like carnival snake-oil pitches. They imply that attendance at the workshop will not only strengthen mind and body, but in all likelihood will clean your garage as well. Sorting through these workshops is much easier if you have friends who have attended them and who can tell you how it was for them. Also, some workshop leaders have written books or articles, or have affiliations with institutions, which can help you to make a preliminary judgment about whether they are likely to run good workshops. Most current cathartic therapies are presented in workshop formats.[3] So are gestalt and psychomotor therapy, both of which contain significant cathartic elements.

The rationale for attending a workshop is to get away from familiar frames of reference and become immersed in a cathartic experience for a significant period of time. This allows time to break down barriers to feeling and provides an opportunity to see others express their feelings fully. You may leave the workshop feeling euphoric and then notice the euphoria gradually dissipate. This is to be expected. Neither the high nor the loss of it has much to do with the real value of the workshop. The important gains from such a workshop are greater comfort with your own and other people's intense feeling-expression, and deeper understanding of how feelings are connected to each other and to personal change.

Even among workshops that emphasize feelings, there are several orientations. Some emphasize body work, some focus on current feelings, and still others stress early feelings. Some are more cognitively oriented than others. Sample several such workshops and take from each what works for you.

The main value of a workshop is the opportunity it provides for immersion in a cathartic system within a supportive community that facilitates feeling-expression.

---

[2] See Chapter 7.
[3] See Chapter 2 for a review of these therapies.

SUPERVISION

So far this chapter has focused primarily on how a therapist not familiar with cathartic approaches can become increasingly fluent and comfortable with intense feeling-expression. Difficult as that may seem, it is in fact, the easy part. The hard part is integrating feeling with thinking and behavior change, and monitoring countertransference feelings so that they do not interfere with clients' progress. We have spoken about these issues in earlier chapters, but getting beyond an intellectual understanding of them to mastery in therapeutic practice requires personal supervision.

First, it is important to realize that supervision does not have to be a one-way process. Peers can provide supervision to each other. Also, supervisory meetings need not occur weekly. Occasional, or even once-only, supervision can be helpful. If you do not live near someone you want supervision from, you may be able to travel to another city for occasional supervisory visits. You may even be able to mail therapy tapes back and forth to a colleague and give each other taped comments about the sessions.

If you do not have a supervisor with whom you are pleased, look around your city for the best therapists by reputation or the therapists whom you think have the most to teach you. Ask them if they want to swap supervision with you or if you can buy supervisory time from them. Since there are important advantages to having supervision in a small group, you might get two or three other therapists to join you in hiring a supervisor or in forming a group of peer supervisors. It is important to be relentless in your search for good supervision and not to let pride, money, or fear interfere with your pursuit of the best possible supervision.

To paraphrase an old milk commercial, "You never outgrow your need for supervision." Bad habits and inattention grow on even the most experienced therapists. It is often remarkable how different one's memory of a session is from the audio or video tape. The therapist often listens to the tape and says, "I didn't realize how angry I was," or "That dead section is a lot longer than I thought," or "Boy! It sounds like I'm doing all the work!"

There are three main foci of supervision: (1) theory and technique, (2) the client, and (3) the therapist. By far the trickiest of these is the therapist. A therapist working alone without supervision can partially offset this handicap by extensive reading and sheer brain power in relation to theory and technique and to the client's dynamics, goals, and needs. It is very hard, however, to supervise your own countertransference. Your feelings toward clients can powerfully affect what you do without you even suspecting their presence. To get help with this part of supervision, you need someone else to listen to your sessions and ask hard questions. It is important that you feel comfortable being open with this person; ideally, the person should know you well. A lot of time can be saved by looking for trouble first in the most obvious place—where you have had trouble before.

Example

The following example occurred at a supervisory meeting at the Center and shows how a therapist's feelings toward a client can impede progress and also how they can be untangled.

Melissa was a therapist who wanted help with a client she was seeing, and the others—Harry, Jean, and Sam—were therapists in her supervisory group.

Melissa: I'm having some trouble with Jake Robbins. It doesn't seem like he's working well. He had a great session about . . . oh . . . a month ago, it must be now. He was able to picture his mother really clearly when he was little and just cried and cried. He said goodbye—the whole thing—perfect session, and he hasn't done anything since!

Harry: He got scared, huh?

Melissa: That's what I figured at first. The next week he didn't feel anything. We talked about how that went, how good sessions were often followed by dead ones, we talked about whether he was scared, etc. But . . . I don't know . . . that might be what was happening then but I don't think it explains the last couple of weeks. I've done everything I can think of to get him going and he just won't give. Last week I called him the Great Stone Face and he just grunted. He won't do anything!

Jean: You sound pissed at him.

Melissa: I guess I am.

Jean: You know why?

Melissa: (Laughing.) You mean other than that he's being an impossible pain in the ass who refuses to get better?

Jean: Yeah. Something a little more personal.

Melissa: (Thoughtful.) I don't know. (Pause.)

Sam: What about that "Great Stone Face" part? You seemed to have a lot of feeling about that phrase.

Melissa: Well, I don't know . . . I do see my father somewhat that way. (She lights up now and looks at Harry, with whom she often peer-counsels.) You remember that? Mount Rushmore? Geez, I'd forgotten about that. (Turning to the group, talking fast.) I was working a while ago with Harry on how cold my father was, how stolid and stony he was. And I remembered going to Mount Rushmore on vacation when we were kids and looking at my father and then at the heads of the presidents on the mountain and thinking to myself, "He's just like them. He just stands there." (Reflective now) Uh-huh, . . . that's right. Poor old Jake has been getting some shit he doesn't deserve.

Jean: Jake could have been shut down the first day 'cause of his fear and then subsequently as a response to pressure from you.

Melissa: That's right.

Jean: It's amazing how sensitive clients are to your need. If the message is, "It's fine with me for you to feel," it's great for them. If it's, "I need you to feel," that takes the safety away. (Melissa nods.) I felt it vaguely the other day. Bill said he'd peer-counsel with me and first I said "yes," and then I didn't know if I had time, and I went back and forth, and he said real casually, "If you want to, I'd be happy to work with you. If you don't, that's okay, too. We can do something else if you want." That easy permission got me out of any sense of having to, and so I worked and had a great session.

Melissa: That makes a lot of sense. I'm sure I've been making him feel pressured. . . . Thanks.

Harry: You're welcome. You have anything else you want to say about Jake?

Melissa: I don't think so. I've got plenty to think about. . . . I feel better about him.

At this point, the group went on to other matters. In succeeding weeks, Melissa reported that her work with Jake was back on track.

In this particular instance, Melissa's countertransference feelings were particularly focused and clear. Typically, a more complicated web of feelings is involved and it is resolved more gradually than in this case. The principle is the same, however; the therapist's feelings toward the client are composed partly of unresolved childhood hurts and needs, and those sometimes interfere significantly with therapeutic progress. A trusted colleague or supervisor is usually needed to help the therapist sort out these complicated feelings.

A different kind of countertransference deals with characterologic issues. Each therapist has certain personality features that cause characteristic difficulties in therapy. Some are too passive, some too critical, and some too casual to work effectively. It usually does not take long to discover where a therapist's Achilles heel is, but it often takes considerably more time to change it. In supervision at the Center, we identify these chronic issues and suggest ways to work against them. However, supervision does not deal with the extensive personal therapeutic work that therapists must do to overcome the roots of these characterologic blindnesses. That is the work of peer-counseling and personal psychotherapy.

SUMMARY

In this chapter, we described ways to become more aware of feelings, more comfortable with expressing them, and wiser about how early family history affects present emotional responses. We described how peer-counseling, personal therapy, and workshops can help therapists to know and express their own feelings better, as well as to gain an understanding of the experience of being a client. We pointed out the importance of supervision in helping therapists to integrate feeling-expression with the other aspects of therapy. We underlined the importance of supervision in helping therapists to grapple with their own countertransference feelings and we suggested ways of finding useful supervision.

The suggestions we made in this chapter for increasing therapists' comfort with feelings and facility at eliciting feeling-expression from clients are no substitute for case-by-case supervision, but we hope they provide a useful start.

10

Research on Feeling-Expressive Psychotherapy

> The split between researcher and therapist is . . . endemic to the entire field of psychotherapy.
>
> Erich Coché & Robert R. Dies

Nothing as important as psychotherapy should be entered into, practiced, or taught uncritically. Clients invest their time, money and hopes; and therapists invest their professional lives in the belief that psychotherapy can bring about significant personal change. But does it?

To date, although there is an extensive body of research about psychotherapy, it does not clearly answer the most frequently asked questions (Bergin & Garfield, 1971; Bergin & Lambert, 1978; Strupp, 1978). There is hardly any evidence that one school of therapy yields better results than any other (Bergin & Lambert, 1978), that individual therapy is more or less effective than group therapy (Meltzoff & Kornreich, 1970), or even that the training and experience of the therapist is related to positive outcomes (Auerbach & Johnson, 1977; Parloff, Waskow & Wolfe, 1978). By far the largest number of predictors of successful outcome deal with client factors; relatively few deal with therapist or treatment variables (Garfield, 1978; Luborsky, Chandler, Auerbach, Cohen & Bachrach, 1971). Unfortunately, these findings are likely to have little impact on practice, since they can be summed up as saying: "Good clients get better."

Psychotherapy is an extraordinarily complex process. Each of its components—patient, therapist, treatment, and outcome—involves a network of interacting variables, such as age, sex, and intelligence, as well as subtle

235

factors, such as motivation, expectations, and attractiveness. Some researchers have responded to the Herculean task of controlling these various elements by throwing up their hands in despair; others have isolated one or two variables in experimental models, or analogues, of treatment. Although some have made a case for the relevance of analogue studies (e.g., Goldstein, Heller & Sechrest, 1966), we believe that research must capture some of the elements of therapy as it is practiced, if it is to have an impact on clinical practitioners.

CATHARSIS AS A THERAPEUTIC TOOL

Literature and Research

If the expression of powerful feelings is therapeutic, then one should be able to demonstrate it empirically and explain it with an adequate theoretical rationale. Unfortunately, neither the evidence nor the rationale is yet available. A recent exhaustive survey of the literature on catharsis (Nichols & Zax, 1977) produced such meager evidence that interpreting it, like a Rorschach blot, depends largely upon the predilections of the reviewer. Nichols and Zax (1977) examined eleven analogue studies of the effect of catharsis in therapylike situations. Seven of these supported the effectiveness of cathartic interventions (Dittes, 1957; Goldman-Eisler, 1956; Gordon, 1957; Haggard & Murray, 1942; Levison, Zax & Cowen, 1961; Martin, Lundy & Lewin, 1960; Ruesch & Prestwood, 1949); one did not support the effectiveness of catharsis (Keet, 1948); and three were ambiguous (Gordon, 1957; Grossman, 1952; Wiener, 1955).

Recently, Arthur Bohart has attempted to demonstrate the therapeutic effects of catharsis in laboratory analogues. In one study (Bohart, 1977), undergraduate volunteers were first asked to recall any incident that had made them angry. Next they were assigned to one of four "treatment" conditions: (1) a *control* group that merely recalled the physical details of the incident; (2) an *intellectual analysis* group that was helped "rationally to analyze the feelings, motives, and events associated with the incident"; (3) a *discharge* group that was instructed to pretend that the person who had angered them was seated with them and to express anger verbally; and (4) a *role-play* group that was told to express anger and then to switch chairs and respond as the person at whom the anger was directed.

Following the various "treatments," all subjects filled out self-report measures and then were given the opportunity to punish an (imaginary) subject in the next room who supposedly had made a mistake on a learning task. Of all the subjects, those in the role-play condition showed the greatest reduction in anger and hostile behavior. Bohart concluded that catharsis works best when combined with insight.

In a subsequent study (Bohart & Haskell, 1978) using a similar analogue paradigm, Bohart found that "catharsis" (hitting a pillow) was less effective than role-play or nondirective counseling in reducing anger. Bohart's data are unconvincing, because he neither used realistic problems nor got subjects to express feelings energetically. Yet his ideas about catharsis are interesting. Personality change, he suggests (Bohart, 1980), is a function of a dual cognitive-affective process. Expressing anger reduces angry feelings only if it leads to coping with the stimulus, i.e., changing the environment or one's perception of it. Bohart extends the same model to sadness. Although this model seems useful, it is not supported by Bohart's data. Bohart's conclusion that emotional expression *may* be therapeutic is contradicted by the data of his most recent study (Bohart & Haskell, 1978).

In fact, none of these analogue studies of catharsis were an adequate test. Experimental subjects lack the distress that motivates actual patients to change significant aspects of their behavior, and they may also lack the emotional blocks that make such changes difficult. Furthermore, it is extremely difficult to simulate techniques as powerful as those of cathartic psychotherapy in a brief laboratory study. No analogue studies of catharsis have produced the intense emotional discharge that occurs in feeling-expressive therapy and in other contemporary emotive therapies. At best, the analogue studies provide suggestive evidence that emotional catharsis leads to tension-reduction. But the power of sustained catharsis to produce behavior change has yet to be tested in the laboratory.

Another body of literature that bears on the effects of catharsis comes from the behavior therapists. Although behaviorists and emotivists seem unlikely bedfellows, they do share a number of things in common, including an interest in catharsis.

Ullmann and Krasner (1965) wrote that "interview-induced emotional responses, including abreaction and emotive imagery," are one of the nine basic procedures of successful behavior modification. Like emotive therapists, behaviorists emphasize the present, new experiences, and changes in behavior. While behaviorists are more interested in learning new responses in social situations, they have also been interested in cathartic expression and have amassed some tentative support for its power to change behavior.

Joseph Wolpe, one of the leading developers of behavior therapy, found catharsis, or abreaction, to be an effective ingredient in the treatment of a wide spectrum of neurotic disorders (e.g., Wolpe & Lazarus, 1966). Wolpe argues that abreaction achieves its effectiveness by reciprocal inhibition, or counterconditioning of anxiety, which he claims is the basis of any psychotherapy's effectiveness.

Notable among other behavior modifiers who have experimented with catharsis is Arnold Lazarus, who found emotive imagery an effective means of treating phobic children (Lazarus & Abramovitz, 1962) and depressed adults (Lazarus, 1968). Like Wolpe, Lazarus suggests that emotive imagery and the catharsis that follows help chiefly by disrupting anxiety, rather than by "getting out" feelings.

The only behavior therapist who has written of the direct therapeutic value of emotional release is Shoben (1960). Shoben found that catharsis is effective in therapy because it allows for the symbolic reinstatement of repressed cues for anxiety within the context of a permissive social relationship. He explained this effect in terms of counterconditioning, a process that entails reactivating traumatic responses in order to extinguish them through catharsis. Shoben found that catharsis provides emotional release, which leads to re-examination and reintegration of formerly traumatic experiences.

Stampfl's "implosive therapy" (Stampfl & Levis, 1973) is without doubt the most dramatically emotional of any treatment not designed specifically to produce catharsis. In theory, implosive therapy consists of extinguishing maladaptive avoidance responses by presenting conditioned stimuli with no reinforcement, no avoidance, and no escape. In practice, it is a highly evocative and expressive form of treatment. As clients are forcefully and repeatedly bombarded with vivid descriptions of their greatest fears and most painful fantasies, they shake with fear, rage, and weep uncontrollably. The most successful sessions are presumed to be the ones with maximum emotional response (Fazio, 1970; Hogan, 1968; Stampfl & Levis, 1973).

The effectiveness of implosive therapy is supported by a number of clinical reports of success (e.g., Hogan, 1968), and several controlled studies of outcome in clinical settings (e.g., Boudewyns & Wilson, 1972; Boulougouris, Marks, & Marset, 1971; Hogan, 1966; Levis & Carrera, 1967; Watson, Gaind & Marks, 1972). Although validation of implosive therapy is only indirect evidence of the effectiveness of catharsis, two studies support the contention that the effects of implosive treatment are due to nonspecific emotional arousal and expression, rather than to extinction of specific phobic images (Hodgson & Rachman, 1970; Watson & Marks, 1971).

Another indirect source of support for catharsis in psychotherapy is evidence from the client-centered tradition that intense emotional focusing characterizes effective sessions (e.g., Bierman, 1969; Gendlin, Beebe, Cassen, Klein & Oberlander, 1968; Howard, Orlinsky & Hill, 1970; Luborsky, Chandler, Auerbach, Cohen & Bachrach, 1971).

A final series of studies deriving from the feeling therapy group are suggestively positive, though they have some methodological problems. Three studies dealt with physiological changes and two with psychological changes. The first (Karle, Corriere & Hart, 1973) used EEG, blood pressure, pulse, and rectal temperature as measures of tension and found reduced levels immediately following primal therapy sessions. The second (Woldenberg et al., 1976) found clients had lower pulse, blood pressure, and rectal temperature following feeling therapy sessions. These changes were again interpreted as signs of reduced tension levels. A third study (Karle et al., 1976) showed that long-term feeling therapy clients had lower postsession blood pressure, pulse, and body temperature than did beginning clients, but neither group was able to maintain the lowered postsession tension level in a 10-day follow-up.

Other feeling therapy studies (Karle et al., 1978, and Karl et al., 1981) showed that long-term clients (up to 5 years in therapy) had better self-actualizing profiles on the Personality Orientation Inventory than did early-stage clients (up to one year in therapy). Although these studies are cross-sectional and make no definitive connection to catharsis, they do seem to show positive changes in clients who have had a great many cathartic experiences over a long period of time.

Catharsis is generally included in lists of the underlying curative factors common to all forms of therapy. For example, Rosenzweig (1936) and Frank (1971) described catharsis as one of the basic ingredients in psychotherapy. Similar claims have been made and supported by quasi-experimental research (e.g., Symonds, 1954).

Psychosomatic Disorders

It is widely believed that emotional suppression plays a major role in a variety of psychosomatic disorders. The combination of chronic emotional restraint and acute stress frequently is seen as playing a role in the etiology of migraine headaches, ulcers, asthma, colitis, arthritis, and hypertension (Lipowski, 1968). Since stress is difficult to predict or control, treatment often has been directed to the predisposing personality style of emotional constraint.

People who have difficulty expressing anger, assertive strivings, or sadness may be particularly prone to psychosomatic symptoms (Bastiaans, 1969; Gitelson, 1959; Groen, 1957). This is due in part to the fact that the autonomic nervous system, which is activated by psychological stress, remains activated for a prolonged period unless the stress is responded to with action and feeling. Instead of showing their feelings, people who develop psychosomatic disorders suffer their fate in silence to the detriment of their bodies.

If suppressed emotional expression is a major contributing factor in psychosomatic illness, then patients with this illness must learn to express their feelings. Therefore, cathartic psychotherapy is widely recommended. Bastiaans (1969) advocates cathartic discharge of feelings and has noted improvement in psychosomatic syndromes as soon as patients are able to discharge some of their inner tension through verbal and nonverbal expressions of feeling. After they achieve catharsis in psychotherapy, he works to help them express their feelings more freely in their daily lives.

It seems clear that emotive psychotherapy can be an important part of the treatment of psychosomatic disorders. Intense somatic-emotional expression can both release the tension of prolonged autonomic arousal and help to resolve the chronically restimulated pain arising from early life experiences. In this way, the psychosomatic patient can learn to respond to the frustrating aspects of daily life without excessive and inappropriate emotional arousal due to generalization from childhood experiences.

Social Psychological Studies

Social psychologists have studied the effects of catharsis on aggression and attitude change. Led by Berkowitz and Bandura, researchers in this field have demonstrated that a wide variety of experiences considered to be cathartic *increases*, rather than decreases, hostile behavior. For example, watching violence on television and playing aggressive games may teach children to be more, rather than less, violent. However, this research is not directly relevant to cathartic psychotherapy because indulging in or observing aggressive behavior is quite different from encouraging cognitive and somatic-emotional discharge of previous distressing experiences. Subjects in these social psychological experiments do not remember and cry about painful experiences in a therapeutic context. Instead, they punish, or watch others punish, real people who appear to be actually hurt. By contrast, the whole emphasis in cathartic therapy is that angry feelings may be recognized and expressed in a context quite removed from any direct confrontation with the instigator of those feelings. We make it clear to our clients that there is a distinction between:

1. Catharsis in a therapy session, which is emotive and expressive, and
2. Confrontation with people outside the therapy session, which is intended to change the other person's behavior or to improve the relationship with the person confronted.

We emphasize that these are different processes and that working on anger in a session is in no way a rehearsal for a real-life confrontation.

The more clearly clients grasp this distinction, the freer they feel to express their feelings fully in therapy. Far from fostering increased hostility, such procedures are likely to run the opposite risk: encouraging patients not to discuss their annoyance with those who anger them. Berkowitz's claim (1973) that "ventilationists" reward unrestricted aggression is simply false.

Although studies of attitude change seem to support catharsis, again, a very limited definition of catharsis is employed. Here, catharsis means allowing subjects to verbalize beliefs that run counter to those that the experimenter is attempting to instill. The idea is that if a listener is first given a chance to express his or her point of view, then he or she may be less preoccupied by it and therefore more receptive to the speaker's arguments. Even when this process is intensely emotional (e.g., Lewin, 1964; Frank & Nash, 1965), it differs from remembering and expressing feelings about important life interactions as a means of better handling such interactions in the future.

Conclusion

The research findings relevant to cathartic therapy are suggestive, but permit few definitive conclusions. In examining both indirect and anecdotal evidence, we found a tendency to support the utility of catharsis as a vehicle for behavior change. This evidence suggests that cathartic therapists need to make explicit the distinction between cathartic discharge in therapy and social behavior outside therapy. If this distinction is blurred, clients might either be unwittingly encouraged to act on their hostile fantasies outside of therapy, or become preoccupied with ventilation in therapy to the exclusion of working out constructive ways of expressing feelings in everyday life. Either of these unhappy possibilities represents a loss of the needed balance between feeling-expression and real-life behavior change.

THREE TYPES OF THERAPEUTIC CHANGE

Empirical answers to the question "What constitutes psychotherapeutic change?" are operationally defined by the measures of outcome selected by researchers. Ideally, measures of outcome should be both rigorous—valid and accurate—and meaningful—relevant to the important dimensions of change.

Several reviewers of psychotherapy research have pointed out that change is multifactorial (e.g., Bergin & Strupp, 1972; Kiesler, 1966), and others have suggested various categories of therapeutic change. We believe that there are three types of therapeutic change: (1) resolution of symptoms or behavioral change, (2) increased happiness or satisfaction, and (3) inner or characterological change.

An unfortunate side effect of Freud's concern with fundamental personality change is a tendency among some therapists to forget that, in addition to other goals, resolution of presenting problems is also important. This happens as therapists translate their clients' goals into theoretical goals, and is exacerbated by a tendency to view therapy as a vague process without a clear rationale or purpose. For example, a therapist may decide that the "real problem" in a family seeking help for a child who is failing in school is poor communication. If the therapist succeeds in helping the family to communicate better, but the child's school performance does not improve, then she/he has failed them in a very important respect.

The second type of change in psychotherapy is increased satisfaction or happiness. This change is the most important from the point of view of the consumer, the client. Unhappiness is the real reason for entering treatment, and without some measure of relief, therapy is not successful. Unhappiness may center around a focal complaint, but resolution of the presenting complaint may occur without relieving the unhappiness. A college student may enter therapy distressed about failing grades, but if the poor grades reflect an unrecognized but powerful disinclination to be in school at all, then therapy that helps to bring up the grades may result in less, rather than more, happiness. Treatment may resolve the symptom while failing the client.

Unfortunately, increased happiness is difficult to evaluate and frequently is transitory. Direct replies to inquiry may be complicated by wishes to terminate treatment or to please the therapist, who may have been more friendly than helpful. "Yes, I feel better" may mean "I don't want to remain in treatment" or "I want to thank the therapist for being such a nice person."

An even greater problem is that happiness and satisfaction tend to fluctuate, and changes may be transitory. This problem is particularly acute with emotionally expressive therapies. For example, many people experience a tremendous emotional exhilaration following participation in a weekend encounter group, only to have their high spirits fade as they return to their daily lives essentially unchanged by what was a moving, but not a profoundly therapeutic, experience. Ventilating feelings usually, though not always, feels good; whether or not it leads to lasting increases in satisfaction with living is more difficult to determine.

Lasting changes in satisfaction can be distinguished from transitory changes by asking clients to describe the satisfaction they derive from several areas of their experience. Evaluating satisfaction at several different times, including some time after therapy has been concluded, is also helpful. Furthermore, a sensitive interviewer can help clients to describe their genuine satisfaction, as opposed to apparent satisfaction presented in order to conclude therapy or praise the therapist.

The third aspect of successful therapy, characterological change, is the most difficult to measure. Furthermore, although it ultimately may predict long-lasting satisfaction, it is often of more concern to the therapist than to the client. In fact, it is quite common for a client to experience symptomatic improvement and increased satisfaction from brief supportive therapy while the therapist feels that not much has been accomplished.

In our work, applying and evaluating feeling-expressive therapy, we are concerned with all three categories of change. As therapists, we tend to view presenting problems as related to chronic and rigid defenses. Many of the problems that are brought to us turn out to be part of a pattern of avoidance of feelings, impulses, and experiences. Typically, we communicate this point of view to new clients and attempt to engage them in relatively long-term reconstructive therapy. In some cases, however, initial problems do not seem to be based on characterological maladjustment; here therapy tends to be brief and not to include personality change as a goal. Even when focusing on basic personality change, we do not lose sight of the fact that character change must be manifested in behavioral change and feelings of well-being. As researchers, we have chosen outcome criteria that reflect all three types of therapeutic change.

THE ROCHESTER PROJECT

Since we began developing and practicing feeling-expressive therapy, we have been concerned with evaluating its effectiveness. First, we wanted to know if feeling-expressive therapy worked. Second, we wanted to know with whom it worked best. Finally, we were interested in examining the relationship between the amount of emotional expression and the therapy outcome.

In planning our research, we were determined to study psychotherapy *as it is actually practiced*, even if doing so meant more work and loss of some experimental control. Thus, we only used real clients, and we limited our evaluations to the work of experienced practitioners. After all, the worth of a particular treatment should not be measured on the basis of how effective it is in the hands of beginners.

We also decided to study the actual dialogues of therapy (as recommended by Mahrer, 1979). Instead of relying on post-hoc reports of what transpired in treatment hours, we recorded and reviewed actual sessions to determine what techniques therapists use to increase feeling, and to measure how much emotional expression occurs in feeling-expressive therapy.

In our first study, we compared the effectiveness of feeling-expressive therapy with traditional dynamic psychotherapy, and we evaluated the effect of catharsis on change in brief psychotherapy. In our second study, we studied the impact of length of sessions and interval between sessions on therapy process and outcome. In our third study, we analyzed the success of feeling-expressive therapy with long-term private patients. Since our methodology was similar in all of our studies, we shall describe our general approach first, and the procedure and results of each of the separate studies second.

Outcome measures were chosen to reflect the perspectives of the client, the therapist, and an outside observer; they tapped all three kinds of therapeutic change (i.e., in behavioral, personal satisfaction, and characterological).

Measures

Improvement was measured by change scores on the Minnesota Multiphasic Personality Inventory (MMPI), Personal Orientation Inventory (POI), Feeling Scale, Personal Satisfaction Form (PSF), and with the Behavioral Target Complaints Form (Goals), and therapists' ratings.

The MMPI scales D (Depression), Pt (Psychasthenia), and Sc (Schizophrenia) are widely accepted as some of the most valid measures of subjective distress and psychopathology, and they have been shown to reflect change in psychotherapy (Bergin & Strupp, 1972). In our project, we summed the scores on all three scales to provide a single self-report index of distress and psychopathology.

The POI is a self-report questionnaire similar to the MMPI, but with an emphasis on positive adjustment, or self-actualization. Only the scores deemed most relevant to improvement in psychotherapy—Time Competent (TC) (living in the present, with full awareness) and Inner Directed (ID) (independent and self-supporting)—were analyzed for this project.

In addition to seeking goals common to all forms of psychotherapy, most approaches try to foster some change that is relatively specific. Just as psychoanalysts prize insight, we hope to produce greater acceptance and expression of feelings. Therefore, we devised a new paper-and-pencil test, the Feeling Scale, to assess changes in receptivity to, and expression of, feelings.

The PSF and Goals, measures of client satisfaction and behavioral change, respectively, were derived from independent ratings of semistructured interviews. For the PSF, clients were asked to describe their subjective experience of satisfaction, citing specific examples, in eight areas of life (e.g., work, love, intimate relationships). The actual scores were produced by an independent rater. The validity of the PSF as a measure of adjustment had been established in previous studies (e.g., Nichols, 1975).

Each client set goals and, in consultation with the therapist, operationalized these goals in order to assure their reliable evaluation later. Therapists checked at regular intervals to see if new goals had emerged. Then, at 6-month intervals and termination, client and therapist discussed the degree of success in achieving goals. Scores for goals were produced by an independent rater using a procedure validated earlier by Battle et al. (1966).

The final measure of outcome was a rating by the therapist of the patient's improvement, using a scale from 1 (much worse) to 5 (much improved).

Clients were described according to age, sex, diagnosis, and defensive style. By listening to tape recordings of initial sessions, an independent clinical psychologist determined a diagnosis and defensive style for each subject. Defensive styles were adapted from Shapiro's categories (1965), and included an obsessive and an hysterical style. The obsessive style is characterized by the use of intellect to avoid feelings. Obsessive people are orderly and controlled, tend to be rigid, and use sharply focused concentration, especially on details. In contrast, the hysterical style is displayed in impressionistic thinking and feeling; cognitions are global and diffuse, and there is a tendency to respond readily with feeling, but feelings tend to be shallow and quixotic.

Diagnoses were made on the basis of major categories in the Diagnostic and Statistical Manual of the American Psychiatric Association (DSM-II, 1968). Treatment sessions were tape-recorded and rated by an independent observer to measure: the amount of emotional catharsis, the number and types of techniques used, and the percentage of time spent on recent and past material. In order to quantify emotional catharsis, we operationally defined it as audible sounds of crying, laughing, or angry shouting. Although other types of expression may have a cathartic effect (e.g., talking with feeling), we limited our estimate to plainly audible sounds that are reliable manifestations of strong feeling. Recent events were defined as those occurring within one year of the session.

Procedure

Our general procedure in these studies was designed to provide as rigorous a test of therapy outcome as possible without interfering with the course of treatment as it is actually practiced.

Following their initial therapeutic contact, clients were asked to volunteer to serve as subjects in our studies. The procedure was explained and clients were assured that their participation was optional. Those who chose to participate (and almost all did) were then tested and interviewed. Tape recordings were made of the first four sessions and once a month thereafter. Testing and structured interviews were readministered at 6-month intervals and at termination.

The First Rochester Study

In our first study (Nichols, 1974), we evaluated the effectiveness of feeling-expressive therapy by comparing its results to those of traditional, dynamic psychotherapy. In addition, we explored the effectiveness of our techniques in producing catharsis, and the relationship between the amount of catharsis and the degree of improvement.

Method

Forty-three clients (30 men, 13 women), ranging in age from 17 to 28 years (median = 20), volunteered to participate in this study. The subjects were sufficiently heterogeneous to make this sample comparable to the populations of many mental health clinics and private practice groups. Diagnoses included: psychosis, neurosis, personality disorder, transient situational reactions, psychophysiological reactions, sexual dysfunctions, and "not warranting psychiatric diagnosis."

The reliability of diagnosis and defensive style judgments was assessed by comparison to a sample of eight sets of duplicate ratings made independently by two advanced clinical psychology graduate students. Percentage-of-agreement scores for the three pairs of raters on diagnosis were 50%, 67%, and 84%. For defensive style, the figures were 84%, 84%, and 100%.

The two treatment groups were evenly balanced on all client variables, as well as on pretherapy criterion measures, as can be seen in Table 10-1. By using the *t* test and *chi-square* tests, we ascertained that there were no significant ($p < .10$) differences on any of these variables prior to therapy. Clients were assigned randomly to one of six therapists and to either feeling therapy or dynamic therapy.

The six therapists had from three to ten years' experience. All had been trained in both dynamic and feeling therapy and therefore were able to practice each form of treatment with alternate clients. Every session was tape-recorded and rated to determine the specific techniques used and to measure the amount of catharsis produced. At the termination of therapy, the structured interviews were repeated and the questionnaires readministered.

Results

ANALYSES BASED ON ASSIGNMENT TO TREATMENT GROUPS

Differences between treatment groups were analyzed with a one-way analysis of variance. However, when variances of treatment groups were significantly heterogeneous (based on Cochran's test), the Mann-Whitney *U* Test was employed. Means and standard deviations, as well as the appropriate tests of significance, appear in Table 10-2.

These analyses indicated significant differences on the three major process variables. First, there were significantly more seconds of emotional discharge (mean seconds over all sessions, as well as the number of seconds in the peak session) in feeling-expressive therapy. Furthermore, therapists used significantly more emotive techniques in the feeling-expressive condition. Of the measures, the PSF was the only one on which the feeling therapy group showed directionally greater improvement ($p < .10$). The dynamic therapy group changed significantly more on the MMPI. This result was contrary to prediction, but may have been a by-product of increased self-disclosure or sensitization in the feeling-expressive group.

Table 10-1
Description of Treatment Groups on Matching Variables

		Treatment Group	
Variable		*Feeling*	*Dynamic*
Age	Mean	21.14	20.52
	SD	2.17	2.86
Pre-treatment MMPI	Mean	86.50	92.95
	SD	19.02	22.98
Pre-Treatment			
Personal Satisfaction	Mean	25.64	26.24
	SD	6.79	5.91
Number of Sessions	Mean	9.09	8.65
	SD	3.95	4.36
Number of Males		16	14
Number of Females		6	7
Diagnosis	Psychotic	0	1
	Neurotic	12	9
	Personality Disorder	2	4
	Transient Situational React.	6	3
	Psychophysiological Reaction	0	0
	Specific Sexual Symptoms	0	1
	Not Warranted	2	3
Defensive Style	Obsessive	19	13
	Hysterical	3	8

Note: SD = Standard Deviation.

This interpretation was evaluated by subjecting the decrement in MMPI K scale (social desirability) scores to a t test. The difference was highly significant ($t = 12.79$, $df = 34$, $p < .001$) and suggested that the feeling-expressive group became more open and self-disclosing.

ANALYSES OF HIGH AND LOW DISCHARGERS

Statistical analysis of the data revealed that the feeling-expressive group had a significantly higher mean number of seconds of discharge than did the dynamic therapy group. However, this statistical difference was accounted for by the contribution of certain subjects with extremely high discharge. In fact, some subjects in the feeling expressive condition discharged relatively little. Therefore, a more sensitive test of the therapeutic value of catharsis was obtained when, as planned, the sample was divided into two extreme groups (thirds) of high and low dischargers.

As would be expected, high dischargers had significantly higher peak discharge sessions, and their therapists used significantly more emotive techniques to generate these high levels of discharge. Table 10-3 shows that the high dischargers improved significantly more on the Goals (Behavioral Target Complaints Form) and showed a directional trend toward greater improvement on the PSF. It should be noted that the Goals was the only operationally defined behavioral measure of improvement.

PROCESS MEASURES AND THEIR RELATION TO OUTCOME

As expected, the correlations among mean and peak discharge, as well as number of emotive techniques, were all highly significant ($p < .01$). In addition, the number of sessions of psychotherapy was highly corre-

Table 10-2
Means, Standard Deviations, and Significance Tests for All Measures Across Treatment Groups

Measures	Feeling Group M	SD	Dynamic Group M	SD	Significance Test (a) F	U
Change MMPI	4.722	13.877	15.611	25.617	—	102.500(c)
Change Satisfaction	6.857	2.988	4.571	4.354	3.934(b)(	—
Change Goals	3.789	0.508	3.658	0.488	c)	—
Mean Seconds					< 1(b)	146.500(d)
Discharge	143.180	194.541	27.695	21.886		
Peak Seconds					—	148.00(d)
Discharge	399.273	508.087	80.191	95.199		
Mean No. of Emotive					—	59.00(d)
Techniques	12.219	11.059	2.334	2.409		
					—	

Notes: (a) Mann-Whitney U Tests were employed where variances were significantly different, as measured by Cochran's test for homogeneity of variance; (b) $df = \frac{1}{41}$; (c) $p < .10$; (d) $p < .05$. M = Mean. SD = Standard Deviation.

lated with both peak discharge and mean number of emotive techniques ($p < .01$).

Correlations between mean discharge and change in both the PSF and Goals scores were statistically significant ($p < .05$). Also significant was the correlation between peak discharge and Goals. These findings partially confirmed the major hypothesis of this study, namely, that catharsis leads to improvement in brief psychotherapy.

PRELIMINARY FOLLOW-UP DATA

The mean change from termination to follow-up on the PSF was 1.36 for the feeling-expressive therapy group and $-.18$ for the dynamic therapy group ($t = 2.92$, $df = 16$, $p < .01$). The feeling-expressive group improved directionally more on the Goals', with a mean of .23, as compared with 0.00 for the dynamic therapy group, but this change was not significant ($t = 1$, $df = 16$, N.S.). The Behavioral Target Complaints Form apparently represented goals that either were or were not achieved by the completion of therapy, whereas the sense of personal satisfaction could continue to increase following therapy.

Discussion

The results of our first study clearly demonstrated the power of feeling-expressive therapy to generate high levels of emotional expression. Recording and scoring the techniques used in every session made it possible to determine that it was the use of emotive techniques per se, rather than assignment to treatment groups, that produced catharsis.

Perhaps the most stringent test of improvement in this investigation was the Behavioral Target Complaints Form. That high-discharge clients

Table 10-3
Means, Standard Deviations, and Significance Tests on All Measures Across High and Low Dischargers

Measures	High Dischargers M	SD	Low Dischargers M	SD	Significance Test (a) F	U
Change MMPI	−9.308	13.313	−13.167	28.032	—	74.500
Change Satisfaction	7.357	3.319	5.077	4.462	2.293(c)	—
Change Behav. Goals	4.018	0.465	3.614	0.555	4.233(c)(	—
Mean Discharge	224.506	205.142	7.461	4.372	e)	0.000(e)
Peak Discharge	642.214	503.710	24.643	22.592	—	1.000(e)
Mean Number of Emotive Techniques	16.029	11.960	3.924	4.113	—	21.000(e)

Notes: (a) Mann-Whitney U Tests were employed where variances were significantly different, as measured by Cochran's test for homogeneity of variance; (b) $df = /24$; (c) $df = /26$; (d) $p < .10$; (e) $p < .05$. M = Mean .SD = Standard Deviation.

changed significantly more on this measure provided partial confirmation of the value of catharsis. Furthermore, the amount of emotional discharge was highly correlated with change on the Personal Satisfaction Form. As the latter test measures subjective experience over a wide variety of areas of living, its positive correlation with catharsis is most relevant to the patients' aspirations.

Three factors may have contributed to the lack of significant differential improvement on the MMPI for feeling expressive therapy clients. First, the time between initial testing and re-testing may have been too short for much systematic change to have been reflected on the MMPI. Second, the range of pathology for patients in this study was relatively constricted; most had only moderate pathology. Many patients' pretherapy MMPI scores were not even pathological and therefore change might have been unlikely or undesirable for them. Finally, emotive psychotherapy focuses on overcoming defensiveness and opening patients to dysphoric thoughts and feelings. In contrast, traditional brief psychotherapy is often supportive and may serve to reassure clients about some of their more troublesome feelings. The feeling expressive group may have become more honest and perceptive, rather than more troubled. This hypothesis was supported by the finding of significantly greater reduction on the K score (social desirability) for the feeling-expressive patients.

The Second Rochester Study

Therapists typically meet with their clients once a week for 45 or 50 minutes (Small, 1971). But some have suggested that longer sessions may be advantageous in cathartic treatment to overcome the resistance most people have to expressing strong feelings (e.g., Hart, Corriere & Binder, 1975). The little systematic research done on the effects of varying session length has been inconclusive (Small, 1971). Similarly, the evidence that meeting either more or less than once a week leads to better outcome is also questionable (Lorr, 1962; Meltzoff & Kornreich, 1970). Thus, we were interested in finding out if frequency and duration of meetings had any effect on the amount of catharsis produced or on the outcome of therapy.

Method

Subjects were assigned randomly to groups that were seen twice a week for half an hour, once a week for one hour, or once every other week for two hours (Bierenbaum, Nichols & Schwartz, 1976). Each therapist was assigned clients alternately in the different conditions. All clients were seen in one-hour sessions for initial and final evaluation interviews, and for approximately nine hours of therapy sessions.

Percentage-of-agreement scores for ratings of defensive style were 72%, 80%, and 93%. For diagnosis, the percentage-of-agreement scores were 53%, 53%, and 60%. Ratings of amount of catharsis were highly correlated ($r = .96$, $p < .01$), as were frequencies of emotive techniques ($r = .98$, $p < .01$). Reliability for PSF scores was high ($r = .97$, $p < .01$), as was reliability on Goals scores ($r = .79$, $p < .01$).

As shown in Table 10-4, there were no significant pretherapy differences among the three groups on any of the measures.

Table 10-4
Description of Combined Samples on Matching Variables

	LENGTH OF SESSION		
	½ Hour	Hour	Hours
Variable	(13)	(12)	(16)
Age			
M	20.62	21.67	21.38
SD	1.44	2.19	2.60
Hours			
M	7.92	9.83	8.75
SD	1.40	3.09	2.04
Sex			
Male	7	8	8
Female	6	4	8
Diagnosis			
Psychotic	—	—	—
Neurotic	6	5	9
Personality disorder	3	1	1
Transient situational	4	4	4
Not warranted	—	2	2
Defensive style			
Obsessive	8	9	12
Hysterical	5	3	4
Pre-treatment MMPI			
M	92.69	89.50	84.69
SD	26.02	15.30	16.73
Pre-treatment Personal Satisfaction			
M	28.62	27.25	30.75
SD	6.17	7.14	6.46

Note: Numbers in parentheses are number of cases. M = Mean. SD = Standard Deviation.

Results

EFFECTS OF SESSION LENGTH ON CATHARSIS

As shown in Tables 10-5 and 10-6, a main effect of session length on catharsis was observed: $F(2,32) = 4.18$, $p < .05$. These results favored the one-hour condition, with a significant difference ($p < .05$) between the one-hour and half-hour conditions.

ANALYSIS OF THE USE OF EMOTIVE TECHNIQUES

Therapists differed in their use of emotive techniques: $F(2,32) = 24.09$, $p < .01$. The same therapist who produced the most catharsis was

Table 10-5
Means and Standard Deviations for All Measures For All Treatment Groups

	LENGTH OF SESSION		
	½ Hour	1 Hour	2 Hours
Measure	(13)	(12)	(16)
Catharsis sec/hr			
M	76.85	220.17	133.44
SD	58.78	222.16	151.75
Catharsis log transformation			
M	1.80	2.09	1.79
SD	.27	.64	.54
Emotive techniques per hour			
M	13.46	14.42	12.79
SD	10.99	8.62	12.46
Change in MMPI			
M	− 16.85	− 7.80	− 5.59
SD	12.08	11.54	10.89
Change in goals			
M	3.85	4.05	3.92
SD	.31	.46	.35
Change in personal satisfaction			
M	3.23	7.75	2.75
SD	4.51	3.05	3.30

Notes: Numbers in parentheses are numbers of cases. M = Mean. SD = Standard Deviation.

also the most active in using emotive techniques ($p < .05$). Furthermore, significantly different amounts of emotional catharsis were produced in the different treatment conditions. The latter differences were related to the time frames themselves, rather than to changes in the therapists' behavior within treatment conditions.

Consistent with findings in the first study, a significant positive correlation was found between the frequency of use of emotive techniques and the amount of emotional catharsis produced ($r = .55$, $p < .01$).

Table 10-6
Summary Table for Treatments by Therapists Analyses on Catharsis, Emotive Techniques, and Three Measures of Outcome

Source		SS(d)	df(e)	MS(f)	F(g)
		Catharsis			
Treatments	(A)	1.85	2	.92	4.18(b)
Therapists	(B)	1.78	2	.89	4.04(b)
A by B		1.33	4	.33	1.50
Within cell		7.07	32	.22	
		Emotive Techniques			
Treatments	(A)	13.18	2	6.59	.12
Therapists	(B)	2,686.64	2	1,343.32	24.09(c)
A by B		91.26	4	22.82	.41
Within cell		1,784.72	32	55.77	
		MMPI Change			
Treatments	(A)	759.48	2	379.74	2.89(a)
Therapists	(B)	538.07	2	269.04	2.05
A by B		192.10	4	48.03	.36
Within cell		3,543.32	27	131.23	
		Goals Improvement			
Treatments	(A)	.71	2	.35	3.09(a)
Therapists	(B)	.29	2	.19	1.69
A by B		1.05	4	.26	2.27
Within cell		3.07	32	.11	
		Personal Satisfaction Change			
Treatments	(A)	211.23	2	105.62	7.72(c)
Therapists	(B)	54.86	2	27.43	2.01
A by B		16.66	4	4.16	.30
Within cell		437.69	32	13.68	

Notes: (a) $p < .10$; (b) $p < .05$; (c) $p < .01$; (d) sum of squares; (e) degrees of freedom; (f) mean squares; (g) F test.

RELATION OF INDEPENDENT VARIABLES TO OUTCOME

Although no differences were found between therapists on any of the measures of outcome (Table 10-6), a significant treatment effect that favored the one-hour group was observed for PSF scores: $F(2,32) = 5.91$, $p < .01$. For this measure, the mean for the one-hour group was significantly different from the means for both the half-hour and two-hour groups ($p < .05$). Further, the one-hour group tended to improve more on Goals ($F(2,32) = 3.09$, $p < .10$), although none of the pairwise comparisons were significant. Finally, clients in the half-hour condition tended to improve more on the MMPI scales: $F(2,27) = 2.89$, $p < .10$. The difference between the half-hour and two-hour groups on this measure was significant ($p < .05$).

Clients seen in the one-hour condition experienced the most catharsis and showed the most improvement on two measures of outcome, with high dischargers showing the greatest improvement. The half-hour condition produced the least catharsis, with more catharsis being negatively associated with change in personal satisfaction. However, this condition was the most conducive to the relief of subjective distress, as reflected in MMPI scores, irrespective of the amount of catharsis produced. Finally, although the two-hour group fell between the other two in terms of amount of emotional catharsis produced, this group showed less improvement than either of the other two.

Discussion

The results of this study support the contention that emotional catharsis leads to improvement in brief emotive psychotherapy. Patients in the one-hour condition, who as a group evidenced the most catharsis, also showed the most improvement in personal satisfaction and behavioral goals, with high dischargers in that group improving the most. On the other hand, for the two-hour group, the amount of emotional catharsis was not significantly related to outcome. High and low dischargers in this group did not differ on any of the measures of outcome and, overall, this group showed less improvement than the other two. Meeting for half an hour twice a week seemed least conducive to the production of emotional catharsis and, for this group, amount of emotional catharsis was negatively related to change in personal satisfaction.

Hence, although emotional catharsis was clearly beneficial for those seen in the one-hour condition, such was not the case for the other two groups. Since the therapists' activity level did not change among conditions, it seems that the time frame itself impeded the production of emotional catharsis and reduced its potential to improve outcome.

For clients in the two-hour condition, the two-week interval between sessions probably detracted from the treatment's continuity and supportiveness. A certain amount of security in terms of frequency of meeting seems to be a prerequisite for the exploration of deeply felt emotions. It could well be that the effect of more frequent two-hour sessions would be more catharsis and better outcomes.

Less catharsis was produced in the half-hour group than in the other two. Perhaps trying to explore deeply felt emotions in only a half hour is too frustrating. One might surmise that treatment in this time frame was more supportive in nature, allowing the patient to "seal over" feelings of distress while delving less into problematic emotions. Meeting for a half hour twice a week does not seem to be a good way to conduct confrontative, emotive psychotherapy.

An anxiety-provoking approach to brief therapy is recommended by several authors (e.g., Bellak & Small, 1965; Sifneos, 1972) for clients who have the integrative capacities to handle the therapists' confrontations. The current findings suggest that, within the context of emotive psychotherapy, the best way to pursue such an approach is to meet for at least an hour, probably once a week or more, and to engage the client actively in the direct expression of suppressed affects relevant to the present difficulty.

The Third Rochester Study

Our third study (Nichols & Bierenbaum, 1978) was an attempt to evaluate the differential effectiveness of feeling-expressive therapy with different types of clients. By combining data from our previous studies of short-term therapy, we were able to examine a sufficient number of cases to begin to answer the question, "With whom does our therapy work best?"

Among the most prevalent criticisms of cathartic therapy are (1) that only those people who cry anyway will do so in this treatment, and (2) that only people suffering from a recent trauma are liable to profit from this treatment. Specifically, it is widely believed that women and persons with an hysterical cognitive style are most likely to cry in any psychotherapy, and that people with transient situational reactions are the only ones apt to profit from emotive treatment.

This opinion may indeed be accurate in reference to traditional psychotherapy, in which catharsis only occurs after emotionally upsetting events and then only in people who are not particularly defended against feelings. However, in feeling-expressive therapy, we use powerful techniques to disrupt even long-standing and firmly held defenses. Therefore, in undertaking our third study, we wanted to test the hypothesis that our treatment would be most effective with those for whom feelings *do not* come easily.

Method
The total sample consisted of 42 clients (28 men, 14 women), who ranged in age from 17 to 28 years (mean = 21.22 years). In addition to age and sex, clients were described by diagnosis and defensive style. Percentage-of-agreement for pairs of ratings of defensive style were 72%, 80%, 84%, 93%, and 100%. For diagnosis, the percentage-of-agreement scores were 50%, 53%, 60%, 67%, and 84%.

Measures of catharsis for each of 20 sessions, times independently by two raters, were highly correlated ($r = .96$, $p < .01$). Reliability of ratings on the PSF, which was assessed by independent ratings of 15 subjects by two graduate students, was found to be quite high ($r = .97$, $p < .01$). The reliability of improvement ratings was cross-checked on a sample of 21 subjects by an independent clinical psychologist and was found to be satisfactory ($r = 79$, $p < .01$).

The three participating therapists were all medical school faculty members on the clinic staff. One was a female psychiatrist with four years of postresidency experience and two were male psychologists with five and eleven years of experience. Clients were seen for an average of 8.80 hours of therapy (SD = 2.14).

Results
Table 10-7 summarizes the frequencies of various descriptive categories for the clients in this study. Thirty had obsessive defensive styles while 12 had hysterical styles. In terms of diagnosis, there were 21 neurotics, 5 personality disorders, 12 transient situational reactions, and 4 without mental disorder.

Each of three client characteristics—sex, diagnosis, and defensive style—was analyzed statistically to determine its effect on the amount of catharsis and on the three measures of outcome.

There was no significant difference between men and women on amount of catharsis ($t = .89$, $df = 40$, $p > .25$). Surprisingly, obsessives generated more catharsis than did hysterics ($t = 2.33$, $df = 40$, $p < .05$), and those diagnosed as without mental disorder produced significantly more catharsis than did any other diagnostic category ($t = 2.06$, $df = 40$, $p < .05$).

Neither sex nor defensive style had any significant effect on any of the measures of outcome (all p values $> .25$). Those diagnosed as having personality disorder, most of whom were obsessive-compulsive, improved more than all other categories on the MMPI ($t = 2.58$, $df = 40$, $p < .05$) and the PSF ($F = 2.20$, $df = 40$, $p < .05$). Most of the clients made substantial progress in achieving their behavioral goals; there were no group-related differences on this measure.

Discussion

These results tend to disconfirm the stereotypes that hysterics and women cry most easily in cathartic therapy. Perhaps hysterics, by virtue of their affective liability, and women, by virtue of cultural acceptance of their crying, cry more readily in daily life. But the data in this study suggest that obsessives are able to maintain a focus on unhappy experiences and are therefore able to generate more emotional discharge in brief cathartic therapy. Furthermore, any social differences between men and women with regard to affective expression seem to disappear when this kind of expression is explicitly encouraged in treatment.

The findings also challenge the notion that cathartic treatment is most useful for transient distresses and least useful for characterological problems. We suggest that cathartic therapy was particularly beneficial for clients with personality disorders because cathartic ventilation is an effective means of disrupting long-held, rigid defenses against emotional experience and expression.

Table 10-7
Description of Client Characteristics

	Frequencies
Sex	
Men	28
Women	14
Diagnosis	
Psychotic	0
Neurotic	21
Personality Disorder	5
Transient Situational Reaction	12
Psychophysiological Reaction	0
Sexual Dysfunction	0
Not Warranted	4
Defensive Style	
Obsessive	30
Hysterical	12

The Fourth Rochester Study

Our fourth study examined the results of long-term feeling-expressive therapy. We were interested to learn if long-term therapy produced significantly more change than brief treatment, and we hoped to discover something about the types of people who profit most from feeling-expressive therapy.

Our previous studies demonstrated the effectiveness of our approach in brief psychotherapy. This was not surprising since most clinicians already accept the usefulness of catharsis for dealing with an acute upset or specific trauma (e.g., Watkins, 1978). Indeed, it may be that any active involvement with clients will help them to make short-term improvements.

Definitive change in long-term treatment is much more difficult to achieve, and few would concede that catharsis is useful as the primary vehicle for long-term, reconstructive therapy. Symptomatic improvement and behavior change are far easier to achieve than personality change. Personality reconstruction occurs in only about 40% of long-term psychotherapy patients. (Bergin & Garfield, 1971; Meltzoff & Kornreich, 1970).

"Long-term psychotherapy" is not simply longer than brief psychotherapy, although some critics make this claim (e.g., Rohrbaugh, personal communication). Instead, long-term (definitive, reconstructive, or uncovering) psychotherapy is aimed at lasting character change. Although a similar process may be begun in short-term psychotherapy, definitive personality change generally requires prolonged treatment. Achieving such change is a complex process that involves resolving resistances; reducing mechanisms of defense; uncovering unconscious thoughts, feelings, and impulses; examining feelings about the therapist; and thoroughly reexamining material from the past.

The subjects of this fourth study were a typical sampling of clients who seek private psychotherapy. They ranged in age from 19 to 50 years (mean = 34); 56% were women, and 44% were men. Of the total (N = 97),11% were diagnosed as psychotic, 13% as neurotic, 37% as personality disorders, 11% as transient situational reactions, and 18% as not warranting psychiatric diagnosis. The diagnostic tapes of seven clients were inaudible. An obsessive defensive style was found in 73% of the subjects while 27% were described as having hysterical defenses. Percentage of agreement on diagnosis was 80%; on defensive style, it was 90%. Data on marital status were available for 94 of the subjects: 47% were married, 35% were single, 15% were separated, 2% were divorced, and 1% were widowed.

Four members of the Center staff served as therapists for this study.

Two were men, two were women, and all were experienced practitioners of feeling-expressive therapy (an average of 7.25 years of clinical practice). Reliability of ratings of catharsis was quite high ($r = .93$, $df = 8$, $p < .01$; $r = .87$, $df = 7$, $p < .01$; $r = .99$, $df = 9$, $p < .01$). Reliability of scorings of "percent recent" (how much time was spent on material from the last year rather than on early memories) were also found to be quite high ($r = .81$, $df = 8$, $p < .01$; $r = .86$, $df = 7$, $p < .01$; $r = .93$, $df = 9$, $p < .01$). For the PSF, reliability was indicated by an interjudge correlation of .74 ($df = 10$, $p < .01$); the rating for Goals was .85 ($df = 23$, $p < .01$).

Results

The findings of this study fall into two categories: the general effects of long-term feeling-expressive therapy, and the differential impact of our treatment on various types of clients. Evaluating the general effects of our procedure was possible by comparing the findings on this long-term sample with those of the short-term feeling and dynamic approaches used on previous samples collected under like conditions. Specifically, we were able to compare the average amount of catharsis generated and the magnitude of therapeutic change in long-term feeling-expressive therapy, brief dynamic therapy, and brief feeling-expressive therapy.

The average amount of catharsis generated in the present long-term study was 418.30 seconds per session. This means that patients averaged about 7 minutes of (primarily) crying per session. There was quite a bit of variability, however, with 8 patients averaging 30 seconds or less per session, and 9 averaging 900 seconds (15 minutes) or more per session. One patient averaged 1847 seconds (over 30 minutes) of crying per session.

The average of approximately 7 minutes of catharsis per session in this study is significantly more than the approximately 30 seconds generated in brief dynamic therapy, or the approximately 2 minutes generated in two samples of brief feeling-expressive therapy. Table 10-8 displays these data.

Table 10-9 displays comparisons between mean change scores for those measures common to this sample and previous samples. Clients tended to change substantially more in long-term feeling-expressive therapy than in either of the brief therapies.

Next we analyzed the differential effectiveness of long-term feeling-expressive therapy with different types of clients. Means and standard deviations of average amount of catharsis by gender, diagnosis, and defensive style are displayed in Table 10-10. The table also shows the correlation between age and amount of catharsis. Women discharged significantly more than men, and hysterics discharged more than obsessives. Although contrary to our findings in the short term studies, neither of

Table 10-8
Comparison of Mean Number of Seconds of Catharsis Long-Term Feeling Therapy versus Brief Dynamic and Brief Feeling Therapy

	Brief Dynamic	vs.	Long-Term Feeling	
Mean	27.66		418.30	$t = 81.37$
SD	21.88		361.50	$df = 98$
				$p < .01$

	Brief Feeling Study #1	vs.	Long-Term Feeling	
Mean	143.18		418.30	$t = 48.43$
SD	194.54		361.50	$df = 99$
				$p < .01$

	Brief Feeling Study #2	vs.	Long-Term Feeling	
				$t = 65.86$
Mean	108.07		418.30	$df = 106$
SD	110.07		361.50	$p < .01$

Note: SD = Standard Deviation.

Table 10-10
Amount of Catharsis for Different Types of Clients

	Women	vs.	Men	
Mean	566.23		219.39	$t = 66.32$
SD	349.81		196.93	$df = 81$
				$p < .01$

	Hysterics	vs.	Obsessives	
Mean	517.66		382.32	$t = 19.75$
SD	419.84		304.93	$df = 77$
				$p < .01$

	Psychotics	Neurotics	Personality Disorders	Trans. Sit. Reactions	Not Warranted
Mean	194.16	419.84	392.84	411.31	548.64
SD	101.72	323.43	404.81	257.16	300.84

	Not Warranted	vs.	Other Diagnoses	
Mean	548.64		382.55	$t = 24.14$
SD	300.84		332.21	$df = 77$
				$p < .01$

	Psychotics	vs.	Other Diagnoses	
Mean	194.16		436.71	$t = 27.07$
SD	101.72		343.85	$df = 77$
				$p < .01$

Correlation of Age and Amount of Catharsis
$$r = -.08$$
$$df = 44$$
NS

Notes: SD = Standard Deviation. NS = Not Significant.

Table 10-9
Comparison of Mean Change Scores Long-Term Feeling Therapy versus Brief Dynamic and Brief Feeling Therapy

	Brief Dynamic	vs.	Long-Term Feeling	
MMPI				$t = 2.03$
Mean	15.61		11.68	$df = 42$
SD	25.61		15.49	$p < .05$
PSF				$t = 4.32$
Mean	4.57		8.46	$df = 45$
SD	4.35		5.24	$p < .01$
Goals				$t = 2.21$
Mean	3.65		4.27	$df = 47$
SD	.48		.52	$p < .01$
	Brief Feeling Study #1	vs.	Long-Term Feeling	
MMPI				$t = 4.32$
Mean	4.72		11.68	$df = 43$
SD	13.87		15.49	$p < .01$
PSF				$t = 1.94$
Mean	6.85		8.46	$df = 46$
SD	2.98		5.24	$p < .10$
Goals				$t = 1.75$
Mean	3.78		4.27	$df = 48$
SD	.50		.52	$p < .10$
	Brief Feeling Study #2	vs.	Long-Term Feeling	
POI				
ID				$t = 6.85$
Mean	5.12		13.61	$df = 45$
SD	6.85		11.38	$p < .01$
TC				$t = 2.36$
Mean	4.62		2.30	$df = 45$
SD	7.82		3.50	$p < .05$
MMPI				$t = .73$
Mean	10.63		11.68	$df = 50$
SD	11.42		15.49	N.S.
PSF				$t = 6.79$
Mean	2.96		8.46	$df = 53$
SD	3.84		5.24	$p < .01$
Goals				$t = 1.77$
Mean	3.88		4.27	$df = 55$
SD	.33		.52	$p < .10$

Note: SD = Standard Deviation.

these findings is surprising; what is of greater interest is how much men and obsessives *improved* in relation to the other groups. As could be expected, those not warranting diagnosis (normals) discharged more, and psychotics less, than did other diagnostic groups. Age was not significantly correlated with amount of catharsis.

Improvement scores were analyzed at 6 months and again at termination. At 6 months, there were few differences in improvement scores between men and women, as Table 10-11 shows. Only on the MMPI was there a significant difference between genders, and that showed greater improvement by women. Table 10-12 shows the same improvement scores

Table 10-11
Comparison of Improvement Scores Women versus Men at 6 Months

	Women	Men	
MMPI			
Mean	11.00	1.00	$t = 4.44$
SD	18.87	17.31	$df = 19$
			$p < .01$
POI			
TC			
Mean	1.57	.18	$t = 1.43$
SD	3.71	2.96	$df = 20$
			NS
ID			
Mean	7.72	5.55	$t = 1.34$
SD	10.95	10.68	$df = 41$
			NS
Feeling Scale			
Mean	1.67	1.64	$t = .04$
SD	2.67	1.80	$df = 30$
			NS
PSF			
Mean	6.50	5.00	$t = 1.27$
SD	6.31	3.74	$df = 29$
			NS
Goals			
Mean	4.11	3.92	$t = .63$
SD	.37	.37	$df = 32$
			NS

Notes: SD = Standard Deviation. NS = Not Significant.

plus therapist's rating for men and women at termination. Here women improved more than men on four of seven measures.

Tables 10-13 and 10-14 display improvement scores at 6 months and termination for clients with hysterical and obsessive cognitive styles. Hysterics improved significantly more on the MMPI at both points and

Table 10-12
Comparison of Improvement Scores Women versus Men at Termination

	Women	Men	
MMPI			
Mean	21.09	2.10	$t = 8.71$
SD	14.77	10.03	$df = 19$
			$p < .01$
POI			
TC			
Mean	3.61	.75	$t = 2.67$
SD	4.07	1.58	$df = 19$
			$p < .05$
ID			
Mean	18.00	9.70	$t = 4.41$
SD	13.31	6.07	$df = 20$
			$p < .01$
Feeling Scale			
Mean	2.85	2.50	$t = .41$
SD	2.41	1.78	$df = 21$
			NS
PSF			
Mean	10.47	5.55	$t = 3.75$
SD	3.31	7.66	$df = 24$
			$p < .01$
Goals			
Mean	4.42	4.06	$t = .97$
SD	.35	.64	$df = 26$
			NS
Therapist's Rating			
Mean	3.88	3.75	$t = .54$
SD	.67	.67	$df = 91$
			NS

Notes: SD = Standard Deviation. NS = Not Significant.

on the POI & PSF at 6 months. It is worth noting that the greater improvement for hysterics is shown primarily on self-rating data (e.g., MMPI and POI) and may reflect real changes or may be partly an artifact of an hysterical tendency to exaggerate self-descriptions.

Next, we examined outcome as a function of diagnosis. Table 10-15 shows outcome scores at 6 months for the different diagnostic categories. By 6 months, there emerged a tendency for neurotics to show greater improvement than the other diagnostic categories (neurotics showed first, second, or third greatest improvement on all measures). When scores for the neurotic group were compared with scores of all other groups com-

Table 10-13
Comparison of Improvement Scores
Hysterics versus Obsessives at 6 Months

	Hysterics	*Obsessives*	
MMPI			
Mean	14.28	5.59	$t = 3.89$
SD	15.55	10.94	$df = 27$
			$p < .01$
POI			
TC			
Mean	2.14	1.00	$t = 1.04$
SD	2.85	3.52	$df = 27$
			NS
ID			
Mean	18.28	7.23	$t = 4.09$
SD	26.07	12.61	$df = 27$
			$p < .01$
Feeling Scale			
Mean	1.14	1.91	$t = .79$
SD	2.60	2.46	$df = 27$
			NS
PSF			
Mean	9.00	5.12	$t = 2.58$
SD	5.89	5.06	$df = 29$
			$p < .05$
Goals			
Mean	4.00	4.01	$t = .03$
SD	.33	.36	$df = 30$
			NS

Note: SD = Standard Deviation. NS = Not Significant.

bined, they showed significantly greater improvement in the MMPI ($p < .01$) and the Feeling Scale ($p < .05$). The group not warranting psychiatric diagnosis (normals) also did well, showing greatest improvement on 3 of 6 measures, two of which were statistically significant (PSF: $p < .01$). At termination, neurotics and those not warranting diagnosis

Table 10-14
Comparison of Improvement Scores
Hysterics versus Obsessives at Termination

	Hysterics	Obsessives	
MMPI			
Mean	19.50	8.05	$t = 3.71$
SD	·17.71	13.01	$df = 19$
			$p < .01$
POI			
TC			
Mean	3.25	2.17	$t = .69$
SD	4.50	3.45	$df = 19$
			NS
ID			
Mean	10.74	13.17	$t = 1.04$
SD	4.92	12.65	$df = 19$
			NS
Feeling Scale			
Mean	1.75	3.00	$t = 1.14$
SD	1.70	2.29	$df = 19$
			NS
PSF			
Mean	10.0	7.79	$t = 1.58$
SD	3.21	6.69	$df = 24$
			NS
Goals			
Mean	4.30	4.26	$t = .09$
SD	.33	.58	$df = 25$
			NS
Therapist's Rating			
Mean	3.72	3.90	$t = .62$
SD	.76	.65	$df = 81$
			NS

Notes: SD = Standard Deviation. NS = Not Significant.

again tended to improve most. The neurotic groups improved more than all others on the Time Competent scale of the POI, the Feeling Scale, the PSF, and the Therapist's Rating, although only one of these measures was statistically significant (TC, POI, $p < .01$). The group not warranting diagnosis showed either first or second greatest improvement on all measures except the Feeling scale where it was third. None of these differences reached statistically significant magnitude.

Table 10-15
Comparison of Improvement Scores for Different Diagnostic Categories at 6 Months

	Psychotic	Neurotic	Personality Disorder	Trans. Sit. Reaction	Not Warranted
MMPI					
Mean	15.00	19.25	4.66	11.00	3.87
SD	0.00	31.91	16.26	7.43	2.45
POI TC					
Mean	1.00	1.75	1.83	−1.00	1.37
SD	0.00	4.42	3.32	1.82	3.77
ID					
Mean	9.00	8.75	4.83	6.75	11.00
SD	0.00	9.10	9.83	10.71	14.90
Feeling Scale					
Mean	0.00	4.00	1.50	1.50	1.25
SD	0.00	2.94	2.54	2.38	2.12
PSF					
Mean	—	7.33	3.92	4.33	10.16
SD		3.66	5.31	3.82	6.24
Goals					
Mean	—	4.09	3.80	4.14	4.16
SD		.41	.27	2.03	.43

Note: SD = Standard Deviation.

Table 10-17 shows the correlation between age and change on all of our measures, both at six months and termination. Although only two of those correlation coefficients are statistically significant, there is a clear trend for age to be negatively correlated with change. On 12 of 14 measures older clients showed somewhat less change.

Comparison of Improvement Scores for Different Diagnostic Groups at Termination

	Psychotic	Neurotic	Personality Disorder	Trans. Sit. Reaction	Not Warranted
MMPI					
Mean	15.00	11.00	7.42	10.33	12.00
SD	0.007	26.96	12.21	5.68	16.12
POI TC					
Mean	1.00	2.00	2.85	1.00	2.85
SD	0.007	3.60	4.14	1.00	4.33
ID					
Mean	9.00	11.00	13.42	9.33	14.71
SD	0.007	7.93	14.71	11.50	12.07
Feeling Scale					
Mean	0.007	4.00	3.14	1.33	2.85
SD	0.007	3.60	1.77	2.08	2.03
PSF					
Mean	4.00	10.20	8.18	6.80	9.75
SD	0.007	6.41	5.63	8.22	5.31
Goals					
Mean	4.33	4.14	4.24	4.16	4.55
SD	0.007	.44	.38	.97	.39
Therapist Rating					
Mean	3.16	4.14	3.86	3.70	3.94
SD	0.40	.53	.68	.67	.74

Note: SD = Standard Deviation.

Table 10-17
Correlation of Age with Improvement Scores

At 6 Months

MMPI	r = −.12	NS
POI		
TC	r = −.28	NS
ID	r = −.03	NS
Feeling Scale	r = −.25	NS
PSF	r = .15	NS
Goals	r = .01	NS
Therapist Rating	r = −.25	NS

At Termination

MMPI	r = −.06	NS
POI		
TC	r = −.32	p < .05
ID	r = −.11	NS
Feeling Scale	r = −.12	NS
PSF	r = −.13	NS
Goals	r = −.29	p < .05
Therapist's Rating	r = −.20	NS

Note: NS = Not Significant.

Discussion

Statistical analysis of this complex and extensive collection of data has yielded some clear and some suggestive findings. First, the results clearly demonstrate that feeling-expressive therapy is effective in generating high levels of emotional catharsis. Second, the findings show that our treatment leads to significant improvement in all three dimensions of personal change: symptoms, satisfaction, and character structure.

The results demonstrate that ours is an effective form of treatment for a wide variety of patients. When it comes to discerning which types of people show the greatest benefit, the results are less clear, but some patterns begin to emerge. Women do generate significantly higher levels of catharsis than men over the course of long-term therapy. On average, women discharged for approximately 10 minutes per session, compared with 4 minutes for men. Although we previously found that women do not cry more than men in brief cathartic therapy—men *do* cry when given permission and encouragement—apparently the sex role differences in emotional expressivity enable women to sustain more catharsis over a prolonged period.

If women cry more in feeling-expressive therapy, do they change more than men? In the short run, probably not; in the long run, they do. At six months, women showed significantly greater improvement on only one of six measures of change. Apparently, although women may express feelings more easily than men, men gain equally in the first six months of an expressive therapy. By termination, however, women began to show greater improvement than men. Four of our seven measures of change showed greater progress for women. This finding is consistent with anecdotal reports of more change for women in a wide variety of psychotherapies. The high levels of improvement for men as well as women in feeling-expressive therapy suggest that we are effective with both sexes, but that women tend to improve more in any type of psychotherapy.

Clients with an hysterical style experienced more catharsis (approximately 8 minutes per session) than did those with an obsessive style (about 6 minutes per session). Like men, obsessives seem to generate high levels of catharsis when given the encouragement in a cathartic therapy. In brief treatment, obsessives cry as much as hysterics, but over a longer period of time, habitual defensive styles *do* show a difference and hysterics are able to cry more consistently.

For obsessives, feeling-expressive therapy involves going against a lifelong pattern of emotional inhibition. Is this an effective therapy for them because it opens new channels of expression, or is it inappropriate because it is too difficult for obsessives to express feelings? The results (Tables 10-13 and 10-14) show that obsessives do gain significantly in feeling-expressive therapy. Their change scores are quite high compared with findings on similar measures in our studies of short term therapy (Table 10-9). Furthermore, they improved about as much as hysterics, especially by termination.

Our findings suggest that emotive therapy may be more of a challenge for obsessives than are more cognitive treatments, but that they do benefit significantly from learning to express feelings. This notion is further supported by the high change scores shown for obsessives on the Feeling Scale (Tables 10-13 and 10-14), which suggest that they become more feelingful people.

In terms of diagnosis, the pattern of results is least clear. This is due in part to the relatively small numbers in each of the diagnostic categories, which makes statistical differences hard to discover. The ability to express feelings, measured in terms of amount of catharsis per session, was related to the seriousness of psychopathology. Those at the normal end of the continuum cried the most; those at the psychotic end cried the least. Not surprisingly, psychopathology is related to defensiveness and estrangement from feelings.

No striking differences in improvement were found for any particular diagnostic group. In fact, all categories showed great improvement on a wide variety of measures. Even our psychotic clients benefited greatly from feeling-expressive therapy. These findings further support earlier findings that demonstrated that the benefits of cathartic therapy are not limited to transient situational reactions. Since we believe that catharsis helps people to become more feelingful, rather than to get rid of "bad," traumatic feelings, this is exactly what we would expect.

Although all diagnostic groups did well, there was a trend for neurotics to improve the most. We believe that this trend is significant for understanding the value of our treatment. There is a substantial group of people who use psychotherapy (as well as workshops and encounter groups) as a substitute for full participation in life, rather than as a means of achieving it. When we encounter these people in our practice, we find that their lack of anxious distress and clearly focused problems makes it difficult to work with them. They want to "be in" therapy more than they want to change in order to "be in" life. The finding that neurotic clients improve the most in feeling-expressive therapy bears out our clinical opinion that we do well with people who have significant and specific problems.

Our approach seems to be particularly effective with people who are depressed. This fact is obscured in the results of our studies because depression cuts across several diagnostic categories. Since depression is a disorder of affect and we work extensively with affect, it is not surprising that we are very successful with depressed clients, whether acute depression is the presenting complaint or chronic depression underlies other problems.

The depressed people we see usually are stuck, because they avoid significant feelings altogether or because they dwell fixedly on sadness and recrimination. When they do show feeling, it typically is limited to guilty sadness. Almost invariably, we discover unexpressed rage behind the guilt, and once we help to mobilize the forceful expression of this anger, significant improvement occurs.

Another problem we seem to be particularly successful with is trouble with intimacy. We see many people who respond to their anxiety by alternately getting overinvolved with, and fleeing from, other people. Because these people are motivated to affiliate with others, we are able to help them complete their relationships by recognizing and appropriately expressing the feelings mobilized by being close to other people.

The consistent, but weak, negative correlation of age with most improvement suggests that age *is* related to outcome, but perhaps not in a linear fashion. Our own subjective impression is that we are most effective with patients from about 30 to 45 years of age. Those under 30 are more likely to deal with their discomfort by seeking to change in their environment than by seeking to change themselves. As they get older and begin to see the limits of this solution, they become more interested in self-examination. After about age 45, people tend to become somewhat more cautious about making changes. By middle age, most people have erected fairly stable, although not necessarily satisfactory, life structures, and they are reluctant to alter them radically.

RELATIONSHIP BETWEEN CATHARSIS AND CHANGE

In previous studies of short-term cathartic therapy (e.g., Nichols, 1974), we found a strong correlation between the amount of catharsis and the extent of personal change. This suggests that improvement is a function of the amount of catharsis: the more the catharsis, the more the improvement. However, experience over a longer period of time has convinced us that this is not the case.

Expressing feelings is a major and probably essential cause of therapeutic change in our work. This is reflected in the positive correlation across subjects between catharsis and change. Those of our clients who do not learn to express feelings tend not to improve, while those who do express feelings do change. But it is not true that those who show the most catharsis show the most change. More significant than the amount of catharsis *per se* are: (1) expressing feelings that previously were avoided, conflict-laden, or unconscious; (2) having a cognitive connection to those feelings, and (3) becoming more expressive than previously.

To be truly cathartic, feeling-expression must involve some breaching of defenses. It is probably more therapeutic for an obsessive-compulsive man to discover and vent long-buried anger at his father, even relatively briefly, than for a chronically melancholic woman to cry for several minutes, week after week. The former catharsis involves a breakthrough; the latter does not. Furthermore, a person with rigid defenses and chronically restrained emotions probably benefits more from learning, in treatment, to laugh and cry than does an already expressive person. A client with hysterical defenses benefits most when the feelings are connected with a web of meaning and insight. Such changes are useful because they go against the grain of the client's usual defenses. Both our empirical and observational data show that patients motivated to change by neurotic (broadly defined) pain tend to benefit more than those people for whom emotive therapy and workshops are more a way of life than a treatment for problems. The latter may cry a lot, but they do not change much.

The occurrence (though not the amount) of catharsis also has an important impact on therapists. Because emotional expression is immediate and observable, it helps to keep therapists actively engaged in what they are doing, aware of progress in overcoming defenses, and empathically attuned to patients. It is far too easy for psychotherapists to lapse into a passive stance in which they listen to their clients, but do not intervene to produce change. However, by noticing the amount and quality of feelings that clients express, therapists have a ready guide that makes it hard to think that something is happening when it is not. A therapist who works with feelings knows that in the absence of catharsis, or when feeling-expression becomes stereotyped and mechanical, resistance is at work and must be grappled with before additional progress can occur.

SUMMARY

The literature is filled with studies of the effects of catharsis. Some are anecdotal, some are experimental, and they come out of social psychology and medicine, as well as clinical psychology and psychiatry. Unfortunately, few of these studies have a direct bearing on the effectiveness of catharsis as a psychotherapeutic tool. Those that do, suggest that cathartic feeling-expression is therapeutic, although for whom and under what circumstances are less clear.

Therefore, when we set out to evaluate the effectiveness of feeling-expressive therapy, we concentrated our attention on the role of catharsis, which is the central ingredient in our approach. In our early studies, we examined brief feeling-expressive therapy as practiced in a clinic setting. We demonstrated that our techniques *do* produce high levels of cathartic expression, and moreover that the occurence of catharsis was directly related to therapeutic improvement. Furthermore, when we compared feeling-expressive therapy to traditional, dynamic psychotherapy, we found significant differences in favor of our approach, especially in the context of weekly sessions of one hour's duration. We also refuted the myth that only women and hysterics cry in cathartic treatment, and that only people with traumatic disorders profit from this type of therapy.

Having demonstrated the power and wide applicability of cathartic therapy in time-limited treatment, we were eager to explore the results of our work as practiced with long-term private patients. In doing so, we resolved to study our therapy as it is actually practiced, applying the most rigorous scientific standards possible within a naturalistic setting. After collecting data on nearly a hundred patients over the course of several years, we were gratified to discover that ours is an effective form of treatment for patients ranging from normal people with problems in living to psychotics. Clients of the Center remained in treatment for a protracted period of time, during which they continued to experience high levels of catharsis week after week. This finding is significant because it tends to belie the notion that feelings are bad "things" to be "discharged" or gotten rid of. Instead, the results support our contention that feelings are dispositions to action, and that cathartic therapy helps people to become more feelingful. Our patients did not get rid of anything, they gained something—a fuller appreciation of themselves as feeling, thinking, and acting people.

That catharsis itself is a major element in the success of our treatment has been amply demonstrated in several studies. In short-term therapy this is reflected in a direct correlation, the more catharsis, the more change. However, over the course of long-term treatment it is not simply the amount of catharsis that produces success, but the fact that the feelings expressed were suppressed and conflicted. The term "catharsis" suggests an emotional epiphany, and our experience has convinced us that feeling expression is most therapeutic when it involves discovery and insight. A corollary of this is that feelings, once expressed, need to be examined.

Although we hoped to learn a great deal about what sorts of people are most helped by feeling expressive therapy, our results yielded only preliminary information on this question. We found that those people with the least social and psychological restraint on their emotions were able to sustain the highest amounts of emotional expression over the course of long-term therapy. We also found that the people who changed most were those suffering from specific and significant problems. For this group catharsis was more than an end in itself. Instead, these people used feeling-expressive therapy to overcome defenses against feeling, and then to examine the feelings to discover parts of themselves that were not being realized and expressed in relation to the important people and events in their lives.

REFERENCES

American Psychiatric Association. *Diagnostic and statistical manual.* DSM-II, 1968.

Auerbach, A. H. & Johnson, M. Research on the therapist's level of experience. In A. S. Gurman & A. M. Razin (Eds.) *Effective psychotherapy: A handbook of research.* New York: Pergamon Press, 1977.

Bastiaans, J. The role of aggression in the genesis of psychosomatic disease. *Journal of Psychosomatic Research,* 1969, *13,* 307-314.

Battle, C. C. et al. Target complaints as a criteria of improvement. *American Journal of Psychotherapy,* 1966, *20,* 184-192.

Bellak, L., & Small, L. *Emergency psychotherapy and brief psychotherapy.* New York: Grune & Stratton, 1965.

Bergin, A. E., & Garfield, S. J. *Handbook of psychotherapy and behavior change.* New York: Wiley, 1971.

Bergin, A. E. & Lambert, M. J. The evaluation of therapeutic outcomes. In S.

L. Garfield & A. E. Bergin (Eds.) *Handbook of psychotherapy and behavior change: An empirical analysis. Second Edition.* New York: Wiley, 1978.

Bergin, A. E. & Strupp, H. H. *Changing frontiers in the science of psychotherapy.* Chicago: Aldine-Atherton, 1972.

Berkowitz, L. The case for bottling up rage. *Psychology Today,* 1973, *7,* 2, 24-31.

Bierenbaum, H., Nichols, M. P. & Schwartz, A. J. Effects of varying session length and frequency in brief emotive psychotherapy. *Journal of Consulting and Clinical Psychology,* 1976, *44,* 790-798.

Bierman, R. I. Dimensions of interpersonal facilitation in psychotherapy and child development. *Psychological Bulletin,* 1969, *72,* 338-52.

Bohart, A. Roleplaying and interpersonal-conflict reduction. *Journal of Counseling Psychology,* 1977, *24,* 15-24.

Bohart, A. Toward a cognitive theory of catharsis. *Psychotherapy: Theory, Research and Practice,* 1980, *17,* 192-201.

Bohart, A. & Haskell, R. The ineffectiveness of a cathartic procedure for anger reduction. Paper presented at the 58th Annual Convention of the Western Psychological Association, San Francisco, April, 1978.

Boudewyns, P. A. & Wilson, A. E. Implosive therapy and desensitization therapy using free association in the treatment of inpatients. *Journal of Abnormal Psychology,* 1972, *79,* 259-268.

Boulougouris, J. C., Marks, I. M. & Marset, P. Superiority of flooding (implosion) to desensitization for reducing pathological fear. *Behavior Research & Therapy,* 1971, *9,* 7-16.

Dittes, J. E. Extinction during psychotherapy of GSR accompanying "embarrassing" statements. *Journal of Abnormal and Social Psychology,* 1957, *54,* 187-191.

Fazio, A. F. Implosive therapy in the treatment of a phobic disorder. *Psychotherapy: Theory, Research and Practice,* 1970, *7,* 228-32.

Frank, J. D. Therapeutic factors in psychotherapy. *American Journal of Psychotherapy,* 1971, *25,* 350-61.

Frank, J. D. & Nash, E. H. Commitment to peace work: A preliminary study of the determinants and sustainers of behavior change. *American Journal of Orthopsychiatry,* 1965, *35,* 106-119.

Garfield, S. L. Research as client variables in psychotherapy. In S. L. Garfield & A. E. Bergin (Eds.) *Handbook of psychotherapy and behavior change: An empirical analysis. Second Edition.* New York: Wiley, 1978.

Gendlin, E. T. et al. Focusing ability in psychotherapy, personality and creativity. In J. M. Schlien (Ed.) *Research in Psychotherapy, Vol. III.* Washington, D.C.: American Psychological Association, 1968, 217-41.

Gitelson, M. A critique of current concepts in psychosomatic medicine. *Bulletin of the Menninger Clinic,* 1959, *23,* 165-178.

Goldman- Eisler, F. A contribution to the objective measurement of the cathartic process. *Journal of Mental Science,* 1956, *102,* 78-95.

Goldstein, A. P., Heller, K. & Sechrest, L. B. *Psychotherapy and the psychology of behavior change.* New York: Wiley, 1966.

Gordon, J. E. Leading and following psychotherapeutic techniques with hypnotically induced repression and hostility. *Journal of Abnormal and Social Psychology,* 1957, *54,* 405-410.

Groen, J. Psychosomatic disturbances as a form of substituted behavior. *Journal of Psychosomatic Research*, 1957, *2*, 85-96.

Grossman, D. An experimental investigation of a psychotherapeutic technique. *Journal of Consulting Psychology*, 1952, *16*, 325-331.

Haggard, E. A. & Murray, H. A. The relative effectiveness of three "therapy" procedures on the reduction of experimentally induced anxiety. *Psychological Bulletin*, 1942, *39*, 441.

Hart, J., Corriere, R., & Binder, J. *Going sane.* New York: Jason Aronson, 1975.

Hodgson, R. J. & Rachman, S. An experimental investigation of the implosion technique. *Behavior Research and Therapy*, 1970, *8*, 21-27.

Hogan, R. A. Implosive therapy in the short term treatment of psychotics. *Psychotherapy: Theory, Research and Practice*, 1966, *3*, 25-31.

Hogan, R. A. The implosive technique. *Behavior Research and Therapy*, 1968, *6*, 423-431.

Howard, K. I., Orlinsky, D. E. & Hill, J. A. Affective experience in psychotherapy. *Journal of Abnormal Psychology*, 1970, *75*, 267-75.

Karle, W., Corriere, R. & Hart, J. Psychophysiological changes in abreaction therapy—study I: Primal therapy. *Psychotherapy: Theory, Research and Practice*, 1973, *10*, 117-122.

Karle, W., Corriere, R., Hart, J., and Klein, J. The Personal Orientation Inventory and the Eysenck Personality Inventory as outcome measures in a private outpatient clinic. *Psychotherapy: Theory, Research & Practice*, 1981, *18*, 117-122.

Karle, W. et al. The maintenance of psychophysiological changes in feeling therapy. *Psychological Reports*, 1976, *39*, 1143-1147.

Karle, W. et al. Preliminary study of psychological changes in feeling therapy. *Psychological Reports*, 1978, *43*, 1327-1334.

Keet, C. D. Two verbal techniques in a miniature counseling situation. *Psychological Monographs*, 1948, *62*, No. 294.

Kiesler, D. J. Some myths of psychotherapy research and the search for a paradigm. *Psychological Bulletin*, 1966, *65*, 110-136.

Lazarus, A. Learning theory and the treatment of depression. *Behavior Research and Therapy*, 1968, *6*, 83-89.

Lazarus, A. & Abramovitz, A. The use of "emotive imagery" in the treatment of children's phobias. *Journal of Mental Science*, 1962, *108*, 191-195.

Levis, D. J. & Carrera, R. N. Effects of ten hours of implosive therapy in the treatment of outpatients: A preliminary report. *Journal of Abnormal Psychology*, 1967, *72*, 504-508.

Levison, P. K., Zax, M. & Cowen, E. L. An experimental analogue of psychotherapy for anxiety reduction. *Psychological Reports*, 1961, *8*, 171-178.

Lewin, K. Quasi-stationary social equilibria and the problem of permanent change. In W. G. Bennis, K. D. Benne& R. Chin (Eds.), *The planning of change.* New York: Holt, Rinehart and Winston, 1964.

Lipowski, Z. J. Review of consultation psychiatry and psychosomatic medicine: III Theoretical issues. *Psychosomatic Medicine*, 1968, *30*, 395-422.

Lorr, M. Relation of treatment frequency and duration to psychotherapeutic outcome. In H. H. Strupp & L. Luborsky (Eds.) *Research in psychotherapy (Vol. 2).* Washington, D.C.: American Psychological Association, 1962.

Luborsky, L., Chandler, M., Auerbach, A. H., Cohen, J., & Bachrach, H. M.

Factors influencing the outcome of psychotherapy: A review of the quantitative research. *Psychological Bulletin*, 1971, *75*, 145-185.

Mahrer, A. R. An invitation to theoreticians and researchers from an applied experiential practitioner. *Psychotherapy: Theory, Research and Practice*, 1979, *16*, 409-418.

Martin, B., Lundy, R. M. & Lewin, M. H. Verbal and GSR responses in experimental interviews as a function of three degrees of "therapist" communication. *Journal of Abnormal and Social Psychology*, 1960, *60*, 234-240.

Meltzoff, J. & Kornreich, M. *Research in psychotherapy*. New York: Atherton Press, 1970.

Nichols, M. P. Outcome of brief cathartic psychotherapy. *Journal of Consulting and Clinical Psychology*, 1974, *42*, 403-410.

Nichols, M. P. Personal Satisfaction Form as a measure of psychotherapeutic outcome. *Psychological Reports*, 1975, *36*, 856-858.

Nichols, M. P. & Bierenbaum, H. Success of cathartic therapy as a function of patient variables. *Journal of Clinical Psychology*, 1978, *34*, 726-728.

Nichols, M. P. & Zax, M. *Catharsis in psychotherapy*. New York: Gardner Press, 1977.

Parloff, M. B., Waskow, I. E., & Wolfe, B. E. Research on therapist variables in relation to process and outcome. In S. L. Garfield & A. E. Bergin (Eds.) *Handbook of psychotherapy and behavior change: An empirical analysis. Second Edition*. New York: Wiley, 1978.

Rosenzweig, S. Some implicit common factors in diverse methods of psychotherapy. *American Journal of Orthopsychiatry*, 1936, *6*, 412-15.

Ruesch, J. & Prestwood, A. R. Anxiety: Its initiation, communication and interpersonal management. *Archives of Neurology and Psychiatry*, 1949, *62*, 527-50.

Shoben, E. J., Jr. Psychotherapy as a problem in learning theory. In H. J. Eysenck (Ed.) *Behavior therapy and the neuroses*. New York: Pergamon Press, 1960.

Shapiro, D. *Neurotic styles*. New York: Basic Books, 1965.

Sifneos, P. E. *Short-term psychotherapy and emotional crisis*. Cambridge, Mass.: Harvard University Press, 1972.

Small, L. *The briefer psychotherapies*. New York: Brunner—azel, 1971.

Stampfl, T. G. & Levis, D. J. *Imposive therapy: Theory and technique*. Morristown, New Jersey: General Learning Corporation, 1973.

Strupp, H. H. Psychotherapy research & practice: An overview. In S. L. Garfield & A. E. Bergin (Eds.) *Handbook of psychotherapy and behavior change: An empirical analysis. Second Edition*. New York: Wiley, 1978.

Symonds, P. H. A comprehensive theory of psychotherapy. *American Journal of Orthopsychiatry*, 1954, 697-714.

Ullman, L. P. & Krasner, L. *Case studies in behavior modification*. New York: Holt, Rinehart and Winston, 1965.

Watkins, John G. *The therapeutic self*. New York: Human Sciences Press, 1978.

Watson, J. P., Gaind, R. & Marks, I. M. Physiological habituation to continuous phobic stimulation. *Behavior Research and Therapy*, 1972, *10*, 269-278.

Watson, J. P. & Marks, I. M. Relevant and irrelevant fear in flooding—A crossover study of phobic patients. *Behavior Therapy*, 1971, *2*, 275-293.

Wiener, M. The effects of two experimental counseling techniques on performance impaired by induced stress. *Journal of Abnormal and Social Psychology*, 1955, *51*, 565-572.

Woldenberg, L. et al. Psychophysiological changes in feeling therapy. *Psychological Reports*, 1976, *39*, 1059-1062.

Wolpe, J. & Lazarus, A. A. *Behavior therapy techniques.* New York: Pergamon, 1966.

[1]Coché, E. and Dies, R. R. Integrating research findings into the practice of group psychotherapy. *Psychotherapy: Theory, research and practice*, 1981, *18*, 410-416.

11

Final Thoughts

26 April: Mother . . . prays now, she says that I may learn in my own life and away from home and friends what the heart is and what it feels. Amen. So be it. Welcome, O life! I go to encounter for the millionth time the reality of experience and to forge in the smithy of my soul the uncreated conscience of my race.

James Joyce
Portrait of the Artist
as a Young Man

In any termination, there are a few last things to say to bring closure. In the epigraph above, Stephen Deadalus is trying to do this as he prepares to leave home; in this chapter, we hope to do the same, although perhaps a trifle less poetically.

We have a few final thoughts on two salient aspects of our approach—our emphases on community and on feeling-expression. Although many contemporary psychotherapies do not emphasize these modalities, they have figured prominently in the history of healing.

COMMUNITY

In their review of ancient healing rituals, Nichols and Zax (1977) make it clear that, from earliest times, the community has been involved in the healing of its members. More recently, community psychology programs staffed by volunteers have provided preventive help or early intervention in a creative use of community spirit.

The one-to-one, private, closed-door therapy session, which today is often taken as a standard, actually began only with Freud and is based on a psychoanalytic theory of change. According to Freud, emotional problems develop as a result of unhappy interactions with significant early figures and treatment to resolve these pathogenic family influences must take place in social isolation. The traditional psychoanalytic model used by many therapists is analogous to a sterile operating room where surgeons excise malignancies. Although isolation in a private client-therapist relationship is helpful in generating a climate of sufficient safety to encourage self-exploration and discovery, it is not enough. People are naturally social creatures, and successful psychotherapeutic outcome depends in part on improved interpersonal relations.

We believe that the best way to enhance people's ability to relate is to include social interaction as a part of the total treatment package. In this, we are not alone. All of the emotive therapies we have studied include significant aspects of group work, and some have elaborate structures of community living as well. There seem to be strong, cohesive forces released by intense feeling-expression which draw people together in positive ways.

The individualistic bias of many traditional psychotherapies is caricatured in the popular culture, where people have been exhorted to "Do your thing" (Perls, 1969) and "Look out for number one" (Ringer, 1977). Indeed, ours has been described as a "culture of narcissism" (Lasch, 1979). Perhaps in reaction to these trends, there have emerged a number of recent movements in which individuals are encouraged to lose themselves in identification with a group. Many quasi-religious groups offer surcease from the lonely isolation of selfhood in union with a powerful leader or an enveloping group. The self-other balance that we need for a fully human life is distorted at both of these extremes.

We believe that community founded on shared, openly expressed feelings maintains this balance. There is closeness in the sharing of common feelings and separateness in the recognition that everyone has a different history, different hurts, and individual styles of meeting needs and handling difficulties.

One of the dangers of any intense therapy is that the therapy can become an end in itself, rather than a means to greater satisfaction in life outside the consultation room. So powerful is the emotional relief of intense psychotherapy that many people are tempted to prolong their dependence on it. Others become so preoccupied with their own problems that they get mired down in introspective self-scrutiny. Finding themselves surrounded with alligators, they forget they are there to drain the swamp. A community can be helpful in reminding its members that, however fascinating they may find their pain, or a particular memory or conflict, the point of the therapy is to be able to enjoy a loving and productive life.

The community at the Therapy Center is partial, open-ended, and composed of interlocking circles of people. It is partial in that very few members of the community live, work, or eat together. It is a voluntary association that, however important, involves only a few hours per week. Everyone at the Center is also a member of several other communities. This greatly reduces the risk that clients will become overly dependent on the community or that the community will become an authoritarian or conformist force in its members' lives.

The community is open-ended in that membership is constantly changing as new clients arrive and old clients leave. Some clients continue to peer-counsel or visit with other members of the community after their formal therapy is over, but active involvement usually ends when therapy terminates.

The community is composed of interlocking circles of people who have met each other through workshops or weekly groups. After a workshop, 30 to 50 participants know each other and most of the therapists. As new clients in this cohort begin to peer-counsel and to join weekly groups, they become members of the community. They gradually get to know more people through other workshops and informal interpersonal contacts at the Center. In addition to circles of acquaintanceship based on attendance at a workshop or membership in a group, there are also circles of more experienced clients who have worked together repeatedly and who have come to know and trust each other deeply.

There is also the circle of therapists, who work together, peer-counsel, and frequently socialize together as well. Even here, however, the community is not total. Although we support each other, take part in the significant events in each other's lives, and enjoy being together, we also enjoy being apart. We do not live together and we often spend time with friends who are not part of the Center. For us, this level of involvement maintains the right balance between self and community. No one needs to be isolated and without help, and no one is smothered or infantilized by an all-consuming group.

Essentially, then, the community provides a safe laboratory for trying out new ways of interacting, and a pool of people with whom one can peer-counsel and exchange practical and emotional support. Since our emphasis on community is greater than that of most current mainstream psychotherapies, the level of involvement we offer may seem excessive when judged by those standards. We believe, however, that mankind's long-term history of healing efforts suggests a level of community involvement greater than that offered by most contemporary psychotherapies and very much in line with that available in our practice.

FEELING-EXPRESSION

Many beginning golfers have a tendency to slice the ball, giving it a spin that makes it veer off to the right. In seeking to correct the slice, many develop a hook, sending the ball far to the left of its target. We believe that something like this has characterized the history of psychotherapy. The ideal blending of thought and feeling, reflection and experience, is often lost.

Most therapists are the products of rigorous graduate programs in social work, medicine, or psychology, where intellect and an obsessive-compulsive character style are virtual prerequisites for graduation. It is not surprising, therefore, that many therapists emphasize thoughts, rather than feelings. From our perspective, most psychotherapy has this rightward slice, characterized not only by too much thought and too little feeling, but also by too little activity and involvement on the part of the therapist.

At various points in the history of psychotherapy, theorists like Lowen and Janov have tried to correct this imbalance, reminding us of the importance of feelings. Often, however, these efforts to correct the bias toward thinking have been equally far from the mark, emphasizing feeling to the exclusion of thought. These movements have been characterized as extremist not only because conservative practitioners are afraid of intense catharsis, but also because the proponents of these systems often have isolated emotion as the only avenue for therapeutic change.

We would love to believe that feeling-expressive therapy is the long, straight shot right down the middle that perfectly combines feelings and insight, but we know better. For example, we know that in our own practice, we sometimes lead clients to think too much and other times to think too little. We know that there is much more to be learned about the ideal blending of thought and feeling, not to mention their integration with behavior change. We do believe, however, that feeling-expressive therapy is a useful way of combining insight and feelings, and represents a *rapprochement* of sorts between the emotive and psychoanalytic camps.

Our connection with the emotive point of view needs no explanation, but our similarity to psychoanalysis may require discussion. Both feeling-expressive and psychoanalytic therapies focus attention on the underlying causes of symptoms, rather than on the symptoms themselves. Both believe the underlying causes are rooted in reactions to past experiences which have created defenses that cut people off from the direct immediacy of their experience. Both also place importance on the present therapeutic relationship and the client's present everyday life outside the consulting room. This combined attention to past and present is in marked contrast to primal therapy's exclusive emphasis on the past and gestalt therapy's total focus on the present.

Those who think of psychoanalytic therapy as merely intellectual have distorted it. Psychoanalytic thinkers no longer believe that making the unconscious conscious is sufficient. To be successful in psychoanalytic therapy, patients must also undergo a profoundly emotional experience (Paolino, 1981, Dauanloo, 1980). Naturally, we agree.

Finally, we share with psychoanalytic therapists the conviction that the success of therapy parallels the success in overcoming resistances. Smashing through defenses may produce brilliant interpretations or emotional pyrotechnics, but only permanently reducing those defenses will produce lasting personal transformation. This is true whether the therapy is analytic or cathartic. In essence, we believe feeling-expressive therapy represents a sane and thoughtful attempt to bring intense emotional expression back into psychotherapy without negating the importance of insight and thought.

SUMMARY

Our hopes for this book will be fulfilled if we can play a part in helping therapists to bridge the gap between thinking and feeling. If the majority of therapists who work mostly with cognition and insight introduce a little more feeling into their work, and if the minority who work mostly with feelings find some new ways to integrate feeling with meaning and understanding, we will have accomplished our goal.

REFERENCES

Davanloo, H. *Short-Term Dynamic Psychotherapy.* New York: Jason Aronson, 1980.

Lasch, C. *The Culture of narcissism.* New York: Norton, 1979.

Nichols, M. and Zax, M. *Catharsis in psychotherapy.* New York: Gardner Press, 1977.

Paolino, J. T., Jr. *Psychoanalytic psychotherapy: Theory, technique, therapeutic relationship and treatability.* New York: Brunner/Mazel, 1981.

Perls, F. *Gestalt therapy verbatim.* Lafayette, Calif.: Real People Press, 1969.

Ringer, R. J. *Looking out for number one.* Beverly Hills: Los Angeles Book Corp., 1977.

INDEX

Ables, Billie S., 204
abreaction, 237
Acculturation, 90
Aguilera, D., 72
Alexander, F., 143
analogue studies, 236
Auerbach, A.H., 235, 238
alliance, 52, 53, 216
alloplastic/autoplastic issue, the, 102
"animal magnetism," 30
Aristotle, 28
art, 226
asthma, 239
Ayer, A.J., 5

Bachrach, H.M., 235
Bandler, R., 59, 63
Bandura, A., 26, 240
Bastiaans, J., 239, 240
Battle, CC, 245
behavior, changes in, 26, 51, 58, 242
  history of catharsis in, 28-29
  goal-directed, 43
behavior-to-feeing connection, 43
Behavioral Target Complaints Form, 244,
  248, 249
Behaviorists, 25, 26, 77
Bellak, L., 255
bereavement, 32
Bergin, A.E., 235, 242, 244, 258
Berkowitz, L., 240, 241
Bierenbaum, H., 250, 255
Bierman, R.I., 238
Binder, J. 37, 250
Bioenergetics, 34, 74
blood pressure, 239
Bohart, Arthur, 236, 237
Boudewyns, P.A., 238
Boulougouris, J.C., 238
Bowen, Murray, 28
Bowlby, John, 32
breathing, attention to, 49, 74-77, 84
Brenner, C., 59
Breuer, J., 4, 30, 31
blocked feelings, 7, 43
Brandsma, J., 204
Brodsky, A., 72
Brown, William, 32

Casriel, Daniel, 41, 46
catatonic schizophrenia, 19
Chandler, M. 235
"character armor," 33
characterological defenses, 15
child-rearing practices, 2, 23
client-centered therapy, 26
coaching, 49, 61

Cohen, J., 235
communication, 203, 206
"complete feelings," 37
complete feeling-expressive cycle, 9, 23
conflict theory, 31
content, variety of, 54
contract, 95, 212
control, fear of losing, 19, 51
"corrective emotional experience," 143
Corriere, R., 37, 239, 250
counterconditioning, 238
counterdependant client, the, 16
countertransference, 52, 54, 69, 158, 231
Cousins, N., 76

Dante, 117
Davanloo, H., 143, 283
defenses, 69
  breaching of, 271
  characterological, 15
  countering, 52-56
dependency, 58, 59
*Diagnostic and Statistical Manual (DSM-
  II)*, 245
direct contradiction, 70, 71
disappointment, voicing of, 155
Dittes, J.E., 236

embarrassment, 189
emotional expression, content of, 22
  process of, 22
emotional suppression, 3, 31
emotions, as evil spirits, 31
  as objects, 5
  nature of, 5
emotive imagery, 238
encouragement, 60, 268
Erickson, M.H., 211
exaggeration, 69, 211-212

failure to fit, 144
"false-self system,", 16
family therapy, 28
family-like system, group as, 181
Fazio, A.F., 238
Feeling-expression, cultural inhibitions of,
  1-4
  encouragement of, 95
  incomplete forms of, 7-15
  intense, 42-43, 56
  role of, 1
feelings, flow of, 19
Feeling Scale, 244, 265, 266
feeling therapy, 22, 37-39, 46
Feeling-to-behavior connection, 43
Fenichel, O., 26
focusing, 62-63